THE LONGMAN LATIN READERS SERIES

THE AULULARIA OF PLAUTUS
Gilbert Lawall and Betty Nye Quinn

CATULLUS AND HORACE
Andrew Aronson and Robert Boughner

CICERO AND SALLUST:
ON THE CONSPIRACY OF CATILINE
E. J. Barnes and John T. Ramsey

CICERO'S SOMNIUM SCIPIONIS
Sally Davis and Gilbert Lawall

LOVE AND TRANSFORMATION:
AN OVID READER
Richard A. LaFleur

SELECTIONS FROM CAESAR'S DE BELLO GALLICO
Andrew Aronson

SELECTIONS FROM OVID'S METAMORPHOSES
William S. Anderson and Mary Purnell Frederick

SELECTIONS FROM VERGIL'S AENEID BOOKS I, IV, VI
Jane Harriman Hall and Alexander G. McKay

LOVE AND TRANSFORMATION

An Ovid Reader

LOVE AND TRANSFORMATION

An Ovid Reader

Second Edition

RICHARD A. LAFLEUR

The University of Georgia

S|F
A|W

Scott Foresman - Addison Wesley

Editorial Offices: Glenview, Illinois • New York, New York
Sales Offices: Reading, Massachusetts • Atlanta, Georgia
Glenview, Illinois • Carrollton, Texas • Menlo Park, California

http://www.sf.aw.com

ACKNOWLEDGMENTS

Text

page 5: poem by A. E. Stallings originally published in *Classical Association News;* **page 31:** poem by A. E. Stallings originally published in *The Beloit Poetry Journal;* **page 43:** "EXIT MUSIC (For a Film)," by Thomas Yorke, Edward O'Brien, Colin Greenwood, Jonathan Greenwood, Philip Selway. Copyright © 1997 Warner Chappell Music Ltd. (PRS) All Rights Administered by WB Music Corp. All Rights Reserved. Used by Permission. Warner Bros. Publications U.S. Inc., Miami, FL 33014

Photographs

cover & page 1: Gian Lorenzo Bernini, *Apollo and Daphne,* 1624—Alinari/Art Resource, NY; **pages 4, 55, 89, 91, 101, 103, 111:** Giraudon/Art Resource, NY; **page 30:** National Gallery, London. Alinari/Art Resource, NY; **page 31:** SINTENIS, Renee. *Daphne.* Bronze, 56 1/2" (143.5 cm) high. The Museum of Modern Art, New York. Abby Aldrich Rockefeller Fund. Photograph © 1998 The Museum of Modern Art, New York; **page 35:** Bridgeman/Art Resource, NY; **page 57:** Foto Marburg/Art Resource, NY; **pages 75, 97, 100, 140, 157, 165, 172:** Alinari/Art Resource, NY; **page 77:** Metropolitan Museum of Art, Gift of Thomas F. Ryan, 1910; **page 88:** Metropolitan Museum of Art, Gift of Louis C. Raegner, 1927 (27.200); **page 121:** Wadsworth Atheneum, Hartford. The Ella Gallup Sumner and Mary Catlin Sumner Collection Fund; **page 131:** Walters Art Gallery, Baltimore; **page 146:** Erich Lessing/Art Resource, NY; **page 156:** Cameraphoto/Art Resource, NY

Series Editor: Professor Gilbert Lawall, University of Massachusetts, Amherst, MA

ISBN: 0-673-58920-X

VXORI SEMPER AMATISSIMAE
FILIOQVE FILIABVSQUE CARISSIMAE

CONTENTS

PREFACE

There are many friends and loved ones to thank for their support of this humble project: my wife Laura and our children, Jean-Paul, Caroline, and Kimberley, for their constant love and support, *sine quibus non . . .* ; Mary Wells Ricks, for her careful work on the manuscript itself, her judicious editorial advice, her friendship, and her unequaled good cheer; former graduate student Catherine Anne Bilow, dear friend as well, for her ever meticulous and enthusiastic research assistance; the many Latin teachers and professors who have field-tested portions of the book in their classes (Edith Black, Bob Burgess, Tom Curtis, Sally Davis, Tim Gantz, Muriel Garcia, Ellen Harris, Gail Polk, and Alysa Ward); Gil Lawall, for his masterful supervision of the Longman Latin Readers Series; the outside readers, Margaret Brucia and Peter Howard, for saving me from many errors (those that remain, as they say, *omnes mei sunt*) and for making this a better book in countless respects; the good folks at Longman, especially Lyn McLean, Aerin Csigay, Janice Baillie, and Winnie Jamison, for their steadfast encouragement and professionalism; the students in my spring, 1994, Ovid class (Amy Arthur, Angela Culpepper, David Hill, Charles McKinley, and Natalie Wilson), for their very helpful suggestions; and others at the University of Georgia who have assisted in important ways, among them Frances Van Keuren, Marshall Lloyd, Connie Russell, Dean Wyatt W. Anderson, and Vice President for Research Joe L. Key.

My most obvious debt, of course, is to Naso himself for what Sir Samuel Garth so elegantly termed (in the preface to his 1711 translation of the *Metamorphoses*) the poet's "infinite variety of inimitable excellencies," an artistry and a passion that have provided me such pleasure these many months. And lastly, with Ovid himself, may I say

IVRE TIBI GRATES, CANDIDE LECTOR, AGO

Tristia, IV.10.132

* * *

PREFACE TO THE SECOND EDITION

Once more thanks are due to my *lectores candidi candidaeque*, students, teachers, and reviewers, for the success of the first edition of this modest *libellus*, and for the many suggestions that have been kindly offered for the book's revision and improvement. In this regard I am particularly grateful to Mary Davisson, Robert Harris, Thomas McCreight, Paul Murgatroyd, Diann

Nickelsburg, Diane Svarlien, and Longman Latin Readers Series editor Gil Lawall.

The most important change in this second edition is the addition of three entirely new selections, "Daedalus and Icarus" and "Baucis and Philemon," from the *Metamorphoses*, and *Amores* I.3. These readings have been included in part to accommodate revisions to the College Board's Advanced Placement: Latin Literature syllabus; selections replaced in that syllabus ("Orpheus and Eurydice" and *Amores* I.2) have been retained here, however, both for their interest and to provide an increased number of readings for those using the book as a general text for college or high-school courses. Also new are detailed discussions in the general Introduction of Ovid's style, meter, scansion, and expressive reading; this last matter is always important, of course, to the study of Latin poetry, but all the more so now with the increased emphasis given to the oral/aural dimensions of the language in the new national *Standards for Classical Language Learning*.

In addition, the notes and discussion questions have been modified here and there, and the end vocabulary expanded. The Latin text was newly edited for the book's first printing, with attention to punctuation, capitalization, and paragraphing, as well as to manuscript variants listed in the principal editions, and has been only slightly revised for this new edition; most frequently consulted were William S. Anderson, ed., *Ovidius: Metamorphoses* (Stuttgart and Leipzig GER: Teubner, 1993), G. P. Goold's revision of the two-volume Loeb edition (Cambridge MA: Harvard University Press, 1977, 1984), and E.J. Kenney, ed., *P. Ovidi Nasonis: Amores, Medicamina Faciei Femineae, Ars Amatoria, Remedia Amoris* (Oxford ENG: Oxford University Press, 1994).

Finally, thanks are due to my former student A. E. Stallings, for her poems appearing on pages 5 and 31, which were previously published in, respectively, *Classical Association News* and *The Beloit Poetry Journal*; to my stalwart graduate research assistant Matthew Payne, for his intelligent and enthusiastic help with matters of bibliography, text, and vocabulary; to Mary Ricks and Yvonne Ramsey, for their expert and genial assistance in preparing the manuscript and dealing with a host of editorial details; to my new friends Bill Fleig and Cathy Wilson, of Scott Foresman-Addison Wesley, for joyfully adopting the Longman Latin Readers Series and its authors and making us their own; and most especially, once more, to my dear wife Laura, for lovingly tolerating my every obsession, authorial, editorial, and otherwise.

ATHENS, GEORGIA
Spring, 1998

INTRODUCTION

Et quod temptabam scribere versus erat, "And whatever I attempted to write became verse." So proclaimed Publius Ovidius Naso in *Tristia* IV.10, an autobiographical poem composed toward the end of his life, while in exile at Tomis on the Black Sea. And although great literature is in truth never easily produced, all that Ovid wrote certainly has given audiences over the centuries an impression of facility and grace, so utterly was his artifice concealed by his art (a quality which the poet himself attributes to the sculptor Pygmalion, a character in one of the transformation tales included in this book).

Born to a wealthy equestrian family at Sulmo, about 90 miles east of Rome, on March 20, 43 B.C., Ovid was sent off to Rome to study rhetoric and then to Athens to further his education. His father planned for him, as for his slightly older brother, a legal career, and as a young man he in fact held a few minor court posts. But his passion was for poetry, not the law; he declined an appointment to senatorial rank, and spent his time with Rome's most notable litterateurs: he had seen Vergil (some 27 years his senior), was well acquainted with Horace, and became a close friend of both Propertius and Tibullus.

Though his father liked to point out that even Homer died in poverty, young Naso could not be dissuaded from his Muse. In his early twenties he published his first poems, the *Amores*, romantic elegies chronicling his affairs with Corinna, a playful fiction constructed on the model of Catullus' Lesbia, Tibullus' Delia, and Propertius' Cynthia, and artfully elaborated out of his own fertile imagination and his immense repertory of poetic techniques. Originally issued serially in five books, the revised and abbreviated edition that survives was published about 20 years later in three volumes, containing 50 poems altogether, seven of them included in this book. In the years immediately before and following this second edition, Ovid produced a seemingly endless series of other elegiac works: the *Heroides*, a collection of letters from famous literary heroines to their lovers or husbands (Ariadne to Theseus, for example, and Dido to Aeneas); the *Medicamina Faciei Femineae*, a sprightly poem on cosmetics; the *Ars Amatoria*, a witty, occasionally risqué "manual of seduction," with two books of lessons for men and a third for women; and the *Remedia Amoris*, a follow-up handbook with advice, clever and sometimes quite sensible, on how to disentangle oneself from the snares of love.

The *Remedia* and some of the other poems of this period present now and then a seemingly apologetic tone; perhaps to be included in this category is *Amores* I.2 (one of the selections in this book), although it is far from certain that Augustus will have appreciated its closing entreaty to Cupid that he exhibit the much propagandized *clementia* of his "kinsman Caesar." What appears certain is that Ovid's erotic poetry had received criticism and that one or more of the poems, most likely the *Ars*, ultimately angered the emperor beyond the point of remedy. In A.D. 8, at age 50 and then recognized as the leading poet of his day, Ovid was exiled to Tomis, leaving behind in Rome his third wife (the first he had divorced, the second had died) and much else that he treasured. The specific reasons for his banishment are not clear to us, but Ovid insists more than once in his exile poetry (the *Tristia* and the *Epistulae ex Ponto*, composed between A.D. 8 and 17, the year of his death) that it was for no crime but only a *carmen* and an *error*. Though speculation has been rampant, the "mistake" we simply do not know. The offending *carmen* certainly included his erotic poetry, the *Ars Amatoria* in particular; while the more sexually explicit sections of his work were probably no more offensive to the Roman intelligentsia than they are to most Americans of the 1990s, the pervasive flippancy in his attitude toward the sanctity of marriage and other traditional mores can have had little appeal to an emperor whose sense of humor was often found wanting and who had become increasingly concerned with reviving, and even legislating, the old Republican morality ("legislating love," his own critics might have said). But by the time of his exile Ovid had nearly finished a far more significant body of work, which, because of its larger importance, had far more potential to offend.

Toward the end of *Amores* III.15, the closing poem of that collection's second edition (and another of the selections included in this book), Ovid proclaimed that he would leave elegy behind and "steer his horses over a greater field." He had in mind two major works whose planning he had already commenced and whose composition continued into his years of exile, the *Fasti* and the *Metamorphoses*. The former, a poetic calendar in elegiac couplets, survives only in the six books composed for the first six months of the year, an invaluable source for all manner of lore on Roman festivals, rituals, and events both historical and legendary. The latter, Ovid's best known and most influential work, was nearly complete by A.D. 8 and itself, despite its epic qualities (or perhaps because of them), doubtless added to the aging Augustus' annoyance with the poet's oeuvre.

In this masterpiece, the *Metamorphoses*, Ovid skilfully weaves together in 15 dactylic hexameter books some 250 tales of transformation, a *carmen perpetuum*, as he calls the work; beginning with the creation of the world out of Chaos, the saga proceeds through a quasi-chronological series of myths of gods and men which culminates in the metamorphosis of Troy into Rome, as it were, and of Julius Caesar, the emperor's adoptive father and a descendant of Venus, into a god and a fiery comet. Far more than a mere handbook of classical mythology (though the poem is our principal, and sometimes exclusive, source for many of the most popular Greco-Roman myths), the *Metamorphoses* has been admired for its animated and animating, highly visual, and often cinematographic narrations; the highly musical "soundtrack" which Ovid created through his manipulation of aural effects; the ingenious linkages both between adjacent stories and among larger groups of episodes; the keen insights into human psychology, both the feminine and the masculine; the kaleidoscopic variation in tone from the grand to the ribald, the tragic to the comic, the pathetic to the ridiculous, the sublime to the grotesque. Indeed, as regards this last point, it could be said that what may have pleased Augustus the least (despite the swelling laudations of the imperial family at the close of Book XV) are some of those "democratic" or "revolutionary" qualities that please us most: the poem's focus on private versus public, which can be seen in this book in the Pyramus and Thisbe story, as well as that of Baucis and Philemon, and its anti-epic burlesquing of gods and heroes, seen here in the tales of Eurydice and the blundering Orpheus (almost an anti-Aeneas) and of Daphne and the tyrannical, blustering Apollo (if Apollo is a "joke," how seriously then can Ovid's reader take Augustus, who claimed that deity as his own special patron?).

LOVE AND TRANSFORMATION

Readers of this text will note some remarkable affinities between the *Amores* and the *Metamorphoses*—first because Ovid has by design "eroticized" the latter work (the noted Ovidian critic Brooks Otis called the poem "an epic of love"), and second because most of the transformation tales selected for this book deal, also by design, with amatory themes. Generically speaking, of course, the works are worlds apart. The poet's *carmen perpetuum*, despite all its eccentricities and anti-epic qualities, is in the form of an epic, a long narrative, or rather a lengthy series of interconnected narratives, with tales of divine and heroic action. The *Amores*, on the other hand, are elegy and are thus—by definition and self-consciously—unheroic. Ovid, however, was among Roman poets a playful iconoclast, a revolutionary unrestricted by formal boundaries. He willfully, and with pleasure (his own and ours!), brings down the walls between the world of the hero and the world of the lover, as we shall see from the selections in this book (each of which is more fully discussed in the separate unit introductions). Throughout the tapestry of his epic from Chaos to Caesar—with its traditional elements of heroism, tragedy, and the cult of reason—he irreverently interweaves the anti-heroic and the comic and indulges the triumph of passion.

In his *Amores* too, Ovid plays at the boundaries of genre, permitting and now and then encouraging the infiltration of elegy's ranks by epic's valiant men-at-arms. In particular, the metaphor of the lover as a soldier in Cupid's camp pervades the selections that follow; indeed, Cupid himself—the youthful, ever potent Lord of Love—makes an appearance in every one of the poems, except I.12 (in which the wretched narrator's erotic expectations are disappointed by a duplicitous love-letter!). In form, of course, the *Amores* are quite different from the *Metamorphoses*: the meter (with thanks, as Ovid complains in I.1, to the mischievous Cupid, who has snatched away one of the hexameter's feet from every other line!) is the elegiac couplet, an often lurching, end-stopped form, better suited to short poems than to longer continuous narratives; each poem is brief (our selections range from 20 to 52 lines) and self-contained, though there are frequently interconnections between one piece and another (as here between I.1 and 2 and especially I.11 and 12); and the structure is generally tripartite, in certain instances (I.9 in this collection is a good example) advancing some thesis, with a rhetorical fervor Ovid had carefully studied, in a prologue, an argument, and an epilogue (which very often comes back, by ring composition, to one or more of the opening points).

In tone the *Amores*, following what Horace called the *lex operis* (the "law of the genre"), are more passionate than the *Metamorphoses*, more personal and egocentric, but the passion is largely artistic pretense and the *ego* that speaks to us throughout is far more a parody of the elegiac lover's persona, as the poet himself makes clear in I.1, than a reflection of Ovid's own, ever-elusive personality. Nevertheless readers have always enjoyed these poems, for their intensity, their sprightly humor, and their brilliant word-games. While a mere seven selections quite obviously cannot fully represent the wide range of themes and stylistic variations exhibited by the entire collection, those included here (among them both the programmatic opening elegy of Book I and the farewell poem that closes out Book III) should provide a delightful, and one hopes enticing, sample of the whole, as well as a compelling counterpoint to the half dozen transformation tales here offered up from the *Metamorphoses*.

ASPECTS OF OVID'S STYLE

Ovid is in general read with facility, and most of the peculiarities of his style are addressed early on in the notes accompanying the text, as well as in the list of poetic and rhetorical devices included at the end of this introduction; as a convenience to readers, however, the following summary comments are provided, along with references to the text (examples are drawn from the *Metamorphoses* selections, unless otherwise indicated) or to the definitions that are included below, along with text references, in the Poetic Devices section (abbreviated below "PD").

WORD ORDER: Word order will certainly be one of the greatest challenges for students coming to Ovid with little or no prior experience in reading Latin poetry. You should be aware from the outset that word order in verse, though by no means random, is nevertheless much freer than in prose and that attention to word-endings which signal such syntactical relationships as adjective-noun agreement is accordingly all the more crucial to comprehension and translation. Noun and adjective are often widely separated (*altam . . . urbem* IV.57–58), and frequently placed just before the caesura and at line's end in a pentameter verse

(*Am.* III.15.2); words are sometimes positioned outside their clauses (I.520); initial conjunctions, and other words that would ordinarily introduce a clause, are frequently delayed (*dum* X.9, *postquam* X.11); speech verbs with direct quotations are also commonly delayed and separated from their subjects (I.463–64); relative clauses sometimes precede their antecedents (I.524); occasionally the antecedent is attracted into the relative clause (IV.158); closely connected or coordinating words often "frame" a verse by being positioned first and last in the line (I.526). Other special arrangements of words are frequently employed for imagistic or rhetorical effect; see PD "anastrophe," "chiasmus," "enjambement," "golden line," "interlocked word order," "word-picture."

ELLIPSIS: Words are more frequently omitted in verse than in prose; sometimes one or more words in one phrase are meant to be supplied in another, usually adjacent phrase (I.458). PD "asyndeton," "ellipsis."

NOUNS: Ovid frequently employs case uses less common in prose, e.g., a descriptive genitive in place of a predicate nominative (*Am.* I.12.28), dative instead of ablative with verbs of mixing (IV.140), ablative in place of locative (IV.121), ablative of route (X.13) and duration of time (X.73), accusative of purpose (*Am.* I.1.22) and accusative of respect (especially with reference to body parts, I.484). The "poetic plural" for singular, and singular for plural, are common (I.527), as are Greek noun and adjective forms, including patronymics (*Daphne* I.452, *Peneide* I.472).

VERBS: Often used are the third-person plural perfect form -*ere* for -*erunt* and perfect-system forms with the intervocalic -*v*- omitted (I.478); simple for compound form (*positos* for *dispositos*, I.477); the so-called Greek middle voice, essentially a passive form with active or reflexive sense (*eripitur* I.538), and the historical present (IV.63); participles instead of clauses or in place of nouns (IV.68), with the future active participle sometimes indicating purpose (IV.98).

OTHER PARTS OF SPEECH: Prepositions are often omitted (I.467); -*que* is extremely common and is often attached to the first word of a quotation rather than to the speech verb (I.456). And see PD, "asyndeton" and "polysyndeton."

RHETORICAL STYLE: Ovid (who, as noted earlier, had trained for the law) often employs a highly rhetorical style, especially in speeches of persuasion, such as Apollo's to Daphne and Orpheus' to Pluto and Persephone; for favorite devices, see PD "anaphora," "apostrophe," "irony," "litotes," "oxymoron," "polysyndeton," "tricolon crescens."

FIGURATIVE LANGUAGE: Ovid is a master of figurative language and imagery, of word-pictures and even cinematographic effect; for some of his favorite devices, defined with passage references, see PD, "allegory," "hendiadys," "metaphor," "metonymy," "personification," "simile," "synecdoche," and "transferred epithet" (and see above on word order).

SOUND EFFECTS: One of the most lyrical of Latin poets, Ovid often manipulates such devices as alliteration and assonance simply to add musical effect to his verse, but in other instances the intent is to enhance meaning onomatopoetically; he frequently employs internal rhyme, especially in his elegiac couplets (*Am.* I.11.12), uses dactyls for rapid action (*Am.* I.11.15) or spondees to slow the pace in a dramatic moment (IV.91). See PD, "alliteration," "assonance," "onomatopoeia," and the section below on meter.

For further details and examples, see the introductions to Deveau and Getty, and Anderson's commentaries on *Metamorphoses* I–V and VI–X, as well as Kenney's "The Style of the *Metamorphoses*" (listed in the Teacher's Guide bibliography).

SCANNING AND READING OVID'S VERSE

Ancient poetry was composed to be read aloud (or, in certain instances, to be sung or chanted to musical accompaniment) and with the listening audience, at least as much as the reading audience, in mind; as J.C. McKeown points out in the prolegomena to his commentary on the *Amores* (vol. I, p. 63—cited in the Teacher's Guide for this text), Ovid himself bitterly laments the fact that in exile he had no proper audience for his *recitatio* (*Tristia* III.14.39–40). The Latin poet hoped to appeal at once to the intellect and to the emotions—in varying proportion, depending upon the particular genre—and his approach to both was through the ear. Both the "music" and the "message" of poetry derived in part from its sound effects and its delivery, which was as important to a poet as to a trial lawyer or a politician; rhythm and assonance and such devices as alliteration and onomatopoeia contributed much to the overall effect of a poem. When we read silently, therefore, or aloud but unexpressively, we are neglecting altogether an important aspect of the poet's artistry, just as surely as if we were to experience an opera of Mozart's without the music or the colorful paintings of Gauguin or Picasso only through the medium of black and white photographs.

Correct Pronunciation

The late Professor Gareth Morgan (in his review of the excellent Latin cassette package by Stephen Daitz, cited in the Teacher's Guide) imagined a student, perhaps reading the *Aeneid* for the first time, who complains to his teacher, "How do I put the meter in?" The wise instructor replies, "You don't: Vergil put it in. All you do is bring it back to life again." This "revival of the text" is the fundamental meaning of *recitatio*, of course; and all that is required, as Morgan suggested, is to read the Latin correctly and with attention to what it means.

The first and most important step in any beginning language course is to learn the sounds of the language, that is the correct pronunciation, and to exercise that knowledge through listening and speaking activities every day. Very straightforward rules for pronouncing Latin are provided in the introduction of every beginning Latin text, and more detailed discussions can be found in W. S. Allen's *Vox Latina* and Stephen Daitz' *Pronunciation and Reading of Classical Latin* (cited in the Teacher's Guide). The first and most important step in reading a Latin poem aloud is simply to read each sentence from beginning to end, following those rules and thinking about what the sentence is saying.

Meter

As you read, and especially if your pronunciation is careful and accurately reflects the differences between long and short vowels, the proper sounds of diphthongs (*ae, oe, ei, ui, au*, and *eu*), and so forth, you should detect a certain rhythmical pattern in the arrangement of the words. This, of course, reflects what Roger Hornsby has called "a vital, indeed a primordial, aspect of poetry," meter (from Latin *metrum*, Greek *metron*, meaning "measure"), which may be defined as the measured arrangement of syllables in a regular rhythmical pattern. In English verse, meter is determined by the patterned alternation of accented and unaccented syllables, an accented syllable being one that is spoken with greater stress or emphasis, such as the syllable *mid-*, in "Ónce upón a mídnight dréary" (which is here "scanned," the "scansion" indicating schematically the accented syllables ['] that alternate with unaccented syllables).

In classical Greek, normal word accent was based upon pitch rather than stress (the language was therefore by nature more "musical" than either Latin or English) and was not the prime determinant in verse rhythm. Rather than being "qualitative" (i.e., based on the stress quality of a syllable), Greek meter was "quantitative" (i.e., based on the quantity, or length, of a syllable); and, though it was not entirely suited to their own language, the Romans abandoned the stress-accented poetry they had at first experimented with and adapted the use of quantitative meter to their verse from the time of the early epic poet Ennius (239–169 B.C.) and throughout the classical period.

That syllables may be defined in terms of quantity, i.e., that some may be "long" and others "short," is clear enough from English: compare the time required to pronounce *e, be, beak, beach, beached*. Though the length of Latin syllables might vary considerably, as in these English examples, the Romans thought in terms of only two grades, short and long; a long syllable was felt to take about twice as long to pronounce as a short syllable (in musical terms, one might compare the half note and the quarter note). Latin quantitative meter is based upon the patterned alternation of long and short syllables, and the second step in reading Latin poetry aloud is to read each verse metrically, with an eye (or one should say, an ear) to this quantitative rhythm.

With practice a student can read a Latin poem metrically at first sight, simply because the quantities are inherent in the language. Beginning students, however, should learn the mechanics of scanning a line on paper, i.e., of marking the long and short syllables and separating off the feet in each verse (a "foot" is the smallest characteristic group of syllables in a particular rhythmical pattern, e.g., a short syllable followed by a long one constitutes a foot in iambic meter—a "verse" is the smallest characteristic grouping of feet in a particular meter, e.g., a series of five iambs is an iambic pentameter verse). Such scansion is a simple, mechanical exercise and involves the following steps:

A. *Mark the long and short syllables using the macron (¯) and the breve (˘), respectively.* In their initial introduction to Latin pronunciation, students learn to identify a syllable as either long or short because syllable quantity determines placement of the stress accent in ordinary Latin speech. The rules are essentially the same in scanning poetry: a syllable is long only if it contains a long vowel or a diphthong or if the vowel, though itself short, is followed by two or more consonants (except where the second of the two consonants is *h*, including the aspirates *ch*, *ph*, and *th*, or where the only two consonants are *qu* or, *sometimes*, a "stop," especially *b*, *c*, *d*, *g*, *p*, or *t*, followed by one of the "liquids," *l* or *r*). In this last instance, however, when attempting to determine the quantity of a syllable occurring *at the end of a word within* (not at the end of) *a verse*, one must take into account any consonants occurring *both* at the end of the word *and* at the beginning of the next word; consider the first line of the "Daphne and Apollo" story (the opening selection in our book):

Prīmus amor Phoebī Daphnē Pēnēia, quem nōn

Here the first syllable *Prī-* is long (as the first syllable of a line always is in Ovid's meters), because of the long vowel (*-ī-*); the *-mus* syllable is short, because the vowel itself is short (as indicated by the lack of a macron) and is followed by only one consonant; and the *a-* syllable is short for the same reasons (thus the opening foot is a "dactyl," i.e., a long-short-short, ¯˘˘). The next syllable, *-mor*, is long, however, even though the vowel *-o-* is short, because the vowel is followed by "two or more consonants" (here *-r* + *Ph-*), when taking into account the ending of *amor* itself and the beginning of the next word *Phoebī*. The same principles make the *quem* long (i.e., the *-e-* is short but is followed by *-m* + *n-*, so the syllable itself is long). The long and short syllables in the entire line would be marked as follows:

¯ ˘ ˘ ¯   ¯ ¯   ¯   ¯ ¯˘˘   ¯   ¯

Prīmus amor Phoebī Daphnē Pēnēia, quem nōn

Note that this line has a total of 14 syllables, one for each vowel and diphthong (remember that *oe* is a diphthong, not two separate vowels, and so makes a single syllable, and that *u* after *q* is always a consonant and so does not create a separate syllable). A line of verse, like an individual word, generally has as many syllables as it has vowels and diphthongs, but there is one exception: when a word in the verse ends with a vowel or a diphthong or a vowel followed by *-m*, and the following word begins with a vowel or a diphthong or a vowel preceded by *h-*, the final syllable of the first word and the beginning syllable of the next were usually collapsed, or "elided," into a single syllable. The quantity of the single syllable resulting from such "elision" was usually that of the second syllable (suggesting that, in some cases at least, the preceding vowel or diphthong was in pronunciation actually dropped altogether, as the term "elision," from *elidere* 'to compress or strike out,' might suggest). In writing out the scansion of a verse, any elided syllables should be connected with a line and the macron or breve should be centered above the space between the two words, as illustrated in these two lines from "Daphne and Apollo" (470 and 532):

$$\bar{\quad} \; \breve{\quad} \; \bar{\quad}\bar{\quad} \; \bar{\quad} \; \bar{\quad} \; \breve{\quad}\breve{\quad} \; \bar{\quad} \; \breve{\quad}\breve{\quad}$$
quod facit aurā<u>tum est</u> et cuspide fulget acūtā

$$\bar{\quad} \; \breve{\quad} \; \bar{\quad}\bar{\quad} \; \bar{\quad} \; \breve{\quad}\breve{\quad} \; \bar{\quad}\bar{\quad}$$
ip<u>se Amor</u>, admissō sequitur vestīgia passū

In line 470 the elided syllable is long because the second syllable *est* is long (the short *e-* being followed by the two consonants *-st*), whereas in 532 the elided syllable is short because the second syllable *A-* is short; the actual classical pronunciation of elided syllables was variable, but here the pronunciations were probably *aurātum'st* and *ips'Amor*. Those familiar with Vergil should note that elisions occur only about half as often in Ovid, one of many characteristics of his style that provide a much quicker, more smoothly flowing verse. Occasionally the conditions for elision will exist but the poet will choose for metrical or other purposes not to elide; this phenomenon is called "hiatus," from the Latin word for "gaping" or "yawning" (a very apt term, as the mouth would remain open from the vowel of the first word, across the minute intervening pause, and on through the vowel of the following word).

B. *Mark off the feet using the slash (/).* In order to do so, one must, of course, recognize the particular metrical pattern in which the poem is composed. In Ovid, however, you will encounter only two patterns, the dactylic hexameter (probably familiar to you from Vergil) and the elegiac couplet (also perhaps familiar from Catullus or Martial).

1. *Dactylic Hexameter.* The "heroic" meter of Ovid's *Metamorphoses* (and Vergil's *Aeneid*), a six-foot line, with a dactyl ($\bar{\quad}\breve{\quad}\breve{\quad}$) in the first five feet and a spondee ($\bar{\quad}\bar{\quad}$) in the sixth (the last syllable of the line, even if apparently short,

can be regarded as long due to the natural pause occurring at the end of each verse). In any of the first four feet (rarely in the fifth), a spondee might be substituted for the characteristic dactyl, often with the intended effect of slowing down the movement of the line. Ovid has fewer such substitutions than Vergil, again making for a more rapidly moving verse; since dactyls are commoner than spondees in Ovid (even in his elegiac couplets), his occasional use of heavily spondaic lines, or series of lines, often carries special emphasis (very helpful tables of Ovid's favorite patterns—the two commonest being dactyl-spondee-spondee-spondee-dactyl-spondee and, to abbreviate, DDSSDS—are included by Anderson in the introductions to his commentaries on *Metamorphoses* I–V and VI–X, cited in the Teacher's Guide). The pattern may be schematized as follows:

$$-\breve{\breve{}}/-\breve{\breve{}}/-\breve{\breve{}}/-\breve{\breve{}}/-\breve{\breve{}}/--$$

The second line of "Daphne and Apollo" would be marked as follows:

$$\bar{\ } \ \bar{\ } / \bar{\ } \ \breve{} \ \ \breve{} / \bar{\ } \ \ \ \bar{\ } / \ \bar{\ } \ \breve{} \ \breve{} \ / \breve{} \ \breve{} / \bar{\ } \ \bar{\ }$$
fors ignāra dedit, sed saeva Cupīdinis īra

As in Vergil, a predominantly dactylic line may be used to suggest speed (see *Met.* I.458, 510–11, and notes), while a heavily spondaic verse, as suggested above, often produces some kind of emphasis (I.526, IV.91, and notes); similar effects are employed in the elegiac couplet as well.

2. *Elegiac Couplet.* Common in epigrams and the standard meter for elegiac poetry, including Ovid's *Amores*, this pattern consists of alternating dactylic hexameter and pentameter lines, each pair called a "couplet," in the following scheme:

$$-\breve{\breve{}}/-\breve{\breve{}}/-\breve{\breve{}}/-\breve{\breve{}}/-\breve{\breve{}}/--$$

$$-\breve{\breve{}}/-\breve{\breve{}}/-//-\breve{\breve{}}/-\breve{\breve{}}/-$$

Note that in the pentameter line spondaic substitutions are allowed only in the first two feet; Ovid's couplets have fewer such substitutions (and also fewer elisions—see McKeown, vol. 1, pp. 108–23, cited in the Teacher's Guide) than his predecessors (especially Catullus) and so again, as in the *Metamorphoses*, individual lines have a quicker pace. But Ovid's couplets in the *Amores* are regularly end-stopped, i.e., the ending of the pentameter verse, with its abruptly ending "clickety-clickety-clack" sound, usually coincides with the ending of a sentence or clause; thus the form has a more halting character than the hexameter, where phrases are frequently "enjambed" or carried over from one line to the beginning of the next, giving the verse a more continuous flow. In Ovid, too, the pentameter verse often reinforces or even restates the point of the preceding hexameter, which adds to the self-contained quality that characterizes his couplets.

C. *Mark the principal pause in each line, using a double slash (//)*. In longer lines of verse such as the dactylic hexameter, the rhythm was usually slowed by one or sometimes two major pauses that generally coincided with the close of some sense unit (i.e., the end of a phrase, a clause, or a sentence) and which, therefore, are often easily noted in a modern text by some mark of punctuation. More often than not the principal pause occurs within a foot, where it is called a "caesura," rather than at the end of a foot, where it is called a "diaeresis"; in fact, in classical Latin poetry, the majority of the word endings in a line are caesurae, or, to put it another way, most words begin in one foot and continue over into the next, a deliberate device intended to interweave the feet more closely and prevent a choppy, sing-song effect. In Ovid's hexameters (both in the *Amores* and the *Metamorphoses*) the principal pause is most commonly a caesura following the first syllable in the third foot, with the next commonest pattern a pair of such caesurae in the second and fourth feet (these are also Vergil's favorite patterns, but in Ovid there is even less variation); in the elegiac couplet's pentameter, the principal pause is always at mid-line, though there is occasionally a strong secondary pause, often resulting from an enjambement (*Am*. I.11.2 and 4, where the adjectives *docta* and *utilis* are enjambed for emphasis). Since diaereses are less common, they are occasionally employed for special emphasis (*Met*. I.470, 520, and notes).

Lines 456–58 of "Daphne and Apollo" are fully scanned as follows:

$$- \;\; \breve{} \;\; \breve{}/-// \;\; - \;\; /- \;\; \breve{} \;\; \breve{}/- // \;\; - \;\; / \;\; - \;\; \breve{} \;\; \breve{} \;\; /- \;\; -$$
Quidque tibī, lascīve puer, cum fortibus armīs?

$$- \;\; \breve{} \;\; \breve{} \;\; //- \;\; \breve{} \;\; \breve{}/- \;\; \breve{} \;\; \breve{}/- \;\; - \;\; /- \;\; \breve{} \;\; \breve{}/ \;\; - \;\; -$$
dīxerat; ista decent umerōs gestāmina nostrōs,

$$- \;\; \breve{} \;\; \breve{}/ \;\; - \;\; \breve{} \;\; \breve{}/ \;\; -// \;\; \breve{} \;\; \breve{}/ \;\; - \;\; \breve{} \;\; \breve{}/ \;\; - \;\; \breve{} \;\; \breve{} \;\; / \;\; - \;\; -$$
quī dare certa ferae, dare vulnera possumus hostī

Note: the 2nd-foot/4th-foot caesurae in 456, setting off the demeaning vocative; the enjambed speech-verb, followed by diaeresis, in 457; the standard 3rd-foot caesura in 458.

The opening couplet of *Am*. I.1 is fully scanned as follows:

$$- \;\; \breve{} \;\; \breve{}/- \;\; \breve{} \;\; \breve{}/-// \;\; \breve{}\breve{}/- \;\; \breve{} \;\; \breve{}/ \;\; - \;\; \breve{} \;\; \breve{}/ \;\; - -$$
Arma gravī numerō   violentaque bella parābam

$$- \;\; \breve{} \;\; \breve{}// \;\; - \;\; \breve{} \;\; \breve{}/-//- \;\; \breve{} \;\; \breve{}/- \;\; \breve{} \;\; \breve{}/-$$
ēdere, māteriā conveniente modīs

Note: the common 3rd-foot caesura and the fully dactylic rhythms (quick, to suit the violent subject-matter) in the hexameter; the secondary pause, a diaeresis after the speech-verb, in the pentameter, with the standard mid-line caesura (always marked, even when, as here, the effect is to separate two closely related words, where in the hexameter a pause would not be expected). See further the terms "caesura," "diaeresis," "diastole," "ictus," and "systole," in the list of poetic, rhetorical, and metrical devices below.

Once you have worked out the scansion of a passage, you are ready to read it aloud. We know that the Romans, while not ignoring the actual word accent, gave additional stress to the first long syllable of each foot in a verse. It is a peculiarity of Latin poetry that this verse accent, or "ictus," did not always coincide with the normal word accent; "conflict" between ictus and accent (i.e., their occurrence on different syllables) was sometimes used by poets to underscore some physical violence or emotional discordance in the subject described (*Met.* X.5, 49, and notes), and words were sometimes arranged so that the ictus would accentuate rhyming syllables (*Met.* IV.92, 127). In reading aloud, you should give at least some stress to the syllable bearing the ictus (i.e., the first syllable of each foot) as well as observe the long and short quantities and the principal pauses (i.e., the ends of phrases, clauses, and sentences). Remember that Ovid, like other classical Roman poets, tended to avoid an excess of end-stopped lines in favor of enjambed or "run-on" lines; the pentameter lines in his elegiac couplets are an exception, of course, but in general the reader should avoid an exaggerated pause at the end of a verse, unless it does in fact coincide with the end of a sense unit.

Expressive Reading

The final step, and this is a challenge in reading English aloud as well as Latin, is to read expressively. The ancient poet, as we have noted already, wrote not only for educated readers but also for recitation, to entertain a listening audience: the poetry recitation was a performance and, if successful, an emotionally and intellectually stirring experience. The opposite could be true as well; Martial complains (in Epigram I.34) of the infelicitous results when his own poems were recited by an inept reader:

> Quem recitās meus est, ō Fīdentīne, libellus:
> sed male cum recitās, incipit esse tuus!

Ovid would never have recited his poetry in a sing-song monotone, but would have read dramatically, varying the tenor of his voice to suit the mood and giving proper emphasis to key words and phrases, speaking sometimes as narrator *in propria persona*, but often performing the roles of both Daphne and Apollo, of Pyramus and Thisbe, of Orpheus and Eurydice, and of the many other characters and individualized narrators who were his *dramatis personae*, just as would an actor in a play. You should begin each unit in this book by reading aloud, and as you complete each unit, once you have read and translated and discussed a passage and savored every nuance, you should read the passage aloud one last time, rhythmically and expressively, in order to approximate as nearly as possible the effect intended by Ovid and, in the true sense of *recitatio*, to bring his verses back to life.

A FINAL NOTE TO THE STUDENT

Readers of this book are likely to have had at least some previous experience with Latin poetry, Vergil or Catullus perhaps, or possibly only selections included in a beginning or intermediate text. This volume, however, should serve even the newcomer to Latin verse: Ovid is one of the easiest of Roman poets (and of Roman authors in general); peculiarities of grammar, diction, and word-order, surveyed above, are generally explained in the notes, at least at their first occurrence, and poetic devices and figures of speech are defined below, along with references to representative examples in the text. Latin words likely to be unfamiliar are glossed in the facing notes, with an asterisk marking those that occur more than once in the book and which should therefore be memorized, and all words in the text (except those that appear only once and are glossed) are listed in the end vocabulary. Finally, the notes together with the discussion questions are intended to assist readers with, and provoke their thinking about, matters of both style and interpretation; explanatory notes are more generously provided for the earlier selections and are sparser later on, where questions are more often asked than answered.

You will very quickly become accustomed to Ovid's Latinity and to the free flow of his narratives (this is especially true of the *Metamorphoses* passages, which for that reason appear first in this collection, though they were of course composed after the *Amores*). A final—and vital—word of advice is to read the selections aloud, aloud and expressively, as Ovid intended them to be read; imagine an opera without music or your favorite film without its soundtrack, and you will have an idea of what is to be missed in only reading silently one of the most animated, passionate, and musical of Latin poets.

Poetic, Rhetorical, and Metrical Devices and Figures of Speech

The following figures of speech and poetic and rhetorical devices (including most of those in the *Teacher's Guide to Advanced Placement Courses in Latin*) occur in the selections from Ovid's poetry included in this book; definitions are followed by references to representative examples that appear early in the text and are commented upon in the notes.

Allegory: a prolonged metaphor, i.e., a type of imagery involving the extended use of a person or object to represent some concept outside the literal narrative of a text (e.g., use of Cupid's victory over Apollo in *Met.* I.452–73 to represent the triumph of passion over reason).

Alliteration: deliberate repetition of sounds, especially initial consonant sounds, in successive words, for musical (and occasionally onomatopoetic) effect (*Met.* I.454, 471–72, 489).

Anaphora: repetition of words or phrases for emphasis; often with asyndeton (*Met.* I.458–59, 470–71, 478).

Anastrophe: the reversal of normal word order, as with a preposition following its object, often with the effect of emphasizing the word(s) placed earlier (*Met.* X.49, *Am.* I.9.22, 44).

Apostrophe: address to some person or thing not present, usually for emotional effect (*Met.* IV.114, 155, *Am.* I.9.24).

Assonance: repetition of vowel or syllable sounds in successive words, for musical (and sometimes onomatopoetic) effect (*Met.* I.471, 489, 499).

Asyndeton: omission of conjunctions where one or more would ordinarily be expected in a series of words or phrases; often employed in connection with anaphora and underscoring the words in the series (*Met.* I.480, 505, X.26).

Caesura: a pause between words occurring within a metrical foot; the effect at the principal caesura in a line of verse (generally within the third foot, or in both the second and fourth, in the dactylic hexameter, and at the midpoint of the pentameter in the elegiac couplet) is often to emphasize the word immediately preceding or following; cf. diaeresis (*Met.* I.460, IV.166, X.11).

Chiasmus: arrangement of words or phrases in an oppositional, ABBA order, often to emphasize some contrast or to create a word-picture (*Met.* I.453, 463-64, 468).

Diaeresis: a pause between words coinciding with the end of a metrical foot, less common than caesura and sometimes employed to emphasize the word immediately preceding or, less often, following (*Met.* I.470–71, 496, 519).

Diastole: lengthening of an ordinarily short vowel (and hence the syllable containing it), usually when it occurs under the ictus and before a caesura; sometimes reflecting an archaic pronunciation (*Met.* X.15, 262).

Ellipsis: omission of one or more words necessary to the sense of a sentence but easily understood from the context; often a form of the verb *sum* (*Met.* I.452, 463).

Enjambement: delay of the final word or phrase of a sentence (or clause) to the beginning of the following verse, to emphasize an idea or create suspense (*Met.* I.487, 496, 519).

Golden Line: a form of interlocked word order (see below) in which a verb is positioned in the middle of the verse, with adjectives preceding and nouns following in symmetrical arrangement (*Met.* I.484, 528–29, IV.113).

Hendiadys: use of two nouns connected by a conjunction (or occasionally a preposition), often instead of one modified noun expressing a single complex idea; the usual effect is to give equal prominence to an image that would ordinarily be subordinated, especially some quality of a person or thing (*Met*. IV.59, X.239, *Am*. I.9.42).

Ictus: the verse accent, or beat, occurring on the first syllable of each foot in the dactylic hexameter and the elegiac couplet; when the ictus coincides with the normal word accent, the rhythm flows more smoothly and rapidly, and when the two conflict (i.e., occur on different syllables) there is a more disjointed effect; assonance and other sound effects can be accentuated by carefully arranging words so that selected syllables fall under the ictus (*Met*. IV.92, 127, 166).

Interlocked Word Order: arrangement of related pairs of words in an alternating ABAB pattern (e.g., adj. A / adj. B / noun A / noun B), often emphasizing the close connection between two thoughts or images (*Met*. I.457, 466, 484).

Irony: the use of language with a meaning opposite that suggested by the context (*Am*. I.12.23).

Litotes: a form of deliberate understatement, generally with a softening effect and usually achieved through describing one quality by denying its opposite (*Met*. X.266, *Am*. I.2.43, I.9.29).

Metaphor: an implied comparison, using one word for another that it suggests, usually with a visual effect (*Met*. I.489, 496, 520).

Metonymy: a type of imagery in which one word, generally a noun, is employed to suggest another with which it is closely related (*Met*. I.483, 538, IV.60).

Onomatopoeia: use of words whose sounds suggest their meaning or the general meaning of their immediate context (*Met*. I.454, 466, 528).

Oxymoron: the juxtaposition of two opposing ideas, usually to underscore an incongruity (*Met*. I.554, X.252).

Personification: a type of imagery by which human traits are attributed to plants, animals, inanimate objects, or abstract ideas (*Met*. I.516, IV.69–70, *Am*. I.1.27–28).

Polysyndeton: use of a greater number of conjunctions than usual or necessary, often to emphasize the elements in a series (*Met*. I.500–01, 516–18, X.4–5).

Prolepsis: attribution of some characteristic to a person or thing before it is logically appropriate, especially application of a quality to a noun before the action of the verb has created that quality (*Am*. I.9.5).

Simile: an explicit comparison (often introduced by *ut, velut, qualis*, or *similis*) between one person or thing and another, the latter generally something more familiar to the reader (frequently a scene from nature) and thus more easily visualized; some of Ovid's similes are quite brief (*Met*. I.483, 499), while others are extended and involve numerous and frequently complex points of comparison (*Met*. I.492–96, 533–39).

Synecdoche: a type of metonymy in which a part is named in place of an entire object, or a material for a thing made of that material, or an individual in place of a class (*Met*. IV.86, 119, *Am*. I.2.42).

Systole: shortening of a vowel which was ordinarily long, sometimes reflecting an archaic pronunciation, and not ordinarily occurring when the vowel was under the ictus; cf. diastole (*Am*. I.2.5, 12.9).

Tmesis: separation of a compound word into its constituent parts, generally for metrical convenience (*Met*. X.66–67).

Transferred Epithet: application of an adjective to one noun when it properly applies to another, often involving personification and focusing special attention on the modified noun (*Met*. I.452, 485, 525).

Tricolon Crescens: a climactic series of three (or more) examples or illustrations, each (or at least the last) more fully developed or more intense than the preceding (*Met*. I.500–01, 512–13, *Am*. I.11.9).

Word-Picture: a type of imagery in which the words of a phrase are arranged in an order that visually suggests the image being described (*Met*. I.468, 533, IV.100).

Zeugma: use of a single word with a pair of others (e.g., a verb with two objects, an adjective with two nouns), when it logically applies to only one of them or applies to them both, but in two quite different ways (*Met*. IV.129, X.50, *Am*. I.9.11).

LOVE AND TRANSFORMATION
An Ovid Reader

DAPHNE AND APOLLO

Metamorphoses I.452–567

"The very first love of Phoebus Apollo was Daphne, daughter of the river-god Peneus." So begins what was also the first story of love and transformation in Ovid's *Metamorphoses*—and what has been over the centuries one of the poet's most popular tales, inspiring paintings by Dürer, Poussin, and Sargent, sculpture by Bernini and Sintenis, poetry by Dante, Swinburne, and Pound, operas by Jacopo Peri (our earliest opera, in fact, first performed in 1597), George Frederick Handel, and Richard Strauss, ballets by Didelot and Kölling, even a gold medallion by Salvador Dali, and countless other literary, musical, and artistic works.

The popularity of the Daphne myth and the range of its influences are hardly surprising. Ovid's narration is dramatic, highly visual, even cinematographic, and—in its use of alliteration, assonance, onomatopoeia, and the many other sound effects available to the Latin poet—splendidly musical.

And the story itself, which Ovid had adapted and ingeniously recreated from a number of earlier sources, is captivating in both plot and nuance. In a chance encounter with Cupid, and in a swaggering mood after his victory over the monstrous Python, Apollo accosted and insulted the young god of love. Angered, Cupid drew from his quiver a golden-tipped arrow designed to arouse passion in its victim, and a lead-tipped arrow that would inspire loathing; with the first he shot Apollo, and with the second the beautiful river nymph Daphne. Apollo fell immediately in love with the nymph, while she on the other hand retreated to the forest (appropriate for one whose name, *daphne*, was the Greek word for "laurel tree"), became a devotee of the virgin goddess Diana, and, with her father's reluctant consent, shunned any prospect of love or marriage.

Overwhelmed by Daphne's beauty and failed by his own oracular powers, by which he ought to have known she was unattainable, Apollo approached the maiden and began pursuing her through the woods toward the river. In the midst of the chase, Apollo delivered a volley of arguments—boasting of his many talents and his status as Jupiter's son—which he hoped might persuade her to give in. Instead, and just as the god was about to seize her, Daphne prayed to her father to rescue her by changing her form. Instantly the girl's hair began to change into leaves, her arms into branches, and her feet into roots, and just as Apollo reached and threw his arms around her, he embraced instead a laurel tree, which even then recoiled from his kisses. Having failed in his attempt to possess the girl, the god declared the laurel to be his tree—a tree whose leaves would garland not only his own hair, but the hair of future triumphant generals of Rome and even adorn the entranceway of Augustus' palace.

2

The tale is in part a typical etiological myth, explaining the origin of the laurel tree, its association with Apollo, and the use of its leaves as garlands for victors in the Greek Pythian Games as well as for victorious Roman generals. But in Ovid's hands there is far more to the story. First is its place in the cosmic panorama of *Metamorphoses* I. The book begins with Ovid's version of creation, the transformation of the world and human society out of chaos; then follow the Four Ages of Man, a degeneration from the Golden Age, to the Silver, and the Bronze, into the criminal Age of Iron; next the battle of gods and giants; then the first transformation of a man, the vicious King Lycaon, into a beast, a ravaging wolf (one of the earliest werewolf stories); and finally the Great Flood, sent by the gods to punish man's vice, a cataclysm which only two mortals survived, Deucalion (the Roman Noah) and his wife Pyrrha.

As the world, thus cleansed, was renewed, Deucalion and Pyrrha repopulated humankind by casting behind them stones that grew and softened and took on the general shape of men and women like unfinished statues (or like the pod-creatures in "Invasion of the Body-Snatchers") and which ultimately became human beings in fact. Other animals were born out of the Earth herself, and out of the slime that remained as the flood waters receded sprang countless creatures, among them the colossal snake-beast Python. In the lines immediately preceding the tale of Daphne and Apollo, the archer-god rescued mankind from the Python's depredations, slaying the beast with a thousand arrows and instituting the athletic competitions known as the Pythian Games, whose first victors wore wreaths not of laurel but of oak, for

> Laurels were still unknown; Apollo then
> The greenery of any tree would wear
> For garlanding his long and lovely hair.

> (*Met.* I.450–51; trans. A.D. Melville)

While the links between tales in the *Metamorphoses* sometimes appear quite tenuous, certainly here Ovid means his readers to keep in mind Apollo conqueror of Python as we read of Apollo conqueror of Daphne. We see the god in the Daphne story in many of his aspects—as god of prophecy, and medicine, and music, and the shepherding of flocks—but he is here too, just as in the preceding tale, the god of sun, and light, and order, and civilization, whose task it is to repress chaos and establish harmony in the world. Like the Python, Daphne is a wild creature, untamed; in her rejection of love and marriage, she is unnatural and a threat to human society. Like the Python, Daphne (a "militant virgin," as Sara Mack has aptly called her) must be subdued, and so Apollo, while he cannot possess her in quite the way he initially desires, ultimately does subject her to order and—with a prophetic, typically Ovidian glance forward into the world of

Rome and the Augustan Age—he even presses her into the service of the state. From the traditional patriarchal Roman perspective, Apollo might be construed as the hero of this tale, a hero whose ultimate *Romanitas* would be praiseworthy, and with whose victimization by Cupid and rejection by Daphne one could sympathize. Thus viewed, the sun-god's triumph is the triumph of reason, essential to the progress of civilization as Ovid depicts it in the ever-evolving fantasy world of his *Metamorphoses*.

But from a different perspective—one that Ovid expects his audience to appreciate—Apollo is a tyrant, arrogant, insensitive, a stalker, a would-be rapist. With all his belief in order and reason, he is himself fully vulnerable to passion, to Cupid's arrows. His posturing ineptitudes are laughable. And in the end, like a spoiled child, what he cannot have he transforms and thus destroys. The true hero here is Daphne, whose virtues (if not wholly the "traditional" Roman virtues) are her filial devotion, her piety toward Diana (Apollo's sister—an undeveloped plot complication), her affinity to nature (she is a country, not a city, girl), and her steadfast resistance to change and seduction (even as a tree she resists Apollo's embrace).

What makes this tale so typically Ovidian is that we are allowed by the poet both these perspectives. We can see order prevail in the end, and at the same time laugh at Apollo's arrogant and stumblefooted progress toward that end. The presentation is characteristically Ovidian in its combination of drama and levity; it is epic in its introduction of divine and heroic action, and comic in the in-

"Apollo and the Nymphs," François Girardon, ca. 1666, Park of Versailles

termittently burlesque treatment of Apollo; it has an affinity in one moment to Vergil's *Aeneid*, in another to the spirit of Roman satire (with its element of *spoudaiogeloion*, the humorous treatment of serious matters), and again to Ovid's own earlier work in its elegiac handling of romantic elements (Apollo "reminds one," as A. G. Lee has remarked, "of the conventional lover of Roman elegy"—and the Cupid of this story is very much the same *saevus puer* we shall see in *Amores* I.1–2 later in this book).

The tale that follows this one immediately in the *Metamorphoses* is another story of a woman raped by a god and transformed (Jupiter turns the beautiful Io into a cow so that he can avoid the wrath of his wife Juno); there is, in fact, a series of such tales in the poem (five in Books I-II alone), and each is characterized by an ambiguity, an ambivalence between the frivolity and *machismo* of the gods' amorous adventures and the darkness of rape and victimization. When Daphne, the laurel tree, nods her "head" at the close of the tale, we would do well to consider whether she is nodding in compliant approval of Apollo's victory or rather out of satisfaction with her own.

Apollo Takes Charge of His Muses

They sat there, nine women, much the same age,
The same poppy-red hair, and similar complexions
Freckling much the same in the summer glare,
The same bright eyes of green melting to blue
Melting to golden brown, they sat there,
Nine women, all of them very quiet, one,
Perhaps, was looking at her nails, one plaited
Her hair in narrow strands, one stared at a stone,
One let fall a mangled flower from her hands,
All nine of them very quiet, and the one who spoke
Said, softly:

"Of course he was very charming, and he smiled,
Introduced himself and said he'd heard good things,
Shook hands all round, greeted us by name,
Assured us it would all be much the same,
Explained his policies, his few minor suggestions
Which we would please observe. He looked forward
To working with us. Wouldn't it be fun? Happy
To answer any questions. Any questions? But
None of us spoke or raised her hand, and questions
There were none; what has poetry to do with reason
Or the sun?"

A. E. Stallings

452   **Prīmus . . . Pēnēia**: supply **fuit**; ellipsis.

   ***Phoebus, -ī,** m., *Phoebus* (in origin a Greek term meaning "shining one," which came to be used as an epithet of Apollo, son of Jupiter and Latona, in his role as sun-god).

   ***Daphnē, Daphnēs,** f., *Daphne* (originally the Greek word for "laurel tree," but in this myth the name of a nymph, daughter of the river god Peneus).

      For the Greek case endings, commonly used by Ovid with proper nouns, cf. **Phoebēs** (476 below) and **Thisbē** and **Eurydicē** in the following stories.

   ***Pēnēius, -a, -um,** *of Peneus, child of Peneus* (god of the river Peneus, which flowed from Mt. Pindus through the vale of Tempe in the Greek district of Thessaly).

   quem: the antecedent is **amor**.

   quem nōn: the abrupt rhythms created by the monosyllables at line's end (and continued with **fors** 453) help to focus attention on the crucial point in the following verse; cf. **quae nōn** (499).

453   ***fors, fortis,** f., *chance, destiny*.

   ***ignārus, -a, -um,** *ignorant, unknowing, unaware*.

      fors ignāra . . . saeva . . . īra: chiasmus underscores the contrast—a favorite device in Ovid and other Latin poets; **dedit** goes with both nouns.

   ***Cupīdō, Cupīdinis,** m., *Cupid* (Venus' son and the god of physical love).

      Cupid was often depicted as a cruel or vindictive child; the transferred epithet in **saeva . . . īra** (452) emphasizes this point (cf. **saeve puer,** *Am.* I.1.5 below).

454   **Dēlius, -ī,** m., *the Delian* (Apollo, so-called from his birth to Latona on the Aegean island of Delos).

   hunc: with **flectentem cornua**, i.e., Cupid.

   ***serpēns, serpentis,** m., *snake, serpent*.

      victō serpente: abl. absolute, probably causal in force (explaining **superbus**), *because he had defeated the Python*; in the preceding passage, Ovid had described Apollo's victory over the monstrous snake Python, in celebration of which the god instituted the sacred Pythian games.

      serpente superbus: alliteration, and perhaps a deliberate onomatopoeia to suggest the snake's hissing.

455   **addūcō, addūcere, addūxī, adductus,** *to lead on, bring; to draw back, pull taut*.

   ***flectō, flectere, flexī, flexus,** *to bend, curve; to turn*.

   ***cornū, -ūs,** n., *animal's horn, object made of horn*; here, *bow*, poetic pl. for sing. (or possibly with reference to the type of bow made of two animal horns connected with a centerpiece).

   ***nervus, -ī,** m., *muscle, nerve; cord* (made of such material), *string* (of a musical instrument or a bow).

      adductō . . . nervō: these words aptly enclose **cornua**, just as the bowstring itself stretched from one end of the bow to the other.

452   Prīmus amor Phoebī Daphnē Pēnēia, quem nōn
453   fors ignāra dedit, sed saeva Cupīdinis īra.
454   Dēlius hunc nūper, victō serpente superbus,
455   vīderat adductō flectentem cornua nervō,
456   "Quid"que, "tibī, lascīve puer, cum fortibus armīs?"
457   dīxerat; "Ista decent umerōs gestāmina nostrōs,

---

*In nova fert animus mutātās dīcere fōrmās
corpora. Dī, coeptīs—nam vōs mutāstis et illās—
adspīrāte meīs prīmāque ab orīgine mundī
ad mea perpetuum dēdūcite tempora carmen.*

My heart compels the tale of shapes transformed.
Oh, gods—for you have wrought those transformations—
inspire my start, and from the world's creation
spin out this song continuing to modern times.

Ovid Met. I.1–4

---

456   **Quid . . . tibī:** supply **est,** *what business do you have* (lit., *what is it to
        you*—cf. the poet's own question to Cupid in *Am.* I.1.5 below).
        que: commonly used by Ovid, especially with quotations, the conjunction
        connects the parallel (and identically positioned) verbs **vīderat** (455) and
        dīxerat (457).
        lascīvus, -a, -um, *playful, mischievous, naughty.*
        cum fortibus armīs: i.e., *with a warrior's weapons,* a deliberate contrast
        with **lascīve puer.** For the application of military imagery to affairs of the
        heart, cf. *Am.* I.2 and 9 below.
457   **iste, ista, istud,** *that, that . . . of yours* (often, as here, with a disparaging
        sense).
        *****decet, decēre, decuit,** *to adorn; to be right for* (+ acc.); impers., *it is right,
        suitable.*
        *****umerus, -ī,** m., *shoulder.*
        gestāmen, gestāminis, n., *something worn/carried on the body, ornament,
        equipment.*
            Ista . . . umerōs gestāmina nostrōs: interlocked word order, a favorite
            device of Ovid's (cf. 466 below) and here appropriate to the image of
            the bow slung over the god's shoulder.
        nostrōs: instead of **meōs,** Apollo uses the "royal plural."

458   **quī . . . / quī (459):** a continuation of the plural in **nostrōs,** *of (gods like) us, who . . . (and) who . . .*; Apollo's point is underscored through placement of the repeated pronoun in the same metrical position in both verses, as well as the anaphora **dare . . . dare.**

     certa . . . vulnera: *inescapable wounds;* take with both **ferae** and **hostī.** The series of dactyls in this verse, and the predominantly dactylic rhythms in 459–60, suggest the swiftness and the sureness of the god's attack.

     ***fera, -ae,** f., *wild animal, beast.*

459   ***modo,** adv., *only recently, just now.*

     modo . . . modo: *at one time . . . at another.*

     pestiferus, -a, -um, *deadly, pestilential* (with **ventre**—adjective and noun are often widely separated in Latin verse, so it is essential to pay careful attention to the endings, which signal adjective-noun agreement).

     ***iūgerum, -ī,** n., *a measure of land;* pl., *an expanse of land, fields, acres.*

     venter, ventris, m., *belly, abdomen.*

     ***premō, premere, pressī, pressus,** *to press, press upon; to cover; to oppress.*

     prementem: the participle modifies **Pȳthōna** and has **iūgera** as its object; again, attention to word endings is crucial in verse, where the word order is much freer than in prose.

460   ***sternō, sternere, strāvī, strātus,** *to lay out, spread; to strike down, defeat.*

     ***innumerus, -a, -um,** *countless, innumerable.*

     ***tumidus, -a, -um,** *swollen* (here, with venom); *enraged, violent.*

     Pȳthōn, Pȳthōnis, acc., **Pȳthōna** (another common Greek case-ending—see on **Daphnē** 452), m., *Python* (the snake-beast slain by Apollo at Delphi).

     ***sagitta, -ae,** f., *arrow.*

     innumerīs . . . sagittīs: adjective-noun and other such pairs are often placed by Ovid at the caesura and at line's end, a device that picks out both the grammatical connection and the end-rhyme (cf. 468, 473, and X.238 below). Another effect of the arrangement here is that the beast is, literally, surrounded by the *countless arrows* that have laid him low (a device of word order often employed by Ovid and other Latin poets).

461   **Tū . . . tuā (462):** an emphatic contrast to **nostrōs** (457).

     ***fax, facis,** f., *torch; material used for a torch; flame of love.*

     nescio quōs . . . amōrēs: *some love affair or other;* **nescio** (with final -o shortened) together with **quis** or **quī** is regularly indefinite and often, as here, contemptuous.

     estō: future imperative of **sum, esse;** commonly this imperative has an almost legalistic tone (cf. IV.154 below).

     contentus: with **irrītāre.**

     ***amor, amōris,** m., *sexual passion, love;* pl., *the object of love, a lover; a love affair.*

462   **irrītō, -āre, -āvī, -ātus,** *to provoke; to excite, kindle.*

     ***laus, laudis,** f., *praise; reputation; praiseworthy act, honor.*

     asserō, asserere, asseruī, assertus, *to lay claim to, claim as one's own* (like **estō,** the verb has a legalistic sense—Apollo is "laying down the law").

     nostrās: i.e., *that are owed to us (me).*

458   quī dare certa ferae, dare vulnera possumus hostī,
459   quī modo, pestiferō tot iūgera ventre prementem,
460   strāvimus innumerīs tumidum Pȳthōna sagittīs.
461   Tū face nescio quōs estō contentus amōrēs
462   irrītāre tuā nec laudēs assere nostrās.''
463   Fīlius huic Veneris, ''Fīgat tuus omnia, Phoebe,
464   tē meus arcus,'' ait, ''quantōque animālia cēdunt
465   cūncta deō, tantō minor est tua glōria nostrā.''

Discussion Questions

1. How do the tale's opening lines (452–62) employ military imagery to anticipate the conflict between Cupid and Apollo?

2. What is the tone of Apollo's speech to Cupid (454–62) and what initial impression does it give you of the god's character?

3. What is the effect of the chiasmus in 463–64?

---

463   *Venus, Veneris, f., *Venus* (goddess of love and Cupid's mother).
        *fīgō, fīgere, fīxī, fīxus, *to drive in, insert; to transfix, pierce; to fix, press.*
        tuus omnia . . . / tē meus (464): chiasmus.
464   *arcus, -ūs, m., *a bow.*
             Fīgat . . . arcus (464): verb and subject neatly frame the purposely
             elliptical clause; the full expression would be **Tuus arcus omnia fīgat**
             et meus arcus tē fīgat.
        ait: with direct quotes the speech verb is often delayed (cf. **dīxerat** 457), but
        it should usually be translated with the subject and before the quotation
        (**Fīlius . . . Veneris . . . ait,** *The son of Venus says*).
        quantō . . . tantō (465): *by as much as . . . by that much* (abl. of degree of
        difference).
        animal, animālis, n., *an animal, any living thing* (including men as well as
        beasts, and even plants).
        *cēdō, cēdere, cessī, cessūrus, *to go, proceed*; + dat., *to yield to, be inferior
        to.*
465   nostrā: supply **glōriā**; abl. of comparison. The word deliberately, and
        contemptuously, echoes the identically positioned **nostrās** (462).

466   **Dīxit**: often used to mark the end of a direct quotation.

    ēlīdō, ēlīdere, ēlīsī, ēlīsus, *to break, shatter, crash through*.

    *****percutiō, percutere, percussī, percussus**, *to strike; to beat, shake violently*.

    *****āēr, āeris**, m., *air*.

    *****penna, -ae**, f., *wing; feather*.

        ēlīsō percussīs āere pennīs: an elaborate abl. absolute; freely, *crashing through the air with his beating wings*. The interlocked word order, with the violent participles first, then the nouns, suits the image of wings beating wildly through the air, and the s/-īs soundplay adds an onomatopoetic effect.

467   **impiger, impigra, impigrum**, *quick, swift* (here, with adverbial force, *swiftly*).

    umbrōsus, -a, -um, *shady*.

    Parnāsus, -ī, m., *Parnassus* (a mountain in Phocis, site of the holy city of Phocis and sacred to the Muses and Apollo).

    *****cōnstō, cōnstāre, cōnstitī, cōnstātūrus**, *to take up a position, stand upon, stand firmly*.

    arx, arcis, f., *citadel; hilltop, summit*.

        arce: supply **in**, and note that prepositions common in prose are frequently omitted in verse.

468   **ēque**: **ē** + **-que**.

    sagittiferus, -a, -um, *arrow-bearing* (cf. **sagittīs** 460).

    prōmō, prōmere, prōmpsī, prōmptus, *to bring forth, pull out*.

    tēlum, -ī, n., *weapon*.

    *****pharetra, -ae**, f., *quiver*.

        sagittiferā . . . duo tēla pharetrā: through a sort of chiastic word-picture, the arrows—or rather the words representing them, **duo tēla**—are actually "contained" within the quiver (and see on **innumerīs . . . sagittīs** 460).

469   *****dīversus, -a, -um**, *opposite; different; separate*.

    *****opus, operis**, n., *work, task; function, purpose*; **opus est** + abl., idiom, *there is need of* (something).

    *****fugō, -āre, -āvī, -ātus**, *to drive away, dispel, banish*.

    amōrem: object of both the preceding parallel phrases (which are in turn echoed in the opening phrases of 470 and 471).

470   **quod facit . . . / quod fugat** (471): understand **tēlum** as antecedent and **amōrem** as object of both clauses, each of which is followed by a strong diaeresis setting up the contrasting images. The contrast is further underscored through the anaphora and soundplay in **quod facit/quod fugat** (the verbs sound alike but have opposite meanings) and the chiasmus in **aurātum . . . acūtā / . . . obtūsum . . . plumbum** (471).

    *****aurātus, -a, -um**, *golden*.

    *****cuspis, cuspidis**, f., *sharp point, tip*.

    fulgeō, fulgēre, fulsī, fulsūrus, *to shine brightly, gleam*.

    *****acūtus, -a, -um**, *sharp, pointed* (cf. *Am.* I.1.11).

471   **obtūsus, -a, -um**, *blunt, dull*.

466   Dīxit et, ēlīsō percussīs āere pennīs,

467   impiger umbrōsā Parnāsī cōnstitit arce,

468   ēque sagittiferā prōmpsit duo tēla pharetrā

469   dīversōrum operum. Fugat hoc, facit illud amōrem;

470   quod facit, aurātum est et cuspide fulget acūtā,

471   quod fugat, obtūsum est et habet sub harundine plumbum.

472   Hoc deus in nymphā Pēnēide fīxit, at illō

473   laesit Apollineās trāiecta per ossa medullās.

Discussion Questions

1.   In what ways may the interaction of Cupid and Apollo in the opening scene (through verse 473) be regarded as allegorical? I.e., what broader, symbolic point is conveyed to the reader in Cupid's victory over Apollo?

2.   Comment on the word order in 473 and its appropriateness to the sense of the verse.

     sub: here, perhaps because arrows were generally stored tip downward in the quiver and then held with the tip downward until shot, *(down) at the tip of.*
     ***harundō, harundinis,** f., *reed; fishing rod; shaft of an arrow.*
     ***plumbum, -ī,** n., *lead.*
         The sound effects, especially alliteration of **b** and the **-um/-un-/-um-/-um** assonance, are aptly dull and leaden, in contrast to the harsher **c/g** alliteration used in describing the sharp arrow in the preceding verse.

472   **Hoc . . . illō**: the words (*the latter . . . the former*) are placed at the ends of the line to further emphasize the contrast between the two arrows.
     ***Pēnēis, Pēnēidos,** abl. sing., **Pēnēide,** voc. sing., **Pēnēi,** acc. pl., **Pēnēidas,** *of the river Peneus, descended from the river-god Peneus;* here, *daughter of Peneus* (see on 452). For the patronymic form and Greek case-endings, see on **Bēlis** (X.44 below).

473   ***laedō, laedere, laesī, laesus,** *to harm, hurt, wound.*
     Apollineus, -a, -um, *of Apollo.*
     trāiciō, trāicere, trāiēcī, trāiectus, *to throw across; to transfix, pierce.*
     medulla, -ae, f., usually pl., *the marrow of the bones* (often used, as in English, of one's innermost soul and emotions).
         illō / . . . Apollineās . . . medullās (473): a neat, lilting alliteration, underscored through the placement of **illō** and **medullās** at lines' end.

474   *prōtinus, adv., *immediately.*
       alter amat, fugit altera: chiasmus again underscores the opposing actions.
       nōmen amantis: *the very word "lover"* (lit., *the name of a lover*).
475   latebra, -ae, f., often pl., *hiding place; refuge.*
       latebrīs . . . / exuviīs (476): supply **in**, with **gaudēns**.
       *captīvus, -a, -um, *captured, captive.*
476   exuviae, -ārum, f. pl., *armor, spoils; the hide stripped from a beast.*
       innūptus, -a, -um, *unwed, maiden.*
       aemula, -ae, f., *(female) rival.*
       *Phoebē, Phoebēs, f., *Diana* (sister of Phoebus Apollo and virgin goddess of
          the moon, wild animals, and woodlands).
          For the root meaning of the name, see on **Phoebus** (452); and for the
            word's Greek case endings (here gen.), cf. **Daphnē** (452).
477   coerceō, -ēre, -uī, -itus, *to restrain, confine; to hold back.*
       positōs: i.e., **dispositōs** (in poetry the simple form of a verb was often used
          in place of a compound), *arranged.*
       *lēx, lēgis, f., *law; rule, regulation, order.*
          sine lēge: i.e., *carelessly;* cf. the description of Daphne's hair at 497.
478   illam petiēre; illa . . . petentēs: anaphora; this and the three quick elisions
       suggest how abruptly Daphne rejected all suitors.
       petiēre: for **petīvērunt**; the alternative 3rd pers. pl. perf. ending -ēre is
          common in Latin verse, as are perf. system forms with the intervocalic -v-
          omitted (cf. **fīnierat** 566 for **fīnīverat**, and **agitāsse** 567 for **agitāvisse**).
       āversor, -ārī, -ātus sum, *to turn away from; to reject.*
479   impatiēns, impatientis + gen., *impatient/intolerant* (of).
       expers, expertis + gen., *inexperienced* (with), *without knowledge* (of).
       virī: construe with both preceding adjectives.
       nemus, nemoris, n., *woodland, forest; (sacred) grove.*
       āvius, -a, -um, *pathless, unfrequented; remote.*
       lūstrō, -āre, -āvī, -ātus, *to move around; to wander through, roam.*
480   quid . . . quid . . . quid: anaphora and asyndeton accentuate the series; the
       indirect questions, with **sint**, depend upon **cūrat**.
       Hymēn, Hymēnis, m., *a refrain shouted at weddings; marriage;* often, and
          probably here (with **Amor**), *Hymen* (the god of marriage—cf. X.2 below).
       Amor: Ovid refers not just to love, but to Cupid himself, who as god of love
          was often called Amor (cf. 532).
       *cōnūbium, -ī, n., often pl. for sing., *marriage, wedding rites.*
481   gener, generī, m., *son-in-law.*
482   saepe pater dīxit: the anaphora suits the point explicit in **saepe**; likewise the
       repetitions and chiastic arrangement of "Generum mihi, fīlia, dēbēs"; /
       . . . "Dēbēs mihi, nāta, nepōtēs" suggest Peneus' insistent tone.
       nāta, -ae, f., *daughter.*
       nepōs, nepōtis, m./f., *grandchild; descendant.*
483   velut, adv., often introducing similes, *just as, just like; as if, as though (it
       were).*

474	Prōtinus alter amat, fugit altera nōmen amantis,
475	silvārum latebrīs captīvārumque ferārum
476	exuviīs gaudēns, innūptaeque aemula Phoebēs;
477	vitta coercēbat positōs sine lēge capillōs.
478	Multī illam petiēre; illa, āversāta petentēs
479	impatiēns expersque virī, nemora āvia lūstrat,
480	nec, quid Hymēn, quid Amor, quid sint cōnūbia, cūrat.
481	Saepe pater dīxit, "Generum mihi, fīlia, dēbēs";
482	saepe pater dīxit, "Dēbēs mihi, nāta, nepōtēs."
483	Illa, velut crīmen taedās exōsa iugālēs,
484	pulchra verēcundō suffunditur ōra rubōre,

Discussion Question

What is the significance of Daphne's emulation of Diana (474–80) and how, in the context of this story, is it ironic?

*crīmen, crīminis, n., *charge, accusation; misdeed, crime.*

exōsus, -a, -um + acc., *hating, detesting.*

iugālis, -is, -e, *of marriage, matrimonial, nuptial.*

taedās . . . iugālēs: by metonymy, *marriage;* torches were carried by the celebrants in Roman weddings.

484   pulchra . . . rubōre: note the line's interlocked word order and axial symmetry, with the adjectives preceding, the verb at center, and the nouns following ($A^1 A^2 V N^1 N^2$)—sometimes called a "golden line," the arrangement was a favorite of Ovid's (cf. 528–29 and X.22 below).

verēcundus, -a, -um, *modest, chaste.*

suffundō, suffundere, suffūdī, suffūsus, *to pour on; to cover, fill.*

ōra: acc. of respect or specification, a Greek construction commonly used in Latin verse, especially of parts of the body; *her face is covered* (lit., *she is covered with respect to her face).* The pl. of ōs was often used for the sing. in verse.

rubor, rubōris, m., *blush.*

485   **inque . . . lacertīs:** interlocked order again—take **in** and **patris** with **cervīce**, and **blandīs** with **lacertīs**.

     *__blandus, -a, -um__, *coaxing, flattering; persuasive, enticing.*

        blandīs . . . lacertīs: a transferred epithet, as it is not, strictly speaking, her arms, but Daphne herself who coaxes her father into a change of heart.

     *__cervīx, cervīcis__, f., often pl. for sing., *the neck.*

     *__lacertus, -ī__, m., *arm,* especially the *upper arm* (as in an embrace—cf. 501).

486   **perpetuā:** with **virginitāte** (487).

     *__genitor, genitōris__, m., *father, creator.*

     cārissime: Daphne's words as well as her embraces are designed to persuade.

487   **virginitās, virginitātis**, f., virginity, maidenhood.

        virginitāte fruī: Daphne's entreaty is given special point through enjambement and the heavy pentasyllabic word.

     fruor, fruī, frūctus sum + abl., *to enjoy.*

        fruī: with **dā mihi**, *grant it to me to enjoy.*

     pater: i.e., Jupiter.

     Diānae: indirect object with **dedit**, paralleling **Dā mihi** in the preceding clause, but also in a possessive sense with **pater**; Daphne again turns to Diana as a model (cf. 476) in her resistance to Apollo.

488   **obsequor, obsequī, obsecūtus sum**, *to comply, obey.*

     tē . . . vetat (489): the prose order would be **iste decor tē esse vetat quod optās**; for added vividness, the narrator addresses Daphne directly.

     decor, decōris, m., *beauty, grace; elegance, charm.*

        Note the parallelism of **Ille . . . obsequitur . . . decor iste . . . vetat** (489), contrasting her father's compliance with what Daphne's own beauty forbids.

     quod optās: *what you desire.*

489   *__vōtum, -ī__, n., *vow; prayer, wish.*

     *__fōrma, -ae__, f., *form, shape; beauty.*

     repugnō, -āre, -āvī, -ātūrus, *to offer resistance, fight back; to oppose, be inconsistent with* + dat.

        esse . . . repugnat: the line's "special effects" are spectacular; the alliterative juxtaposition of the antithetical **vetat** and **vōtō**, the harsh repetition of **t** (six times), the mournful assonance of long **ō** at the center of the verse, the chiasmus **vōtōque tuō tua fōrma**, and the strong, metaphorical verb **repugnat** at line's end all dramatize the impossibility of the maiden's prayer.

490   **vīsae . . . Daphnēs:** with both **amat** and **cupit cōnūbia**; freely, *as soon as he has seen Daphne, he loves her and desires to marry her.*

     cupit . . . cupit (491): the word is repeated for emphasis, and perhaps as a reminder of Cupid's role (the god's name and the verb **cupere** are, of course, from the same root).

     Daphnēs: gen., whereas in English we might say *marriage with Daphne.*

491   **quod . . . cupit:** object of **spērat**, *he hopes (to achieve)*; cf. **spērandō** (496).

     ōrāculum, -ī, n., *oracle;* here, *oracular ability.*

485 inque patris blandīs haerēns cervīce lacertīs,
486 "Dā mihi perpetuā, genitor cārissime," dīxit,
487 "virginitāte fruī; dedit hoc pater ante Diānae."
488 Ille quidem obsequitur; sed tē decor iste, quod optās,
489 esse vetat, vōtōque tuō tua fōrma repugnat.
490 Phoebus amat vīsaeque cupit cōnūbia Daphnēs,
491 quodque cupit, spērat, suaque illum ōrācula fallunt.
492 Utque levēs stipulae dēmptīs adolentur aristīs,

Discussion Questions

1. How is the interlocked order of 485 suited to the sense?

2. Comment on the vignette of Daphne and her father Peneus (481–88); how are his demands typical of any Greek or Roman father, and by what devices does Daphne persuade him to set them aside?

---

*fallō, fallere, fefellī, falsus, *to deceive, trick; to disappoint*; (of time) *to while away, beguile*.

   illum ōrācula fallunt: the lilting alliteration adds to the mood; the point here is that a god with Apollo's prophetic powers (sua here is especially emphatic) should not be "hoping" for anything, since he ought to know precisely what the future holds.

492   Ut ... / ut (493) ... / sīc ... (495): *Just as ... just as ... so. ...*; these words set up the first of two extended similes in the story.

*levis, -is, -e, *light* (in weight); *nimble; gentle; unsubstantial, thin*.

*stipula, -ae, f., *stalk* (of a grain plant); *stubble* (left in a field once the grain has been harvested), *straw*.

*dēmō, dēmere, dēmpsī, dēmptus, *to remove, take away; to cut off*.

adoleō, adolēre, adoluī, adultus, *to burn ritually, cremate; to destroy by fire, burn*.

   adolentur: fields were burnt off to increase their fertility, but the flame that consumes Apollo has an opposite effect (see sterilem 496); Ovid may intend the reader to think of the verb's association with ritual.

arista, -ae, f., *grain, kernel*.

493   **facibus**: antecedent of **quās**; cf. the effect of Cupid's torch, **face** (461).

    saepēs, saepis, f., *hedge.*

    viātor: travelers used torches to light their way at night.

494   **nimis**: with **admōvit**, *too close.*

    sub lūce: sc. **prīmā**, *just before dawn.*

    relīquit: i.e., which he *has left* unextinguished and still smoldering.

495   **in flammās abiit**: *became totally inflamed* (lit., *passed into flames*).

    pectore tōtō: sc. **in.**

496   ***ūrō, ūrere, ussī, ustus**, *to destroy by fire, burn* (here, metaphorically, *with passion*—cf. *Am.* I.1.26 below).

    sterilis, -is, -e, *barren, sterile* (here literally and figuratively, as Apollo's love will be unfulfilled and his hoped-for lover forever chaste).

    spērandō: cf. **spērat** (491); Ovid emphasizes again the futility (and, for a god with oracular powers, the folly) of Apollo's hopes.

    ***nūtriō, -īre, -īvī, -ītus**, *to feed at the breast; to support, nourish.*

        ūritur . . . nūtrit: the u/t/r soundplay that runs through the line underscores the antithesis between these two verbs, the first of which (enjambed and with a strong diaeresis following) connotes destruction and the other sustenance.

497   **inōrnātus, -a, -um**, *unadorned, dishevelled.*

        inōrnātōs . . . capillōs: cf. **positōs . . . capillōs** (477); the word order here suggests Daphne's tresses of hair falling all around her neck. The -ll- alliteration adds an aptly delicate touch.

    ***collum, -ī**, n., *neck* (here sc. **in**).

    ***pendeō, pendēre, pependī**, *to be suspended, hang; to hang down* (upon or over).

        pendēre capillōs: acc. + infin. dependent on **spectat.**

498   ***cōmō, cōmere, cōmpsī, cōmptus**, *to make beautiful, adorn; to dress, arrange, comb.*

        Quid, sī cōmantur: sc. **capillī** as subject; Apollo imagines the nymph as even more beautiful with a proper "hairdo."

    ait: again the speech verb is delayed but should precede the quotation in English translation; cf. 464.

    ***ignis, ignis**, m., *fire.*

499   ***sīdus, sīderis**, n., *star, planet*; usually pl., *the stars.*

        sīderibus . . . satis (500): the gasping alliteration of **s**, the stunned assonance of **oculōs . . . ōscula** (*Oh . . . oh . . .*), and the rushing dactyls interrupted at line's end by the succession of monosyllables **quae nōn / est**, all suggest Apollo's quickening pulse and his breathlessness at the sight of the nymph's overpowering beauty.

    ***ōsculum, -ī**, n., diminutive of **ōs, ōris**, n., lit., *little mouth*; most commonly *kiss* or, pl., *lips* (but generally with a kiss in mind!).

    quae: object of **vīdisse**; the infin. phrase is in turn subject of **est**, *which it is not enough (merely) to have seen* (and not, i.e., to have tasted).

500   **digitōsque manūsque / bracchiaque et . . . lacertōs** (501): polysyndeton, used here to "visualize," almost cinematographically, how Apollo shifts his

493   ut facibus saepēs ardent, quās forte viātor

494   vel nimis admōvit vel iam sub lūce relīquit,

495   sīc deus in flammās abiit, sīc pectore tōtō

496   ūritur, et sterilem spērandō nūtrit amōrem.

497   Spectat inōrnātōs collō pendēre capillōs,

498   et "Quid, sī cōmantur?" ait; videt igne micantēs

499   sīderibus similēs oculōs; videt ōscula, quae nōn

500   est vīdisse satis; laudat digitōsque manūsque

Discussion Questions

1.   What is the intended emotional effect of the anaphora in 495?

2.   What are the several points of comparison in the extended simile in verses 492–96. How is the simile appropriate to a description of Apollo as god of the sun? How is it appropriate in view of the reference to Cupid in 461?

And as in empty fields the stubble burns,
Or nightly travellers, when day returns,
Their useless torches on dry hedges throw,
That catch the flames, and kindle all the row;
So burns the god, consuming in desire,
And feeding in his breast a fruitless fire.

John Dryden, 1693

gaze from one part of Daphne's body to another, and another, and yet another. Note too the progression—a variant of the tricolon crescens (cf. 512–13)—from fingertips and hands, to forearms, and on to *her more than half-bare upper arms* (and then, tantalizingly, to **sīqua latent**); the god's passion is heating up here, but a further point of this focus on appendages becomes clear later in the story (cf. **bracchia** 550).

501   *bracchium, -ī, n., *forearm.*

      *nūdus, -a, -um, *naked; unadorned.*

      nūdōs mediā plūs parte: *more than half exposed* (lit., with abl. of degree of difference, *exposed by more than the middle part*), i.e., bare almost to the shoulder.

502   sī qua latent: *whatever (charms) lie hidden.*

      *ōcior, ōcior, ōcius, compar. adj., *swifter, more fleeting* (here with adverbial sense).

      ōcior aurā / illa levī (503): interlocked order.

      *aura, -ae, f., *breath of air, breeze.*

503   revocantis: *as he* (i.e., Apollo) *calls her back* (lit., *of him calling her back*).

      *resistō, resistere, restitī, *to pause in one's journey, halt, stop.*

504   Nympha . . . manē . . . / nympha, manē (505): anaphora underscores the god's urgency.

      *precor, -ārī, -ātus sum, *to pray for, beg*; parenthetically in the 1st pers. sing., *I beseech, pray.*

      Pēnēi: Greek voc. form, *daughter of Peneus* (see on Pēnēis 472).

      *īnsequor, īnsequī, īnsecūtus sum, *to pursue, chase.*

      hostis: *as an enemy.*

505   Sīc: supply ut mē fugis, *just as you are fleeing me, so. . . .* ; anaphora and asyndeton mark out the series of comparisons.

      agna, -ae, f., *ewe lamb.*

        agna lupum . . . aquilam . . . columbae (506): chiasmus.

      cerva, -ae, f., *female deer, doe.*

506   aquila, -ae, f., *eagle.*

      *trepidō, -āre, -āvī, -ātus, *to panic; to tremble, quiver.*

      *columba, -ae, f., *pigeon, dove.*

        fugiunt trepidante columbae: the clattering dentals and quick dactyls suggest the birds' alarm.

507   *quisque, quaeque, quidque, *each* (here, *each creature*; sc. fugit).

      amor . . . sequendī: i.e., not an enemy's hostile intent. Note the phrase's parallelism to sim tibi causa dolōris (509); Apollo's point is that amor should not beget dolor.

508   Mē miserum: acc. of exclamation.

      nē: with all three jussives, cadās, notent, and sim.

      *indignus, -a, -um, *unworthy (of), not deserving (to)* + infin.; *innocent.*

        indigna: probably n. acc. pl. with crūra (509), though it might, like prōna, modify the understood subject of cadās (Daphne); the sense is much the same either way.

509   crūs, crūris, n., *leg, shin.*

      *notō, -āre, -āvī, -ātus, *to mark, brand; to scar; to notice; to inscribe.*

      sentis, sentis, m., *thorny bush, bramble, briar.*

510   *asper, aspera, asperum, *rough, harsh* (to the touch); *wild, uncultivated.*

      quā, adv., *in which part, where.*

      *properō, -āre, -āvī, -ātus, *to act with haste, be quick; to hurry, rush* (either

501   bracchiaque et nūdōs mediā plūs parte lacertōs;
502   sī qua latent, meliōra putat.

Fugit ōcior aurā

503   illa levī neque ad haec revocantis verba resistit:
504   "Nympha, precor, Pēnēi, manē! Nōn īnsequor hostis;
505   nympha, manē! Sīc agna lupum, sīc cerva leōnem,
506   sīc aquilam pennā fugiunt trepidante columbae,
507   hostēs quaeque suōs; amor est mihi causa sequendī.
508   Mē miserum—nē prōna cadās, indignave laedī
509   crūra notent sentēs, et sim tibi causa dolōris!
510   Aspera, quā properās, loca sunt: moderātius, ōrō,
511   curre fugamque inhibē; moderātius īnsequar ipse.
512   Cui placeās, inquīre tamen; nōn incola montis,
513   nōn ego sum pāstor, nōn hīc armenta gregēsque

Discussion Question

How does the poet's language in 497–502 compel readers to visualize the scene?

---

with a direct object or intransitively).

    properās: the breathless dactyls of 510–11 match Apollo's rapid pace.

*moderātus, -a, -um, *temperate, moderate, restrained*; here, *slow*.

    moderātius . . . moderātius (511): another urgent repetition (cf. **manē**
       . . . manē 504–05 and **Nescīs . . . nescīs** 514), but a humorous one;
       Apollo pleads with Daphne, not to stop, but just to slow down, and he
       promises (do we believe him?) that he will do likewise.

511   ***fuga, -ae**, f., *running away, flight*.

    inhibeō, -ēre, -uī, -itus, *to restrain, hold back*.

512   **Cui placeās**: subjn. indirect question with **inquīre** (which in standard prose
    order would precede).

    inquīrō, inquīrere, inquīsīvī, inquīsītus, *to search out, inquire, ask*.

    nōn . . . / nōn . . . nōn (513): anaphora, use of the pronoun subject **ego**,
       and the tricolon crescens all emphasize Apollo's indignation.

513   **pāstor, pāstōris**, m., *shepherd*.

    armentum, -ī, n., *herd of cattle*.

    grex, gregis, m., *herd, flock (of sheep)*.

       Apollo was himself god of shepherds, but he does not want this lovely
       girl to mistake him for one of them.

514   **horridus, -a, -um**, *having a rough surface; rough, wild, uncouth.*

515   **ideō**, adv., *for that reason, therefore.*

     Mihi . . . servit (516): the pronoun's position adds to the impression of the god's arrogance, as does his enumeration of the several shrines at which he was worshiped (the last three of them in Asia Minor); polysyndeton and the rapid dactylic rhythm add to the effect.

     Delphicus, -a, -um, *Delphic, of Delphi* (a town of Phocis known as the site of Apollo's oracle—see on **Parnāsī** 467).

     ***tellūs, tellūris**, f., *land, earth.*

516   **Claros, Clarī**, f., *Claros* (an Ionian town sacred to Apollo).

     Tenedos, Tenedī, f., *Tenedos* (an Aegean island off the coast of Troy where there was also a temple dedicated to the god).

     Patarēus, -a, -um, *of Patara* (a coastal city in Lycia, site of another oracle of Apollo).

     ***rēgia, -ae**, f., *palace, royal house;* here, *shrine.*

     serviō, -īre, -īvī, -ītūrus + dat., *to serve* (a master), *be the servant of.*

         servit: sing. to agree with the nearest noun in the series, but also because all these lands and their shrines are thought of collectively, and through personification, as slave to the god's dominion.

517   ***Iuppiter, Iovis**, m., *Jupiter* (the Roman sky-god, father of Apollo by Latona).

     Iuppiter est genitor: assonance underscores the boast.

     per mē . . . per mē (518): again the pronouns (cf. **mihi** 515), anaphora, and polysyndeton punctuate the deity's boast.

518   ***pateō, patēre, patuī**, *to be open; to be visible/revealed.*

     concordō, -āre, -āvī, -ātūrus, *to live in harmony; to be in harmony, harmonize.*

     ***carmen, carminis**, n., *ritual utterance, chant, hymn; song, poem.*

         concordant carmina: an aptly harmonious assonance.

     nervīs: *with the strings (of a lyre)*; see on **nervus** (455). Apollo was the god of music.

519   **Certa . . . nostra est**: sc. **sagitta** from the next clause (and in that clause sc. **est** from here); Apollo was the archer god (cf. **sagittīs** 460).

     Certa . . . nostra . . . nostrā . . . / certior (520): chiasmus emphasizes the contrast, as do the enjambement of **certior** (to the same metrical position as **certa**) and the diaeresis following.

520   **in vacuō**: with **pectore**; in prose the relative pronoun would precede.

     ***vacuus, -a, -um**, *empty, hollow; carefree, fancy-free* (cf. *Am.* I.1.26 below); + abl., *devoid (of), free (from).*

     vulnera: this wound metaphor sets up the reference to Apollo's association with the healing arts in 521–24; Apollo was patron of medicine, but he could not heal his own wounds (just as, though a prophet, he could not foresee his own future—see 491).

521   **inventum, -ī**, n., *discovery, invention.*

     opifer, opifera, opiferum, *bringing help, aiding*; here an epithet of Apollo, *bringer of aid.*

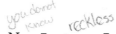

514 horridus observō. Nescīs, temerāria, nescīs
515 quem fugiās, ideōque fugis. Mihi Delphica tellūs
516 et Claros et Tenedos Patarēaque rēgia servit;
517 Iuppiter est genitor; per mē quod eritque fuitque
518 estque patet; per mē concordant carmina nervīs.
519 Certa quidem nostra est, nostrā tamen ūna sagitta
520 certior, in vacuō quae vulnera pectore fēcit.
521 Inventum medicīna meum est, opiferque per orbem
522 dīcor, et herbārum subiecta potentia nōbīs;
523 ei mihi, quod nūllīs amor est sānābilis herbīs,

"Daphne and Apollo," Wilhelm Baur, 1639

---

*orbis, orbis, m., *disc, any disc-shaped object; wheel; orb* (of the sun or moon); *the world.*

522 *herba, -ae, f., *small plant, herb; grass.*

  herbārum . . . nōbīs: the prose order would be **potentia herbārum nōbīs** (dat. with compounds) **subiecta (est).**

  subiciō, subicere, subiēcī, subiectus, *to cast upward*; + dat., *to place beneath, place under the control of.*

  *potentia, -ae, f., *power, potency*; here, *healing power.*

523 ei, (monosyllabic) interj. expressing anguish and used commonly with **mihi**, *oh miserable me!*

  nūllīs: set far in advance of **herbīs** for emphasis; the point Apollo makes is in one sense invalid, since Ovid himself had authored a tongue-in-cheek poetry book titled *Remedia Amoris* ("Cures for Love")!

  sānābilis, -is, -e, *curable, remediable.*

524 ***prōsum, prōdesse, prōfuī** + dat., irreg., *to be of use to, benefit, help*; +infin., *to be beneficial* (to do something).
  quae: the antecedent, **artēs**, follows the relative clause, rather than preceding it, an arrangement common in verse.
  artēs: i.e., of medicine.
  nec . . . artēs: the parallel ABCABCD structure, with the subject **artēs** delayed to line's end, effectively closes Apollo's plaint.

525 **locūtūrum**: supply **Apollinem** (object of **fūgit**); English would use a clause rather than the participial phrase, *as he was about to say more.*
  *timidus, -a, -um, *fearful, timorous* (though sometimes applied to situations rather than persons, the word here is, strictly speaking, a transferred epithet—cf. IV.100 below).
  cursus, -ūs, m., (the act of) *running, flight; course.*

526 **fūgit . . . relīquit**: the line's clipped spondees, elisions, and framing verbs underscore the abruptness of Daphne's flight from the god's impassioned appeal; **fūgit** here is not just *fled*, but *outdistanced* or (nearly) *escaped.*
  cum . . . ipsō: sc. **deō.**
  imperfectus, -a, -um, *incomplete, unfinished.*

527 **Tum quoque**: i.e., even as she quickened her flight.
  vīsa: supply **est** (ellipsis—forms of the verb **sum, esse** are frequently omitted in Latin prose and verse).
  decēns, decentis, *fitting, appropriate; graceful, attractive.*
  nūdō, -āre, -āvī, -ātus, *to strip, lay bare, expose.*
    nūdābant . . . vibrābant (528) . . . dabat (529): the near-rhyming and similarly positioned "continuous action" imperfects, each with object/subject or subject/object following, provide a sort of motion picture of the nymph's flight.
  corpora: pl. for sing., to suggest the parts of her body.

528 **obvius, -a, -um,** *in the way, opposing*; here, *at her face* or *oncoming.*
    obviaque . . . vestēs: with its v/s alliteration the line onomatopoetically suggests the whooshing sounds of Daphne's flight through the winds—the audio-track, as it were, to Ovid's video (cf. on *Am.* I.2.46 below).
    obvia . . . capillōs (529): two golden lines (cf. 484), with interlocked word order and verbal axial symmetry; the effect here is that we see the actions first, before the objects themselves.
  *adversus, -a, -um, *opposite (to), facing, turned toward.*
  vibrō, -āre, -āvī, -ātus, *to wave, (cause to) flutter.*
  flāmen, flāminis, n., *blast, gust (of wind); wind, breeze.*

529 **et levis . . . capillōs**: another highly musical verse, with alliteration of the sibilant s, the l/r liquids, and the assonant -ōs/-ō/-ōs, sounding almost like the shrieking of the wind as its breezes course around the nymph's body.
  levis: not *gentle* here, but *quick, fleeting.*
  *impellō, impellere, impulī, impulsus, *to strike, beat against; to motivate.*
    impulsōs . . . capillōs: Latin often uses a participle where English would use a finite verb; with **retrō dabat**, translate *struck against her hair*

524	nec prōsunt dominō, quae prōsunt omnibus, artēs!"
525	Plūra locūtūrum timidō Pēnēia cursū
526	fūgit, cumque ipsō verba imperfecta relīquit.
527	Tum quoque vīsa decēns: nūdābant corpora ventī,
528	obviaque adversās vibrābant flāmina vestēs,
529	et levis impulsōs retrō dabat aura capillōs,
530	auctaque fōrma fugā est. Sed enim nōn sustinet ultrā
531	perdere blanditiās iuvenis deus, utque monēbat

Discussion Questions

1. In lines 504–24, Apollo argues a number of different points in his effort to persuade Daphne to stop fleeing. What are his principal arguments and how do they reflect upon his character? Is this characterization consistent with his behavior in the story's opening scene?

2. Remembering that Apollo is racing madly after Daphne as he delivers the speech in 504–24, would you say that the overall effect of the scene is serious or comic? How does the content of the speech support your view?

and sent it streaming behind her.
*retrō, adv., *toward the rear, backwards, behind.*
530   enim: with sed, *but in fact*; i.e., despite Daphne's growing attractiveness, Apollo intends no more imploring speeches (like the one in 504–24) but will quicken his pursuit.
*sustineō, sustinēre, sustinuī, *to hold up, support; to sustain*; + infin., *to be able* (to do something) *without relenting.*
ultrā, adv., *on the far side, beyond; further, any longer.*
531   *perdō, perdere, perdidī, perditus, *to destroy, ruin; to waste.*
*blanditia, -ae, f., often pl. with sing. meaning, *flattery, alluring speech.*
monēbat: some manuscripts have movēbat, *was stirring* (for the idea cf. amor est mihi causa sequendī 507), but Amor here, with the intensive ipse, likely refers to Cupid himself (cf. 480) and monēbat is the livelier reading.

532 **admittō, admittere, admīsī, admissus**, *to admit, receive; to give rein to, direct.*

　*****passus, -ūs**, m., *step, pace, stride.*

　　admissō . . . passū: *with quickened pace.*

533 **Ut . . . cum . . . / sīc . . .** (539): *just as when . . . so . . .*; another extended simile (cf. 492–96).

　Gallicus, -a, -um, *Gallic, of Gaul* (a region of Europe north of Italy noted for its hunting dogs).

　*****arvum, -ī**, n., *field.*

　　canis . . . arvō: the interlocked order produces a neat word-picture with the rabbit actually situated in the middle of the desolate field and "trapped," so to speak, by the **canis . . . Gallicus**; Horace (*Odes* I.37.18–20) similarly compares Cleopatra, in her flight from Octavian after Actium, to a hunted rabbit.

534 **hic praedam . . . petit, ille salūtem**: note the ABCAB arrangement (which is replicated in 539), the quick dactyls, and the harsh **d/t/p** alliteration; take **pedibus petit** with both subjects (**hic**, the hound, and **ille**, the hare) and with both objects.

　*****praeda, -ae**, f., *booty, plunder; prey, game.*

　salūs, salūtis, f., *safety, well-being.*

535 **alter . . . / alter** (537): the two pairs of lines (535–36, 537–38) are neatly balanced, with the hound hoping to catch hold of its prey and snapping at it with its mouth, and the rabbit uncertain whether or not it has already been caught and ripping itself free from the hound's jaws.

　inhaereō, inhaerēre, inhaesī, inhaesūrus, *to be attached to, stick to*; (of an animal) *to hold on (to) with its teeth.*

　　inhaesūrō similis: *like an animal about to grab its prey with its teeth.*

　iam iamque: anaphora; this adv. is commonly repeated for emotional emphasis.

536 **spērat . . . rōstrō**: the verse is highly alliterative, and the series of harsh dentals (eight **t**'s) and the snarling **r**'s and **s**'s may be deliberately onomatopoetic.

　extentō . . . rōstrō: the parallelism with **admissō . . . passū** (532) reinforces the simile; here, with the wide separation of participle and noun, the phrase is stretched out across the verse, just as the dog's snout is extended in the direction of its prey—possibly an effect intended by Ovid.

　*****stringō, stringere, strīnxī, strictus**, *to bind, secure; to draw tight; to draw close to, touch.*

　rōstrum, -ī, n., *snout, muzzle.*

537 **ambiguum, -ī**, n., *ambiguity.*

　　in ambiguō, idiom, *in a state of uncertainty, uncertain.*

　*****an**, conj., often introducing indirect questions, *whether, or, if.*

　comprēndō, comprēndere, comprēndī, comprēnsus, *to seize, catch.*

538 *****morsus, -ūs**, m., *bite* (of an animal); pl., by metonymy, *teeth, jaws.*

　ēripitur: passive but with a reflexive sense (a usage comparable to the Greek middle voice and common in Latin poetry), *rips itself from.*

532	ipse Amor, admissō sequitur vēstīgia passū.
533	Ut canis in vacuō leporem cum Gallicus arvō
534	vīdit, et hic praedam pedibus petit, ille salūtem—
535	alter inhaesūrō similis iam iamque tenēre
536	spērat, et extentō stringit vēstīgia rōstrō;
537	alter in ambiguō est an sit comprēnsus, et ipsīs
538	morsibus ēripitur, tangentiaque ōra relinquit—
539	sīc deus et virgō; est hic spē celer, illa timōre.
540	Quī tamen īnsequitur, pennīs adiūtus Amōris,
541	ōcior est, requiemque negat, tergōque fugācis

Discussion Question

Compare the simile in 533–39 with those at 492–96 and 505–07; in what
respects are they alike and in what respects different? Which is more
sympathetic to Apollo? How does Ovid's comparison of Daphne with a
hunted animal relate to his depiction of her earlier in the story?

*tangō, tangere, tetigī, tāctus, *to touch.*
relinquit: here, *escapes from.*

539 hic spē celer, illa timōre: celer belongs with both phrases, just as pedibus
petit connects hic praedam and ille salūtem in 534; the repetition of
structure and diction between that line and this helps make the equation,
while the two couplets intervening describe first the hic (535–36), then the
ille (537–38).

*spēs, speī, f., *hope.*

540 Quī: supply is (i.e., Apollo) as antecedent.
Amōris: with pennīs adiūtus we are again meant to think not only of love
but of Cupid, who is controlling the action behind the scenes.

541 *requiēs, requiētis, acc. usually requiem, f., *rest, respite.*
*negō, -āre, -āvī, -ātus, *to say (that) not; to refuse, deny.*
tergō: dat. with imminet.
fugāx, fugācis, *evasive, fugitive* (used here as a noun).

542   **immineō, imminēre**, *to rise up, overhang*; + dat., *to press closely (upon); to threaten.*

    ***crīnis, crīnis**, m., *lock of hair*; pl. or collective sing., *hair.*

    ***spargō, spargere, sparsī, sparsus**, *to scatter, strew; to allow to stream out.*

    cervīcibus: supply **in**; here, as often with this word, pl. form with sing. meaning.

    afflō, -āre, -āvī, -ātus, *to breathe on, blow on.*

543   ***absūmō, absūmere, absūmpsī, absūmptus**, *to use up; to wear out, exhaust.*

    ***expallēscō, expallēscere, expalluī**, *to grow pale.*

       expalluit illa: the alliterative **-ll-** lends a delicate, perhaps even pathetic effect.

    ***citus, -a, -um**, *swift, rapid.*

545   ***ops, opis**, f., *power, ability; resources; aid.*

    ***flūmen, flūminis**, n., *stream, river.*

       flūmina . . . habētis: Daphne addresses the river's streams as the very spirit of her father, *if you streams have. . . .*; note the internal rhyme in **flūmina nūmen ha-.**

    ***nūmen, nūminis**, n., *nod (of assent); divine power, supernatural influence.*

547   **Quā:** again the antecedent (**figūram**) follows.

       There are interpolations and other corruptions in the manuscripts at this point in the text; the best solution seems to be to omit verse 546.

    ***nimium**, adv., *too much, excessively.*

    ***mūtō, -āre, -āvī, -ātus**, *to exchange; to change, replace; to transform.*

    ***figūra, -ae**, f., *form, composition; outward appearance.*

548   ***prex, precis**, f., *entreaty, prayer.*

    torpor, torpōris, m., *numbness, paralysis.*

    ***artus, -ūs**, m., *joint of the body; arm, leg, limb.*

549   ***mollis, -is, -e**, *soft, tender; gentle.*

    ***cingō, cingere, cīnxī, cīnctus**, *to surround, encircle.*

    ***tenuis, -is, -e**, *slender, thin.*

    praecordia, -ōrum, n. pl., *chest, breast.*

    liber, librī, m., *inner bark of a tree* (cf. **cortice 554**); *book.*

       mollia . . . librō: the line's interlocked order neatly suits its meaning.

550   ***frōns, frondis**, f., *leafy part of a tree, foliage.*

    ***crescō, crēscere, crēvī, crētūrus**, *to be born, arise; to increase, change into (by growing); to grow, bud.*

551   **vēlōx, vēlōcis**, *rapid, swift.*

    piger, pigra, pigrum, *sluggish, inactive; motionless, inert.*

    ***rādīx, rādīcis**, f., *root (of a plant or tree).*

    pēs . . . vēlōx pigrīs rādīcibus: chiasmus.

552   **ōra cacūmen habet:** Ovid's cinematographic eye moves quickly from foot to head in 551–52; the image here is elaborated in 567.

    ***cacūmen, cacūminis**, n., *peak, top (especially of an object that tapers upward to a point)*; here, *treetop.*

    remaneō, remanēre, remānsī, remānsūrus, *to remain; to persist, endure.*

    nitor, nitōris, m., *brightness, splendor; beauty.*

542	imminet, et crīnem sparsum cervīcibus afflat.
543	Vīribus absūmptīs, expalluit illa, citaeque
544	victa labōre fugae, spectāns Pēnēidas undās,
545	"Fer, pater," inquit, "opem, sī flūmina nūmen habētis!
547	Quā nimium placuī, mūtandō perde figūram!"
548	Vix prece fīnītā, torpor gravis occupat artūs;
549	mollia cinguntur tenuī praecordia librō,
550	in frondem crīnēs, in rāmōs bracchia crēscunt;
551	pēs modo tam vēlōx pigrīs rādīcibus haeret,
552	ōra cacūmen habet; remanet nitor ūnus in illā.
553	Hanc quoque Phoebus amat, positāque in stīpite dextrā
554	sentit adhūc trepidāre novō sub cortice pectus,

Discussion Questions

1. What is the effect of the polysyndeton in 541–42?

2. What is the purpose of the chiasmus in 551?

3. It has been said that meter is to a poem what the soundtrack is to a film. How does Ovid's manipulation of the meter in 548–52 enliven the images he describes? Think specifically of the alternation of dactyls and spondees in 549; how does this suit the action of 548–49? Comment on the striking metrical differences between 550 and 552; and what is the effect of the shift after the first foot in 551?

4. How is the meter in 553–54 appropriate to the action described?

---

      remanet nitor: i.e., in the sheen of the tree's leaves.

553   **Hanc:** the shift from **illā** (552) to **hanc** shows the transformation is complete.
      stīpes, stīpitis, m., *trunk of a tree.*

554   **trepidāre . . . pectus:** acc. + infin. with **sentit.**
     *****cortex, corticis,** m., *bark* (of a tree).
      novō sub cortice: there is perhaps a deliberate oxymoron in the description
        of something that is old and tough with an epithet meaning *fresh and new.*
      pectus: here, *her heart.*

555   **complector, complectī, complexus sum**, *to hold in the arms, embrace, hug.*
    *membrum, -ī, n., part of the body, limb, member.

556   **ōscula dat . . . refugit . . . ōscula:** chiasmus.
    lignum, -ī, n., firewood; wood; stump; shaft.
    refugiō, refugere, refūgī, refugitus, *to flee, run away; to recoil from.*

557   *coniūnx, coniugis, m./f., spouse (husband or wife).*

558   **mea:** repeated from 557 and suspensefully delayed to add emphasis (along
      with **certē** and **semper**) to Apollo's pronouncement.
    habēbunt: in a dual sense, *will possess* and *will display*; Apollo cannot
      actually have the nymph herself, but his hair and his various accoutrements
      will ever be adorned with the leaves and wood of the tree into which she
      has been transformed.

559   *coma, -ae, f., hair.*
    nostrae: with **coma** and **citharae** as well as **pharetrae**.
    laurus, -ī, f., laurel tree, bay; sprig/branch of laurel; garland of laurel (as a
      ritual object, especially one sacred to Apollo, or a sign of victory).
    laure: in applying this name to the tree, Apollo thus identifies his
      "invention." She who was the nymph **Daphnē**, and whose name was
      the Greek word for the laurel tree, has become now **laurus**, with its
      new Latin name, a laurel tree only, subject not only to the control of
      Apollo but even, as the following lines imply, to the triumphant *lords
      of Latium* (**ducibus Latiīs** 560).

560   **Latius, -a, -um,** *of Latium, Latin.*
    ducibus Latiīs: dat. with the compound verb **aderis**; Ovid Romanizes
      his story by having Apollo foresee the Roman empire and the
      triumphal processions in which Roman generals wore laurel garlands in
      their hair when celebrating their military victories.
    triumphus, -ī, m., the ritual shout "triumphe" (cf. *Am.* I.2.25, 34 below);
      triumph (the ritual procession of a victorious general through the streets of
      Rome); *victory celebration; victory.*

561   *canō, canere, cecinī, cantus, to sing, chant; to sing about, celebrate.*
    vīsō, vīsere, vīsī, *to look at, view.*
    Capitōlium, -ī, n., *the Capitoline Hill* (site in Rome of the temple of Jupiter
      Capitolinus, where triumphal processions generally concluded).
    Capitōlia: the pl. form of this noun is often used for the sing. in Latin
      verse, but here, along with **pompās**, Ovid may intend to suggest a
      great series of triumphs over the generations, all of which Apollo can
      foresee because of his prophetic powers (one might compare the
      prophecies of Jupiter to Venus in *Aeneid* I and Anchises to Aeneas in
      Aeneid VI).
    pompa, -ae, f., ceremonial procession.
    triumphum / vox canet et vīsent . . . Capitōlia pompās (561): an
      elaborate and sonorous chiasmus, appropriate to the ritual train
      described.

562   **Postibus Augustīs:** dat. with **fīdissima custōs** (and a further Romanization);
      the entrance to Augustus' imperial palace was adorned with laurel, a

555 complexusque suīs rāmōs, ut membra, lacertīs
556 ōscula dat lignō; refugit tamen ōscula lignum.
557 Cui deus "At quoniam coniūnx mea nōn potes esse,
558 arbor eris certē," dīxit, "mea! Semper habēbunt
559 tē coma, tē citharae, tē nostrae, laure, pharetrae.
560 Tū ducibus Latiīs aderis, cum laeta triumphum
561 vōx canet et vīsent longās Capitōlia pompās.
562 Postibus Augustīs eadem fīdissima custōs
563 ante forēs stābis, mediamque tuēbere quercum,

Discussion Questions

1. How does the word order in 555 suit the action described?

2. What is the emotional effect of the anaphora in 559?

3. What are the purposes of the "Romanizing" elements in 560–63? How would Ovid's audience respond to them? How are the specific Roman elements Ovid has chosen appropriate to the story itself and to the ultimate outcome of Apollo's pursuit of Daphne?

       symbol of victory and of the emperor's special reverence for Apollo.

    Augustus, -a, -um, *of Augustus; imperial.*

    eadem: here, *ever the same, immutable.*

    *fīdus, -a, -um, *faithful, loyal, devoted.*

563   **foris, foris*, f., *door, entrance* (of a building or room); pl., *double-doors.*

    *tueor, tuērī, tuitus sum, *to look at, observe; to watch over, protect.*

      tuēbere: = **tuēberis.**

    mediam: *in the middle*, i.e., hanging suspended over the middle of the palace's entranceway.

    *quercus, -ūs, f., *oak tree*; here, *oak garland* (the **corōna cīvica**, an oak garland traditionally awarded by the Roman government for acts of heroism, also adorned the door to Augustus' palace).

564   **meum . . . capillīs**: interlocked word order.

    intōnsus, -a, -um, *uncut, unshorn* (usually of the hair or beard, but also of the foliage of trees).

        intōnsīs . . . capillīs: descriptive abl.; long hair was a mark of youth, and Apollo, of course, was perpetually young.

    *****iuvenālis, -is, -e**, *youthful*.

565   **perpetuōs**: *everlasting*, because the laurel tree is evergreen.

    honor, honōris, m., *high esteem, honor; mark of grace, beauty* (here pl. for sing. with **frondis**, *the loveliness of your foliage*).

566   **Fīnierat**: i.e., **Fīnīverat** (see on **petiēre** 478); the short clause effectively punctuates Apollo's lengthy prophecy.

    Paeān, Paeānis, m., *Paean* (an epithet of Apollo in his aspect as god of healing).

    factīs modo . . . ramīs: abl. of means, *with her recently created branches*.

    laureus, -a, -um, *of laurel, laurel*; here a substantive, *the laurel tree*.

567   **adnuō, adnuere, adnuī, adnūtus**, *to beckon, nod* (the verb means sometimes, but not always, *to nod assent*).

        adnuit . . . cacūmen: with its fluttering alliteration of the hard **d/t/q/c/g** consonants and the sibilant **s**'s, the line provides a sonorous, even onomatopoetic closure to Ovid's tale.

    ut caput: *as though it were her head*; for the image cf. 552.

    agitō, -āre, -āvī, -ātus, *to move, shake, stir*.

        agitāsse: = **agitāvisse** (see on **petiēre** 478).

"Apollo and Daphne"
Antonio Pollaiuolo, ca. 1475
National Gallery
London, England

564 utque meum intōnsīs caput est iuvenāle capillīs,
565 tu quoque perpetuōs semper gere frondis honōrēs!"
566 Fīnierat Paeān; factīs modo laurea rāmīs
567 adnuit, utque caput vīsa est agitāsse cacūmen.

Discussion Questions

1. What is the point of addressing Apollo in 566 as "Paean"?

2. What is your response to the story's outcome and Daphne's fate? Would a Roman's response be the same? Is there any ambiguity (compare the closing scene of the *Aeneid*)?

3. What further insights might a feminist analysis of this tale provide?

Daphne

"Daphne"
Renée Sintenis, 1930
Museum of Modern Art
New York

Poet, Singer, Necromancer—
I cease to run. I halt you here,
Pursuer, with an answer:

Do what you will.
The blood you've set to music I
Can change to chlorophyll,

And root myself, and with my toes
Wind to subterranean streams.
Through solid rock my strength now grows.

Such now am I, I cease to eat,
But feed on flashes from your eyes;
Light, to my new cells, is meat.

Find then, when you seize my arm
That xylem thickens in my skin
And there are splinters in my charm.

I may give in; I do not lose.
Your hot stare cannot stop my shivering,
With delight, if I so choose.

A.E. *Stallings*

PYRAMUS AND THISBE

Metamorphoses IV.55–166

This second selection from the *Metamorphoses* is quite unlike the first. The story of Daphne and Apollo was one of unreciprocated love, of power and violence, of male (and divine) aggression, and feminist resistance, told in variously epic and comic tones, and, though set in a primordial epoch, resonating in its final scene with the Roman world of imperialism and Augustan order. Ovid's tale of Pyramus and Thisbe comes in Book IV of the *Metamorphoses*, much later in his cosmic scheme; civilization has advanced from its emergent state in Book I; we are now in the exotic, mystical world of the East, in the Babylon of Queen Semiramis.

And although the unhappy circumstances of our hero and heroine are reminiscent of the frustrated lovers of Roman comedy, as well as of elegy (with its *amatores exclusi* and its secret encounters), and while Ovid's drama certainly does have some lighter moments, the action is ultimately not comic at all, but unexpectedly tragic. Pyramus and Thisbe have many admirable and heroic traits (Thisbe in particular is strikingly courageous and perceptive—like Daphne in certain respects), but their story lacks the divine action and heroic conflict of epic and the ambiguous political associations with Roman empire and emperor of the poet's Daphne tale; it is instead a purely human and private drama, a sentimental story of youthful romance that comes to a dark and bloody conclusion. In a reversal of the point made at the outset of "Daphne and Apollo," the crisis here is created, not by "the savage wrath of Cupid," but by "blind chance," the impetuousness of two innocent young lovers, and the stern prohibitions of their doubtless well-intended but overly protective parents.

We have no literary sources for this story earlier than Ovid, who describes it as "a little-known tale" (*vulgaris fabula non est, Met.* IV.53). Because of its Babylonian setting and the fact that there were rivers named "Pyramus" and "Thisbe" in Cilicia and elsewhere in the eastern Mediterranean, the tale is generally supposed to have originated in the East. Like many of Ovid's episodes, this one is presented as a tale within a tale (hence the quotation marks enclosing the entire Latin text that follows), the first of three love stories narrated in the first half of *Metamorphoses* IV by the three daughters of Minyas, king of Orchomenos in Boeotia. While their fellow townspeople are celebrating a festival in honor of Bacchus, the Minyades, ignoring the example of the Theban king Pentheus (whose destruction for a similar impiety had just been recounted at the end of Book III), reject the god's divinity and remain at home, spinning wool and exchanging stories to pass the time. Of their three amatory tales, only this first one tells of an untainted love—the "ideal" Ovidian love, as Brooks Otis has remarked and as we can see both from the progress of the narrative itself and from the sympathetic comments interjected along the way by Ovid's own "partisan narrator" (as distinguished by Otis from the vile daughter of Minyas who tells the tale and who, in effect, deliberately contrives its unhappy ending). When all three of the tales were concluded, Bacchus' spirit descended on the palace, causing grapevines and ivy to grow out of the sisters' tapestries and looms, and transforming the Minyades themselves into hideous bats.

The tale may be summarized as follows: Pyramus, a handsome Babylonian youth, and his beautiful young neighbor Thisbe (we should imagine them in their teens) fall in love, but are forbidden by their parents to marry or even to meet. At first they communicate only by whispering through a crack discovered in the wall connecting their two houses; like the elegiac lover who reproaches the door that keeps him from his mistress, both Pyramus and Thisbe often scold their wall as though it were alive, but then thank it for the passage it has given to their speech. Eventually, however, longing to share more than just words, the two conspire to leave their homes by night and to meet under a mulberry tree—a tree whose berries were in those days white—near the tomb of king Ninus on the outskirts of the city. Arriving first, Thisbe sees a lioness, drenched with blood from a recent kill and drinking from the nearby stream; she rushes to take refuge in a dark cavern and, in her flight, drops her veil, which the lioness soon finds, shreds with her bloody maw, and then leaves behind. When Pyramus arrives, he sees the animal's tracks and Thisbe's mutilated, blood-stained garment, and mistakenly concludes the worst; blaming himself and rushing to the tree where the two had planned to rendezvous, the youth first kisses Thisbe's veil, then plunges his sword into his groin, spattering the tree's berries and soaking its roots with his blood as he lies dying. Soon Thisbe emerges from the cave, still fearful but determined to see her beloved. When she discovers his body instead and realizes what has happened, she tries at first to arouse him, but then, failing in that, commits suicide with Pyramus' own sword. But before plunging the sword into her breast, Thisbe utters two final prayers, first to their parents, that they allow the cremated remains of both lovers to rest in a single urn, and then to the mulberry tree where they had made their fatal rendezvous, that its own "offspring," its berries, should be forever altered from white to the dark-red hue of blood, to serve both as the tree's own cloak of mourning and as a perpetual reminder of the lovers' suicides. In the story's closing lines we see both of Thisbe's prayers realized—one fulfilling the myth's etiological function (explaining the origin of the purplish-red mulberry), the other bringing the folktale's plot to closure by joining the two lovers at last in death as their parents had forbidden them in life.

With its implicit warnings for young people who may exercise too little control over their passions, and for parents who try to exercise too much, Ovid's story is a folktale rather than a myth in the usual Greco-Roman sense, one that quickly transcends its eastern setting and assumes, as the poet intended, a universal quality that has insured its appeal to subsequent generations. One of Ovid's most beautiful tales of love, and beautifully told, "Pyramus and Thisbe" has inspired countless imitations and adaptations over the centuries. An early version appears in the *Fabulae* of the 2nd-century A.D. mythographer Hyginus. Dante alludes to the tale, which is retold later in the 14th century by both Boccaccio and Chaucer (in his "Legende of Goode Women") and which provides the subject of several plays, both comic and tragic, the best known of them the burlesque play-within-a-play performed by the "mechanicals" in Shakespeare's *Midsummer Night's Dream* (and of course *Romeo and Juliet* takes up the themes of parental restriction and the suicide of young lovers). Other poets have been captivated by the tale, among them John Donne in an epigram composed in 1631, the year of his death. Countless representations have appeared in the visual arts as well, including paintings, woodcuts, and engravings, among them a series of drawings by both Rubens and Rembrandt from the 17th century and even, from the same period, an etching by Stefano Della Bella for a set of playing cards. We have besides, from the 18th into the 20th century, several cantatas, more than half a dozen ballets, and about 20 operas, including Federico Ghisi's *Piramo e Tisbe*, composed in the 1940's and based upon Shakespeare's adaptation.

Like so many others over the centuries who have treasured the story of "Pyramus and Thisbe," modern readers of Ovid's original will appreciate the easy, dynamic flow of his narrative, the brilliant effects of sound and sight (not least the poet's manipulation of dark/light imagery and sexual metaphor), and especially the humanity of his star-crossed hero and heroine, the tenderness of their love, the depth of their courage, and the intensity of passion that compels both, inexorably, to the act of suicide.

At every tyme whan they durste soo,
Upon the o syde of the walle stood he,
And on that other syde stood Tesbe,
The swoote soune of other to receyve.

Chaucer, Legende of Goode Women, lines 749-52

"Thisbe," J. W. Waterhouse, 1909

55   ***Pȳramus, -ī**, m., *Pyramus* (a Babylonian youth).
    *Thisbē, Thisbēs, f., *Thisbe* (a Babylonian maiden, Pyramus' neighbor and
      inamorata; for the Greek case endings, see on **Daphnē**, *Met.* I.452).
    iuvenum pulcherrimus alter, / altera . . . praelāta puellīs (56): chiasmus;
      the entire phrase is in apposition to **Pȳramus et Thisbē**, the subjects of
      tenuēre (57).

56   **quās**: the antecedent is **puellīs**.
    oriēns, orientis, m., *the rising sun, dawn; the eastern world, the orient.*
    praelāta: with **altera**; here, *preferred.*

57   **contiguus, -a, -um**, *adjacent, connected.*
    tenuēre: = **tenuērunt**, *had* or *occupied.*
    ubi . . . urbem (58): an epic periphrasis for the ancient city of Babylon;
      positioning of the adjective/noun pair **altam / . . . urbem** at the ends of
      the verses adds to the epic effect.

58   **coctilis, -is, -e**, *baked; made of fired bricks.*
    mūrīs: the vast walls and gardens of Babylon were among the wonders of the
      ancient world.
    Semīramis, Semīramidis, f., *Semiramis* (legendary queen of Assyria, wife of
      Ninus, and founder of Babylon).

59   **nōtitia, -ae**, f., *acquaintance.*
    *gradus, -ūs, m., *step, pace; phase, stage* (in a process).
        Nōtitiam prīmōsque gradūs: supply **amōris**, *their acquaintance and the*
          first steps (of their love); or possibly a hendiadys, *the first stage of*
          their acquaintance.
    *vīcīnia, -ae, f., *nearby area, vicinity; nearness, proximity.*

60   **Taedae . . . iūre**: *in the bond of marriage* (metonymy— lit., *with the*
    sanction of the [wedding] torch).
    *iūs, iūris, n., *law, legal sanction; legal authority, right.*
    *coeō, coīre, coiī, coitus, *to come together, meet; to form an alliance* (here,
      of marriage).
        coīssent: potential subjn., *they would have come together.*

61   **vetuēre patrēs . . . potuēre vetāre**: understand **patrēs** with **potuēre**, and
    note the sound-play and chiastic arrangement.
    quod: the entire clause in 62 is the antecedent (*but—what they could not*
    prevent—they both burned. . . .).

62   **aequus, -a, -um**, *level, even.*
      ex aequō: idiom, *at the same level, equally.*
    *mēns, mentis, f., *mind.*

63   **cōnscius, -ī**, m., *accomplice, witness.*
    abest . . . aestuat (64): here and often throughout the story (cf. 84–92) Ovid
      lapses into the historical present to engage the reader and add vividness to
      his narrative.
    nūtus, -ūs, m., *nod of the head* (especially a nod of assent).

64   **quōque**: i.e., **quō + -que**; **quō . . . magis . . . (eō) magis**, *the more . . .*
    the more.

55   "Pȳramus et Thisbē, iuvenum pulcherrimus alter,
56 altera, quās oriēns habuit, praelāta puellīs,
57 contiguās tenuēre domōs, ubi dīcitur altam
58 coctilibus mūrīs cīnxisse Semīramis urbem.
59 Nōtitiam prīmōsque gradūs vīcīnia fēcit;
60 tempore crēvit amor. Taedae quoque iūre coīssent,
61 sed vetuēre patrēs; quod nōn potuēre vetāre,
62 ex aequō captīs ardēbant mentibus ambō.
63 Cōnscius omnis abest, nūtū signīsque loquuntur,
64 quōque magis tegitur, tēctus magis aestuat ignis.
65   "Fissus erat tenuī rīmā, quam dūxerat ōlim,
66 cum fieret, pariēs domuī commūnis utrīque.
67 Id vitium nūllī per saecula longa notātum—

Discussion Questions

1. How is the chiasmus in 55–56 appropriate to the description of Pyramus and Thisbe and the houses in which they lived?

2. How is the symmetry of 62 appropriate to the circumstance described? And what may the series of spondees and hard consonants be intended to suggest?

3. Comment on the metaphor in 62–64. How is the image enhanced through the anaphora and word order in 64?

4. Explain the aptness of the interlocked word order in 66.

---

*tegō, tegere, tēxī, tēctus, *to cover; to hide, conceal.*
aestuō, -āre, -āvī, -ātūrus, *to burn fiercely, blaze; to burn with desire.*
ignis: subject of both tegitur and aestuat.
65 findō, findere, fidī, fissus, *to split apart; to open up.*
   dūxerat: *it had developed*; pariēs . . . commūnis is subject of all three verbs
     in the sentence.
66 *pariēs, parietis, m., *wall.*
   domuī . . . utrīque: dat. with commūnis.
67 *vitium, -ī, n., *defect, fault; flaw, imperfection; vice.*
   nūllī: dat. with notātum, *known to nobody.*
   saeculum, -ī, n., *generation, age* (i.e., a long period of time).

68   **quid . . . amor**: the question, out of the narrator's own sense of excitement, anticipates the discovery in **prīmī vīdistis amantēs**.

        prīmī: as often in Latin, the adj. has adverbial force (cf. **tūtae** 69).

        amantēs: the participle of **amō** often functions as a noun, *lovers* (cf. 73, 108, and *Am.* I.9.25 below).

69   **iter facere**, idiom, *to clear a way, grant passage*; with **vocis**, *to create a pathway for speech*, a personification elaborated in **tūtae . . . blanditiae . . . trānsīre solēbant** (70).

        tūtus, -a, -um, *safe, secure.*

            tūtae . . . minimō (70): interlocked order.

        illud: i.e., **iter**.

71   ***hinc***, adv., *from this place; from/on this side.*

        illinc, adv., *from that place; from/on that side.*

        hinc Thisbē, Pȳramus illinc: the chiastic arrangement brings the two lovers together, but the strong diaeresis (like the wall) keeps them apart—more marvelous Ovidian wordplay!

72   **in vicēs**, idiomatic adv., *(each) in turn, alternately.*

        fuerat captātus: = **captātus erat**; not just *had been felt* or *listened for*, but far more passionately, *had been seized at and inhaled*—the lovers' lips cannot quite touch (see lines 75, 79–80), but each frantically gasps in the other's breath through the tiny crack.

        anhēlitus, -ūs, m., *gasping, panting; breath, breathing.*

73   **invidus, -a, -um**, *malevolent, hateful; envious, jealous* (the wall itself has become an enemy!).

        quid, here an adv., *why?*

        obstō, obstāre, obstitī, obstātūrus + dat., *to face; to stand in the way (of), obstruct.*

74   **Quantum erat: esset**, a potential subjunctive, might be expected; the construction takes a result clause, *How great a matter would it be to . . . ?* Diaeresis punctuates the query.

        tōtō nōs corpore iungī: the lovers' desire is made explicit, and the ō/ō/ō assonance perhaps onomatopoetically mimics their cries of longing.

75   **vel**: here, *at least.*

        ad ōscula danda: a gerundive phrase expressing purpose; freely, *for us to kiss.*

76   **ingrātus, -a, -um**, *ungrateful, thankless, unappreciative.*

        fateor, fatērī, fassus sum, *to acknowledge, admit, confess; to accept.*

77   **quod**: here, *the fact that*; the entire **quod** clause is object of **dēbēre** (76).

        amīcus, -a, -um, *friendly, loving; of a friend/lover.*

        trānsitus, -ūs, m., *passage, path.*

            The noun here looks back to **trānsīre** (70) and continues the personification of 69–70; the line's repeated sibilants (s six times) suggest the sounds of the lovers' whispering.

        auris, auris, f., *ear.*

78   **Tālia**: object of **locūtī**.

        nēquīquam, adv., *with no effect, to no avail, in vain.*

68   quid nōn sentit amor?—prīmī vīdistis amantēs,
69   et vōcis fēcistis iter; tūtaeque per illud
70   murmure blanditiae minimō trānsīre solēbant.
71   Saepe, ubi cōnstiterant hinc Thisbē, Pȳramus illinc,
72   inque vicēs fuerat captātus anhēlitus ōris,
73   'Invide,' dīcēbant, 'pariēs, quid amantibus obstās?
74   Quantum erat, ut sinerēs tōtō nōs corpore iungī
75   aut, hoc sī nimium est, vel ad ōscula danda patērēs?
76   Nec sumus ingrātī: tibi nōs dēbēre fatēmur,
77   quod datus est verbīs ad amīcās trānsitus aurēs.'
78   Tālia dīversā nēquīquam sēde locūtī,
79   sub noctem dīxēre, 'Valē,' partīque dedēre

Discussion Questions

1. Why does the narrator suddenly shift to the use of second person verbs in 68-69? What is the effect?

2. Why is the personification in 69-70 especially appropriate in this context?

3. What is the effect of the **m/n** alliteration in 70?

4. How does the imaginative view of the inanimate world expressed by the two lovers in 73-77 coincide with the poet's own fantasizing images? In light of the overarching imagery of the *Metamorphoses* (think, for example, of Daphne's transformation into a tree that can hear and communicate), how is it perfectly "logical" that Pyramus and Thisbe should "often" (**saepe** 71) address the wall shared by their two houses? Once you understand how Ovid "animates" the inanimate world, what seems to be the best translation of **amīcās . . . aurēs** (77)?

5. How is the word order in 78 a perfect construct for the situation described?

*sēdēs, sēdis, f., *seat; home; place, position.*
    sēde: supply ē.
79 sub: here, *just before.*
    dīxēre . . . dedēre: = dīxērunt . . . dedērunt; the subject quisque (80) often takes a pl. verb, *they each.*
    partī . . . suae (80): *their own side* (of the wall); the interlocked order (partī . . . / ōscula . . . suae . . . nōn pervenientia) matches the complications of their kissing!

80   **nōn pervenientia**: English would use a rel. clause, *that did not come through*.

    contrā: here adv., *on the opposite side*.

81   **Postera . . . ignēs**: interlocked order.

    nocturnōs . . . ignēs: a metaphor for the stars.

    aurōra, -ae, f., *dawn, daybreak;* here personified, *Aurora* (goddess of the dawn).

82   *__sōl, sōlis,__* m., *the sun;* here personified (as in the tale of the Sun's loves that follows this story in the *Metamorphoses*), *Sol* (god of the sun).

    pruīnōsus, -a, -um, *frosty.*

    __radius, -ī,__ m., *ray of light.*

    siccō, -āre, -āvī, -ātus, *to dry.*

        pruīnōsās . . . siccāverat herbās: the word order replicates, and to an extent rhymes with, **nocturnōs . . . remōverat ignēs** (81).

83   **solitus, -a, -um,** *usual, accustomed.*

        Note the assonance of **-tum/-cum/Tum/murmure** and cf. line 70.

    parvō: here, *gentle, quiet.*

84   **multa . . . silentī**: note the s/t alliteration and the internal rhyme, which is accentuated by the pauses after **questī** and **silentī**.

    __queror, querī, questus sum,__ *to complain (about), protest.*

    statuō, statuere, statuī, statūtus, *to set upright, stand;* with **ut** + subjn., *to decide (that).*

    ut . . . temptent (85) **. . . relinquant** (86) **. . . conveniant . . . lateant** (88): jussive noun clauses (indirect commands) after **statuunt**.

    silēns, silentis, *quiet, silent.*

85   **fallere custōdēs foribusque excēdere**: chiasmus, and a neat **f/c/d/f/c/d** alliteration; the infinitives are complementary to **temptent**.

    foribus: supply **ex** (prepositions expected in prose are often omitted in verse).

86   **tēctum, -ī,** n., *roof, ceiling; house, building* (a common synecdoche).

87   *__nēve__* or **neu,** conj., *nor; and so that . . . not.*

    sit errandum: negative purpose clause with a pass. periphrastic, following **nēve** and with **spatiantibus** as dat. of agent, *so that they would not go astray* (lit., *so that it would not be gone astray by them*), as they wander about.

    lātus, -a, -um, *broad, wide; extensive, vast.*

    spatior, -ārī, -ātus sum, *to walk/wander about.*

88   *__conveniō, convenīre, convēnī, conventūrus,__* *to assemble, meet;* + dat., *to be suited (to), befit, harmonize (with).*

    bustum, -ī, n., often pl. for sing., *funeral pyre, ash; grave-mound, tomb.*

    Ninus, -ī, m., *Ninus* (king of Assyria, founder of Nineveh, and husband of Semiramis—see on 58 above).

89   **arboris**: the diaeresis, the word's enjambement, and its repetition as first word of the following parenthesis purposefully focus our attention on the tree which will be central to the story.

80   ōscula quisque suae nōn pervenientia contrā.
81   "Postera nocturnōs Aurōra remōverat ignēs,
82   Sōlque pruīnōsās radiīs siccāverat herbās;
83   ad solitum coiēre locum. Tum, murmure parvō
84   multa prius questī, statuunt ut nocte silentī
85   fallere custōdēs foribusque excēdere temptent,
86   cumque domō exierint, urbis quoque tēcta relinquant,
87   nēve sit errandum lātō spatiantibus arvō,
[88 conveniant ad busta Ninī, lateantque sub umbrā
89   arboris (arbor ibī niveīs ūberrima pōmīs,
90   ardua mōrus, erat, gelidō contermina fontī).
91   Pacta placent; et lūx, tardē discēdere vīsa,

Discussion Question

Comment on the onomatopoeia in 83. How may the alliteration in the following verse also be onomatopoetic?

---

*niveus, -a, -um, (consisting) *of snow; snow-white, snowy.*
ūber, ūberis, *copious, abundant*; + abl., *rich* (in).
*pōmum, -ī, n., *fruit-tree; fruit.*
90 *arduus, -a, -um, *tall, towering; steep, precipitous.*
mōrus, -ī, f., *mulberry tree.*
*gelidus, -a, -um, *cold, cool, chilly.*
*conterminus, -a, -um + dat., *bordering* (upon), *close* (to).
*fōns, fontis, m., *spring, spring-water.*
91 pactum, -ī, n., *agreement, plan.*
      Pacta placent: supply eīs, i.e., the lovers, although from the next verse
         and a half it appears that even nature is in accord with the plan; the
         short, alliterative sentence effectively punctuates the detailed plan
         preceding and introduces the scene shift following.
   et lūx . . . ab īsdem (92): a brilliantly economical description of sunset, with
         the sluggish spondees of 91 aptly giving way to the plummeting dactyls in
         92, the lūx/nox/exit soundplay, and the highly visual (and sonorous)
         chiasmus of praecipitātur aquīs et aquīs . . . exit.
   vīsa: *having seemed* (at first), i.e., to the lovers, who were eager for
         nightfall.

92   **praecipitō, -āre, -āvī, -ātus**, *to plunge/hurl downward* (in contrast to **tardē discēdere**).

      praecipitātur aquīs: sc. **in**.

    aquīs, et aquīs: placement of **-quīs** under the ictus accentuates the rhyme.

    nox: the abrupt monosyllable (which echoes **lūx** in 91) and the diaeresis that follows deliberately disturb the rhythm before bringing the scene to closure.

    īsdem: = **eīsdem;** *the same*, since in the mythic world ocean surrounded the lands in a continuous stream, out of which rose and set both daylight and darkness; cf. Vergil *Aeneid* II.250.

93   ***callidus, -a, -um**, *expert, wise; clever, crafty* (here perhaps with adverbial force, *cunningly*).

    tenebrae, -ārum, f. pl., *darkness*.

    *versō, -āre, -āvī, -ātus, *to turn, spin; to turn back and forth, twist*.

    cardō, cardinis, m., *pivot, axis; door-hinge*.

      versātō cardine: *turning the door on its hinges* (lit., *with the door-hinge turned*).

94   **suōs:** i.e., her family (cf. **fallere custōdēs** 85).

    adopertus, -a, -um, *covered, veiled*.

      adoperta: with **vultum**, acc. of respect, and modifying **Thisbē**, *with her face concealed* (by a shawl, see 101).

95   **pervenit . . . sēdit:** chiasmus.

    *tumulus, -ī, m., *burial mound, tomb*.

    dictā . . . arbore: *the tree which they had spoken of*.

96   **audācem faciēbat amor:** supply **eam**; this clause, one of Ovid's many epigrammatic **sententiae**, anticipates the boldness Thisbe will need for the action that follows.

    ecce, recentī / caede (97): the harsh alliteration helps compel our attention to the scene Ovid means us to visualize.

    *recēns, recentis, *recent, newly arrived; newly shed; recently caught*.

97   ***caedēs, caedis**, f., *killing, slaughter; blood, gore*.

    leaena, -ae, f., *lioness*.

    boum: gen. pl. of **bōs**, objective gen. with **caede**.

    spūmō, -āre, -āvī, -ātūrus, *to foam, be covered with foam*.

    oblinō, oblinere, oblēvī, oblitus, *to smear, cover*.

    rictus, -ūs, m., *the open mouth, jaws*.

      spūmantēs . . . rictūs: acc. of respect with **oblita**, *her foaming jowls smeared*.

98   **dēpositūra:** fut. act. participle, here with the force of a purpose clause, *to slake, satisfy*.

    *sitis, sitis, acc. **sitim**, f., *thirst*.

99   **Quam:** = **Eam**, the lioness.

    ad: here, *by the light of*.

    lūna, -ae, f., *the moon*.

    Babylōnius, -a, -um, *Babylonian*.

92 praecipitātur aquīs, et aquīs nox exit ab īsdem.
93   "Callida per tenebrās, versātō cardine, Thisbē
94 ēgreditur, fallitque suōs, adopertaque vultum
95 pervenit ad tumulum, dictāque sub arbore sēdit—
96 audācem faciēbat amor. Venit, ecce, recentī
97 caede leaena boum spūmantēs oblita rictūs,
98 dēpositūra sitim vīcīnī fontis in undā.
99 Quam procul ad lūnae radiōs Babylōnia Thisbē
100 vīdit et obscūrum timidō pede fūgit in antrum,

Discussion Questions

1. How much time elapses between verses 81 and 92?

2. Comment further on the several ways in which Ovid uses meter and word order to enhance the imagery in 91–92; what movements of light and darkness do we actually see and hear in these two lines?

3. How does Ovid's description of the time and place of the lovers' rendezvous in 88–95 help to establish a mood of foreboding? How does the poet use images of light and dark in these lines; what, specifically, may be the symbolism of the **lūx/nox** antithesis in 91–92?

> wake from your dreams
> the drying of your tears
> today we escape
> we escape
>
> *"Exit Music (For a Film)," Radiohead*

100 *obscūrus, -a, -um, *dark, obscure; shadowy; hidden from sight.*
     timidō pede fūgit: for the transferred epithet cf. **timidō Pēnēia cursū / fūgit** (I.525–26 above).
     antrum, -ī, n., *cave, cavern, grotto.*
          obscūrum . . . antrum: in a neat word-picture, the rest of the clause is actually "enclosed," like Thisbe herself, within *the shadowy cave*; again word order enhances imagery (cf. I.468 above). Note too the chiaroscuro effect, as Thisbe flees out of the shadows of the moonlit night into the cave's profounder darkness—an unpropitious omen of things to come.

101   **dumque fugit . . . relīquit**: the present indicative was often used with **dum**, where in English we might expect another tense; translate here as an imperf.

        tergō . . . lapsa: supply **dē**; again English would use a clause (*which had slipped from her back*) rather than a participial phrase (*having slipped from her back*).

        vēlāmina: here (as often) pl. for sing. (cf. **tenuēs . . . amictūs** 104).

102   **lea, -ae**, f., *lioness*.

        lea saeva . . . multā . . . undā: chiasmus.

        compēscō, compēscere, compēscuī, *to confine, restrain; to subdue, quench.*

103   **inventōs . . . amictūs** (104): notice how the noun and its modifier frame the lengthy clause (cf. **lētī . . . tuī** 151–52); for translation of the participle, see on **tergō . . . lapsa** (101).

        ipsā: i.e., Thisbe.

104   **cruentō, -āre, -āvī, -ātus**, *to stain with blood.*

        *lanio, -āre, -āvī, -ātus, *to wound savagely; to tear, shred, mutilate.*

        *amictus, -ūs, m., *mantle, cloak.*

105   **ēgressus**: with **Pȳramus** (107).

106   **pulvis, pulveris**, m., *dust.*

        certa ferae: with **vēstīgia**, delayed for suspense.

        tōtō . . . ōre: supply **in**, but English would make *face* the subject (*his whole face grew pale*).

107   *tingō, tingere, tīnxī, tīnctus, *to wet, soak, moisten; to dye, stain, color.*

108   *reperiō, reperīre, repperī, repertus, *to find, discover; to find* (someone, something) *to be.*

109   **ē quibus**: partitive abl., *of whom.*

        illa: Thisbe.

        *dignus, -a, -um, *suitable, appropriate;* + abl., *worthy* (of).

110   **nostra**: = **mea** (cf. **nostrum** 112, **nostrī** 118).

        nocēns: here, *guilty*, predicate adj.; and note the assonance with **nostra**.

        *anima, -ae, f., *air, breath; soul, life; spirit, ghost.*

        Ego tē: looking back to **illa** (109) and **nostra** (110), the pronouns are emphatically juxtaposed.

        miserandus, -a, -um, *pitiable.*

        perimō, perimere, perēmī, perēmptus, *to destroy, kill.*

111   **in loca plēna metūs**: with **venīrēs**; cf. **per . . . loca plēna timōris** (X.29 below).

        quī: **ego** (110) is the antecedent.

        venīrēs: supply **ut**; a jussive noun clause with the subjunctive, instead of the infinitive usual with **iubeō**.

112   **dīvellō, dīvellere, dīvellī, dīvulsus**, *to tear apart, tear to pieces.*

113   **scelerātus, -a, -um**, *accursed; criminal, sinful.*

        scelerāta . . . morsū: the interlocking order, with the powerful imperative at center, produces a symmetrical golden line—and the **scelerāta . . . viscera** are separated quite aptly, in view of the violence imagined in the equally powerful (and symmetrical) **Nostrum dīvellite corpus** (112).

101   dumque fugit, tergō vēlāmina lapsa relīquit.

102   Ut lea saeva sitim multā compēscuit undā,

103   dum redit in silvās, inventōs forte sine ipsā

104   ōre cruentātō tenuēs laniāvit amictūs.

105   "Sērius ēgressus, vestīgia vīdit in altō

106   pulvere certa ferae, tōtōque expalluit ōre

107   Pyramus; ut vērō vestem quoque sanguine tīnctam

108   repperit, 'Ūna duōs,' inquit, 'nox perdet amantēs,

109   ē quibus illa fuit longā dignissima vītā;

110   nostra nocēns anima est. Ego tē, miseranda, perēmī,

111   in loca plēna metūs quī iussī nocte venīrēs

112   nec prior hūc vēnī. Nostrum dīvellite corpus,

113   et scelerāta ferō cōnsūmite viscera morsū,

114   ō quīcumque sub hāc habitātis rūpe leōnēs!

Discussion Questions

1.   How does Ovid make the scene in 96–101 more vivid and even visual? Consider his choice and manipulation of the verbs in the passage.

2.   What is especially effective about the poet's handling of Pyramus' name in the scene change at 105–07?

3.   What is the effect of the word order in 108 (**Ūna . . . amantēs**), and how does **nox perdet amantēs** continue the light/dark symbolism of 88–93? If you have read Catullus 5, what connections of theme and imagery do you see between that poem and these verses, especially 108?

       ferus, -a, -um, *wild; ferocious, savage.*
       cōnsūmō, cōnsūmere, cōnsūmpsī, cōnsūmptus, *to destroy; to devour.*
       viscus, visceris, n., usually pl., *flesh, entrails.*
114   ō, interj. used in direct address or exclamations, *oh* (here introducing a dramatic apostrophe).
       quīcumque, quaecumque, quodcumque, *whoever, whatever.*
          quīcumque: with leōnēs.
       rūpēs, rūpis, f., *rocky cliff, crag.*

115   **timidī est**: gen. of characteristic, *it is (the mark) of a cowardly (man)*.
    *nex, necis, f., *death, murder*.
116   **pactus, -a, -um**, *agreed upon, settled upon* (with **arboris**).
    umbram: again the poet focuses on the dark shadow cast beneath the tree, to intensify the atmosphere of foreboding (cf. 88–89 above).
117   **nōtae . . . vestī**: indirect object with the repeated verb and both direct objects; for the anaphora (here with a pathetic effect) and the word order, cf. I.458 above.
118   **haustus, -ūs, m.**, *drink, draft*.
119   **Quōque**: = rel. pron. **quō** (with **ferrum** as antecedent) + **-que**.
    accingō, accingere, accīnxī, accīnctus, *to gird, equip*.
    dēmīsit: here, *plunged*.
    īlia, īlium, n. pl., *groin, genitals; entrails*.
    *ferrum, -ī, n., *iron*; by synecdoche, *weapon, sword*.
    ferrum: with both **dēmīsit** and **trāxit** 120.
120   *mora, -ae, f., *delay*; **nec mora**, idiom, *and without delay* (cf. *Am.* I.11.19 below—and note the assonance here with **moriēns**).
    *fervēns, ferventis, *boiling; warm* (here, with freshly shed blood).
121   **resupīnus, -a, -um**, *lying flat on one's back*.
    humus, -ī, f., *earth, ground*.
    humō: supply *in*; abl. instead of the usual loc. **humī**.
    *cruor, cruōris, m., *blood* (from a wound); *slaughter*.
    ēmicō, -āre, -āvī, -ātūrus, *to move suddenly outward/upward; to spurt out/upward*.
122   *aliter, adv., *otherwise, differently*.
    nōn aliter quam cum, *no differently than when* (= *just as when*), a conventional formula for introducing a simile (cf. *Met.* X.64–65 below).
    vitiātus, -a, -um, *faulty, defective* (like the wall that separated the lovers' houses—cf. **vitium** 67).
    *fistula, -ae, f., *tube, pipe* (especially, as here, *water-pipe*); *shepherd's pipe*.
123   **scinditur . . . / ēiaculātur . . . rumpit** (124): the strong verbs are emphatically positioned, the last two in a chiastic arrangement with their objects.
    strīdō, strīdere, strīdī, *to hiss*.
    forāmen, forāminis, n., *hole, perforation*.
    longās / . . . aquās (124): *long streams of water*.
124   **ēiaculor, -ārī, -ātus sum**, *to shoot out, discharge*.
    ictus, -ūs, m., *stroke, blow*; here, *spurt, pulsing*.
125   **arboreus, -a, -um**, *of a tree*.
    *fētus, -ūs, m., *giving birth; fruit; offspring* (*fruit* here, but in view of the overt sexual imagery of the preceding lines, there is clearly a double entendre suggesting the children the two lovers will never have).
    adspergō, adsperginis, f., *sprinkling, spattering*.
    *āter, ātra, ātrum, *black, dark*.
126   *vertō, vertere, vertī, versus, *to (cause to) turn, spin; to reverse, change*.
    vertuntur: intransitive in the passive, *change* (into).

115   Sed timidī est optāre necem.' Vēlāmina Thisbēs
116   tollit, et ad pactae sēcum fert arboris umbram,
117   utque dedit nōtae lacrimās, dedit ōscula vestī,
118   'Accipe nunc,' inquit, 'nostrī quoque sanguinis haustūs!'
119   Quōque erat accīnctus, dēmīsit in īlia ferrum,
120   nec mora, ferventī moriēns ē vulnere trāxit,
121   et iacuit resupīnus humō. Cruor ēmicat altē,
122   nōn aliter quam cum vitiātō fistula plumbō
123   scinditur, et tenuī strīdente forāmine longās
124   ēiaculātur aquās, atque ictibus āera rumpit.
125   Arboreī fētūs adspergine caedis in ātram
126   vertuntur faciem, madefactaque sanguine rādīx

Discussion Questions

1. What is Pyramus addressing in 118? What is the point of **quoque**? What is the emotional effect of this and the preceding line?

2. Comment on the effect of the **c/q** alliteration in 118–19.

3. One commentary (DeVeau and Getty) calls the comparison in 122–24 "certainly one of Ovid's least attractive similes." Is the simile effective or not? Why?

Pyramus: Now am I dead,
                    Now am I fled;
           My soul is in the sky:
             Tongue, lose thy light;
             Moon, take thy flight:
       Now, die, die, die, die, die.

William Shakespeare
A Midsummer Night's Dream
Act V, Sc. I

*****faciēs, -ēī**, f., *outward appearance; face; shape, form.*
madefactus, -a, -um, *drenched, soaked.*

127 *purpureus, -a, -um, *purple.*
 mōrum, -ī, n., *mulberry.*
 *color, colōris, m., *color.*

   purpureō . . . colōre: the adjective/noun pair frame the line,
     emphasizing the dark transformation of the fruit and vividly bringing
     the scene to closure; the assonance of ō/ō/ō (under the ictus in each
     instance) adds a suitably doleful tone.

128 positō: = dēpositō.
 nē fallat: the purpose clause is dependent on redit (129).

129 animō: here, *heart.*

   requīrō, requīrere, requīsīvī, requīsītus, *to try to find, search for; to need,
     miss, long for* (here, through zeugma, the first sense is required with oculīs
     and the second with animō).

130 vītārit: = vītāverit, perf. subjn. in the indirect question (for the syncopated
     form, cf. agitāsse I.567 above).
 gestiō, gestīre, gestīvī, *to desire eagerly, long.*

131 Utque . . . / sīc (132): here, as often, with an implied contrast, *And although
     . . . at the same time.*
 vīsā: with arbore; English would use a clause, *once she has seen it.*
 in arbore fōrmam: = fōrmam arboris.

132 facit: supply eam.
 *incertus, -a, -um, *not fixed; uncertain, doubtful; disarranged.*
 color: suspensefully held to the end of the clause and followed by a strong
     diaeresis.
 haeret: here, *she is uncertain* (cf. the similar English idiom, *to be stuck,* i.e.,
     puzzled, over some problem).

   haeret an haec sit: supply arbor; the harsh sounds (like the c's in the
     first part of the line) and the uneven rhythm caused by the closing
     series of monosyllables help suggest Thisbe's hesitation to approach the
     tree.

133 *dubitō, -āre, -āvī, -ātus, *to be in doubt/be uncertain* (with an + indirect
     question); *to waver, hesitate.*
 tremebundus, -a, -um, *quivering, trembling.*
 *pulsō, -āre, -āvī, -ātus, *to strike, beat (against).*
 cruentus, -a, -um, *bloody.*

134 membra: at first Thisbe notices merely the body itself, only later (137)
     recognizing it as that of her lover.
 solum, -ī, n., *base, foundation; ground, earth.*

   tremebunda . . . cruentum / membra solum (134): interlocked order,
     with the epithets first, to focus on the grisly aspects of the scene.
     While tremebunda could refer to Thisbe as subject of dubitat and
     videt (cf. tremit 136), the connection with pulsāre makes its
     application to membra more likely—or, through a common poetic
     device, Ovid might well intend us to take the word in both ways.
 retrōque pedem tulit: i.e., *she stepped back.*

127	purpureō tingit pendentia mōra colōre.
128	"Ecce, metū nōndum positō, nē fallat amantem,
129	illa redit, iuvenemque oculīs animōque requīrit,
130	quantaque vītārit narrāre perīcula gestit.
131	Utque locum et vīsā cognōscit in arbore fōrmam,
132	sīc facit incertam pōmī color; haeret an haec sit.
133	Dum dubitat, tremebunda videt pulsāre cruentum
134	membra solum, retrōque pedem tulit, ōraque buxō
135	pallidiōra gerēns exhorruit aequoris īnstar,
136	quod tremit, exiguā cum summum stringitur aurā.

Discussion Questions

1. Ancient epic often contained seemingly gratuitous descriptions of physical violence; how is Ovid's graphic depiction of Pyramus' suicide (in 118–27), on the other hand, quite essential to the story-line?

2. The tree's berries turn dark from two different causes in 125–27; comment on the two images and their "believability."

3. How does Ovid introduce an element of bittersweet irony in the scene-change at 128–30?

4. In what way is the meter in the first half of 133 appropriate to the actions described? Comment on the line's other sound effects.

5. How is Ovid's description of Thisbe's face in 134–35 especially apt in this context?

6. Comment on the simile in 135–36.

ōraque . . . gerēns (135): *and with her face* (lit., *and wearing a facial expression*).

buxus, -ī, f., *box-tree; boxwood* (noted for its pale color).

135   **pallidus, -a, -um,** *pale, colorless.*

exhorrēscō, exhorrēscere, exhorruī, *to shudder, shiver* (with fear).

aequor, aequoris, n., *smooth, level surface; surface of the sea* (especially when calm).

īnstar, indecl. n. noun + gen., *the equivalent* (of), *just like.*

136   *****exiguus, -a, -um,** *small, slight.*

cum: in prose this conjunction (*when*) would introduce the clause.

summum: here substantive, *its surface.*

137 **remoror, -ārī, -ātus sum,** *to delay, pause.*

138 **clārus, -a, -um,** *loud, sonorous; clear.*

plangor, plangōris, m., *beating of the breast* (as a sign of grief); *lamentation, wailing.*

139 **comās:** acc. of respect with **laniāta.**

140 **vulnera . . . lacrimīs, flētum . . . cruōrī:** chiasmus.

suppleō, supplēre, supplēvī, supplētus, *to fill up* (with a liquid).

flētus, -ūs, m., *weeping, lamentation; tears.*

cruōrī: prose would have the abl. case.

142 **Pȳrame . . . tē . . . / Pȳrame . . . tē** (143): the repetitions, identically placed in the two verses, intensify the pathos, and the names in particular help create an incantatory effect as well.

quis: with **cāsus,** instead of the interrogative adj. **quī.**

mihi: dat. of reference, with the sense of separation.

*__cāsus, -ūs,__ m., *fall; mishap, misfortune, accident;* pl., *experiences, fortune.*

adimō, adimere, adēmī, adēmptus, *to remove, take away.*

143 **respondē . . . iacentēs** (144): the **-dē/tē/-bē** assonance, the strong **d/t** alliteration in both verses, and the series of spondees following **nōminat,** all lend a forceful sound effect to Thisbe's imperatives.

144 **exaudiō, -īre, -īvī, -ītus,** *to hear; to listen to, heed.*

*__attollō, attollere,__ *to raise, lift up.*

iacentēs: lit., *lying (still);* here, *motionless, lifeless.*

145 **Ad nōmen Thisbēs:** Thisbe had repeatedly called her lover's name to arouse him (note the careful positioning of **Pȳrame . . . / Pȳrame . . . / nōminat** 142–44), but it was the sound of her own name (also deliberately set at line's end in 143) that momentarily revived him.

nōmen . . . oculōs . . . gravātōs: again the ō/ō/ō assonance adds a mournful sound effect (cf. on 127).

oculōs . . . gravātōs: object of both **ērēxit** and **recondidit** (146).

morte: in order to appreciate fully the mystique of this scene, it is important to note that Pyramus is now dead (cf. **gelidīs in vultibus** 141) or at least hovering very near the brink of death.

gravō, -āre, -āvī, -ātus, *to make heavy, weigh down; to oppress, overwhelm.*

146 **Pȳramus:** again the name is emphatically positioned (cf. 142–43).

ērigō, ērigere, ērēxī, ērēctus, *to raise, lift up.*

vīsā . . . illā: abl. absolute.

recondō, recondere, recondidī, reconditus, *to put away, store; to put back, close again.*

147 **Quae:** = **Illa** (cf. **illā** preceding), subject of **inquit** (148).

postquam vestemque suam: placement of **-am/-em/-am** under the ictus accentuates the assonance.

postquam . . . suam cognōvit: an echo of 137, where the words appear in the same metrical position.

vestem . . . cognōvit . . . / vīdit ebur (148): chiasmus.

-que . . . et: = **-que . . . -que,** *both . . . and.*

*__ēnsis, ēnsis,__ m., *sword.*

ēnse / . . . vacuum (148): abl. of separation, *empty of its sword.*

137   Sed postquam, remorāta, suōs cognōvit amōrēs,
138   percutit indignōs clārō plangōre lacertōs
139   et, laniāta comās amplexaque corpus amātum,
140   vulnera supplēvit lacrimīs, flētumque cruōrī
141   miscuit, et gelidīs in vultibus ōscula fīgēns
142   'Pȳrame,' clāmāvit, 'quis tē mihi cāsus adēmit?
143   Pȳrame, respondē! Tua tē, cārissime, Thisbē
144   nōminat; exaudī vultūsque attolle iacentēs!'
145   Ad nōmen Thisbēs oculōs iam morte gravātōs
146   Pȳramus ērēxit, vīsāque recondidit illā.
147   "Quae, postquam vestemque suam cognōvit et ēnse
148   vīdit ebur vacuum, 'Tua tē manus,' inquit, 'amorque

Discussion Questions

1. What sound is most strikingly repeated in 137–38 and how is the effect onomatopoetic? How does Ovid's manipulation of ictus enhance this effect?

2. How is the chiastic arrangement in 140 suited to the image being described?

3. In Roman magic (officially discouraged, but in fact practiced from the earliest times and throughout the imperial period), personal names were felt to have a special power and so they were often repeated in curses and other incantations; control of the name suggested potential control of the person. With this in mind, consider carefully the scene in 142–46 and discuss how it may be construed, at least on one level, as a kind of magical rite.

The headie force of frentick love whose end is wo and payne . . .

Arthur Golding, from the dedication to his 1567 translation

---

148   **vīdit . . . amorque**: the quick dactyls are appropriate to Thisbe's agitated state.

    *ebur, eboris, n., *ivory*; by synecdoche, *an object made of ivory* (here, *an ivory scabbard*).

    Tua tē: an echo of the identically positioned **Tua tē** in 143.

    manus . . . amorque: the two instruments of Pyramus' death are one concrete and the other abstract.

149   **perdidit**: sing. to agree with only the nearer of the two subjects.

      ***īnfēlīx, īnfēlīcis**, unfertile, unproductive; disastrous, ill-fated, unfortunate.*
Most editors set the adjective off with a comma here, regarding it as
vocative, but **amor . . . īnfēlīx** is more effective and likelier what
Ovid intended.

      Est . . . manus (150): freely, *My hand too has the courage for this one act.*

      et: = **etiam** (likewise in the next verse).

      in ūnum / hoc (150): i.e., for suicide.

150   **est et amor**: the phrase, like **Est et . . . manus**, is to be taken with **mihi
fortis in ūnum / hoc**, a dat. of possession construction; the anaphora
focuses our attention back on **manus . . . amorque** (148).

      dabit . . . vīrēs: thus Thisbe's love (**hic**) is likewise **īnfēlīx**, i.e., it will
beget death and not new life—except, of course, in the **fētūs** (161) of the
mulberry tree.

      hic: though the vowel is short, the syllable was often treated in verse as long
(owing to an earlier form **hicc**); cf. **hoc** in *Am.* I.1.5 below.

      in vulnera: i.e., like **in ūnum / hoc**, *for death.*

151   **persequor, persequī, persecūtus sum**, *to follow to the end; to pursue.*

      exstīnctum: here, *dead* or *in death*; supply **tē** (i.e., Pyramus).

      ***lētum, -ī**, n., *death, destruction.*

            lētī . . . tuī (152): noun and adj. frame the clause (cf. **inventōs . . .
amictūs** 103–04).

152   **quīque**: **quī** + **-que**; supply **tū** as antecedent.

      revellō, revellere, revellī, revulsus, *to tear away, remove forcibly.*

153   **sōlā**: with **morte** not **mē** (152).

      nec: here, *not even.*

154   **Hoc . . . estōte rogātī, / . . . / ut** (156): the pronoun is object of this rare
future imperative construction, which has a solemn, almost ritualistic tone,
You shall be asked this one request . . . that.

      ambōrum: i.e., of both Pyramus and Thisbe.

155   **multum**: adv. with **miserī**.

      meus: m. sing. because she thinks only of her father's prohibition (cf.
vetuēre patrēs 61); alliteration of **m** in the first half of the line adds a
somber tone to the pitiful apostrophe.

156   **ut . . . eōdem** (157): the entire clause is in apposition to **hoc** (see on 154),
elaborating Thisbe's entreaty; note the heavy assonance of **ō** in these two
verses.

      quōs: supply **nōs** (the two lovers) as both antecedent of this relative pronoun
(which is repeated for pathetic effect) and subject of the infin. **compōnī**
(157); the request is essentially **ut nōs, quōs amor iūnxit, in eōdem
tumulō compōnī nōn invideātis.**

      certus amor . . . hōra novissima: chiasmus underscores the ironic contrast
between the steadfastness of the lovers' affection and their sudden reversal
of fortune.

      novissima: here, *most recent, last.*

157   **compōnī**: here, with **nōs** understood, *us to be placed together*, i.e., *buried.*

149   perdidit īnfēlīx! Est et mihi fortis in ūnum

150   hoc manus, est et amor; dabit hic in vulnera vīrēs.

151   Persequar exstīnctum, lētīque miserrima dīcar

152   causa comesque tuī; quīque ā mē morte revellī

153   heu sōlā poterās, poteris nec morte revellī.

154   Hoc tamen ambōrum verbīs estōte rogātī,

155   ō multum miserī meus illīusque parentēs,

156   ut quōs certus amor, quōs hōra novissima iūnxit,

157   compōnī tumulō nōn invideātis eōdem.

158   At tū, quae rāmīs arbor miserābile corpus

159   nunc tegis ūnīus, mox es tēctūra duōrum,

Discussion Questions

1. What is the intended effect of the anaphora **Est et . . . manus, est et amor** (149–50)?

2. What is most striking in the language of 152–53 and what is the poet's purpose?

3. What is unusual in the meter of 158 and how is the rhythm suited to the action at this point in the narrative?

---

invideō, invidēre, invīdī, invīsus, *to envy; to be unwilling to allow, refuse, begrudge.*
    nōn invideātis: with **ut**, a jussive noun clause (where **nē** would be the usual negative), *that you not be unwilling to allow.*

158   **At tū, quae rāmīs arbor**: having addressed first Pyramus, then (by apostrophe) their parents, Thisbe now suddenly turns to the tree itself, which had become their rendezvous for death, and speaks to it as though it were a sentient being; the direct address and the feminine modifiers (**quae** 158, **tēctūra** 159) create an impression of the tree as a woman. In prose (and in English translation) **arbor** would ordinarily precede **quae**, but here the antecedent is attracted into the relative clause.
    miserābile corpus: object both of **tegis** and (with the pl. **corpora** understood) of **es tēctūra** (159).

159   **es tēctūra**: fut. act. periphrastic, essentially = **tegēs**.

160 **signa tenē . . . habē fētūs** (161): chiasmus.

pullus, -a, -um: *dark, dreary-colored* (used especially of the clothing worn by mourners).

lūctus, -ūs, m., *(the expression of) grief, mourning, lamentation.*

*__aptus, -a, -um__, *tied, bound;* + dat., *suitable* (for).

161 **fētūs**: the object is held suspensefully to the end and has an array of connotations; the tree's fruits are "her" offspring (see on **fētūs** 125 and **īnfēlīx** 149) and, with **pullōs . . . et lūctibus aptōs** (160), they are also her dark cloak of mourning.

*__geminus, -a, -um__, *twin-born, twin; twofold, double.*

monimentum, -ī, n., *monument; token, reminder.*

162 **aptātō . . . īmum**: interlocked order.

mūcrō, mūcrōnis, m., *sharp end of a sword, point.*

*__īmus, -a, -um__, *lowest, bottommost; lowest part of, bottom of, base of;* n. pl. substantive, *the Underworld.*

163 *__incumbō, incumbere, incubuī__ + dat., *to bend over; to throw oneself (on), fall (on), lie down (on).*

*__tepeō, -ēre__, *to be warm; to have the warmth of a human body.*

    incubuit . . . tepēbat: strong verbs frame the line, and the harsh **c/d/t** alliteration suggests the violence of the act.

164 **deōs . . . parentēs**: in an elaborate chiasmus, line 165 presents the gods' response, and line 166 the parents', to Thisbe's two entreaties, the first in 156–57 directed to the lovers' parents, and the second in 158–61 directed to the tree itself but answerable only through divine agency.

165 **permātūrēscō, permātūrēscere, permātūruī**, *to become fully ripe.*

    permātūruit, āter: the **-ātūr-/āter** soundplay is deliberate and typically Ovidian.

166 **quod**: supply **id** (i.e., the lovers' cremated remains) as both antecedent of **quod** and subject of **requiēscit**.

rogus, -ī, m., *funeral pyre.*

    rogīs . . . urnā: alliteration of **r** and the assonance of **ūnā/urnā** lend a composed sound effect to the tale's closing verse; supply **ex** with **rogīs**.

supersum, superesse, superfuī, irreg., *to be above; to remain, be left over.*

    superest: the word's final syllable, coming before the principal caesura and under the ictus, produces a deliberate internal rhyme with the identically positioned **est** in the preceding verse.

*__requiēscō, requiēscere, requiēvī, requiētūrus__, *to rest, lie at rest.*

*__urna, -ae__, f., *pitcher, urn;* here, *cinerary urn.*

Two, by themselves, each other, love and feare
Slaine, cruell friends, by parting have joyn'd here.

John Donne

160   signa tenē caedis pullōsque et lūctibus aptōs

161   semper habē fētūs, geminī monimenta cruōris.'

162   "Dīxit et, aptātō pectus mūcrōne sub īmum,

163   incubuit ferrō, quod adhūc ā caede tepēbat.

164   Vōta tamen tetigēre deōs, tetigēre parentēs:

165   nam color in pōmō est, ubi permātūruit, āter,

166   quodque rogīs superest, ūnā requiēscit in urnā."

Discussion Questions

1.   Comment on the structure, metrics, and other special effects in 164.

2.   In what ways do the story's closing lines (165–66) aptly conclude the darkness/death imagery which Ovid has developed throughout the narrative?

3.   What similarities do you see between the ending of this tale and that of Daphne and Apollo? And what are some of the most significant differences?

4.   In what respects is this story more believable than the Daphne tale? How does it reveal Ovid's interest in "private versus public"?

"Pyramus and Thisbe"
Lucas Cranach the Elder, 1520-25
Staatsgalerie
Bamberg, Germany

ORPHEUS AND EURYDICE

Metamorphoses X.1–77

The tragic story of the singer Orpheus (son of the Muse Calliope) and his beloved wife Eurydice, twice lost to death, is certainly one of the best known of ancient myths. Ovid's version is told, with remarkable (and intentionally ill-proportioned) economy, in fewer than 80 lines: On the couple's wedding day, the hero's new bride falls dead, stricken by the bite of a serpent. Having mourned Eurydice "sufficiently" and "so that he might not neglect to try the shades of Hell"—two of several deliberately curious details in the narrative—Orpheus descends into the Underworld and appeals to Persephone and the prince of darkness to allow his wife's return to the land of the living. With a rambling, highly rhetorical lyric that takes up nearly a third of the entire tale, the minstrel, who could charm animals and even stones with his song, literally stupefies all the bloodless souls of Hades (the Danaids leave off carrying their urns and Sisyphus sits down on his rock!) and instantly compels Hades' king and queen to his will, on the condition, however, that in leading Eurydice out of their realm he should never look back at her face. Just as they reach the edge of upper earth, of course, Orpheus does steal a fateful backward glance, only to see Eurydice at that moment, "dying again," tumbling downward and for eternity into the abyss. Briefly stupefied himself at the calamity, and then thwarted in his attempt at a second crossing of the river Styx, Orpheus retreats to the mountains of his homeland Thrace (despite the implications of an earlier pledge to join his wife in death should he fail in his mission).

The story was in antiquity widely known from several versions, in particular from Vergil's *Georgics* (IV.452–546), and modern readers ought to consider carefully the differences between the two accounts, just as Ovid expected his contemporary audience to do. Suffice it here to say that Vergil's protagonist is at once more heroic and more sympathetic, his Eurydice far more dimensional (in Ovid's telling, the hapless bride is a mere sketch of a character and has but a single word to say, *Vale*), his rendering of Hell more fearful (and never verging on the comic, like Ovid's Sisyphus perched on his stone). In Vergil's concluding scene, Orpheus' head, torn from his shoulders by a throng of crazed Bacchantes and hurled into the Hebrus river, cried out the name of his beloved Eurydice again and again as it floated downstream, a pitiable lament re-echoed by the river's banks. In Ovid's anti-epic version, a clever undercutting of the traditional tale, Eurydice, "sufficiently mourned," seems insufficiently loved, and his magniloquent Orpheus seems closer in his ineptitudes to Daphne's blustering Apollo than to Thisbe's Pyramus, whose actions speak, as properly they should, far louder than his words.

Like the other transformations in this book, Eurydice's ill-fated marriage to the mystical lord of song and her tragic metamorphosis from dead to dead again have fascinated musicians, poets, and artists over the centuries. The story has inspired verse by Wordsworth and Shelley (both of whom looked to Vergil's account), Swinburne and Robert Browning, Rilke, D.H. Lawrence, Robert Lowell, and James Dickey; operas by Jacopo Peri (our earliest surviving opera, first performed in 1600) and Claudio Monteverdi (1607), by Gluck and Haydn and Mozart in the 18th century, by Offenbach in the 19th, and even the modern Japanese opera, *Hiroshima no Orfe (Orpheus in Hiroshima)*, by Yasushi Akutagawa (1967); other musical compositions by Schubert and Liszt and Stravinsky; numerous dramatizations, including Henry Fielding's farce, *Eurydice, or, The Devil Henpeck'd* (1737), Jean Anouilh's *Eurydice* (1941), and Tennessee Williams' *Orpheus Descending* (1955); paintings by Titian, Poussin, Rubens, and Feuerbach (seen below); sculpture by Bandinelli and Rodin; and a wide range of other artistic productions, among them three choreographed dances by Isadora Duncan and the films *Orphée* (1949) and *Le Testament d'Orphée* (1959) by Jean Cocteau and Marcel Camus' *Black Orpheus* (1959).

"Orpheus and Eurydice"
Anselm Feuerbach, 1869
Österreichische Galerie
Vienna, Austria

1   **Inde**: Book IX had ended with the wedding of Iphis and Ianthe on the island of Crete; the marriage god Hymenaeus (line 2) now makes his way from that event to the wedding of Orpheus and Eurydice.

    *immēnsus, -a, -um, *boundless, vast.*

    croceus, -a, -um, *of saffron; saffron-colored, yellow* (the color worn by brides in Roman weddings).

        croceō . . . amictū: the words surround **vēlātus** just as the cloak itself was wrapped around the god.

    vēlō, -āre, -āvī, -ātus, *to cover, clothe.*

        vēlātus: with **Hymenaeus** (2).

2   ***aethēr, aetheris**, acc., **aethera**, n., *the upper regions of space, heaven.*

    dīgredior, dīgredī, dīgressūrus, *to go away, depart.*

    Cicones, Ciconum, m. pl., *the Cicones* (a tribe of southern Thrace).

    Hymenaeus, -ī, m., *the Greek wedding refrain; the god of marriage* (cf. **Hymēn** I.480).

    ***ōra, -ae**, f., *shore, coast.*

3   ***tendō, tendere, tetendī, tentus**, *to extend, stretch forth; to proceed.*

    Orphēus, -a, -um, *of/belonging to Orpheus.*

        Orphēā . . . vōce: Ovid uses the adjective instead of Orpheus' name, in order to focus on the man's most remarkable attribute, his mesmerizing voice (which in this case fails to achieve the effect he desired).

    nēquīquam: because, while Hymenaeus did appear, his epiphany proved most unpropitious.

4   **ille**: Hymenaeus.

    nec . . . / nec . . . nec (5): an effective polysyndeton.

    sollemnis, -is, -e, *ceremonial, ritual; traditional.*

        sollemnia verba: i.e., the wedding hymn.

5   **nec . . . fēlīx**: a heavy spondaic line, with conflict of ictus and accent.

    ***ōmen, ōminis**, n., *omen, augury, sign.*

6   **quoque, quam**: note the alliteration and cf. **ūsque/-ōsque** in the next line.

    lacrimōsus, -a, -um, *tearful; causing tears.*

        lacrimōsō . . . fūmō: the repeated ō's provide a mournful sound effect.

    strīdulus, -a, -um, *shrill, high-pitched.*

        strīdula: here, *hissing* or *sputtering*, a sound further suggested by the repeated s's in 6–7.

7   ***ūsque**, adv., *all the way to/from; continuously.*

    nūllōs . . . ignēs: i.e., the torch was sputtering and smoking (irritating the eyes of the celebrants) and never thoroughly caught fire, even as it was waved back and forth to ignite the sparks.

    mōtus, -ūs, m., *movement.*

        mōtibus: i.e., *even with shaking.*

8   **exitus, -ūs**, m., *departure, exit; outcome.*

        Exitus . . . gravior: sc. **fuit**; brevity, ellipsis, and the quick dactyls add point to the **sententia**.

1   Inde per immēnsum, croceō vēlātus amictū,
2   aethera dīgreditur Ciconumque 'Hymenaeus ad ōrās
3   tendit, et Orphēā nēquīquam vōce vocātur.
4   Adfuit ille quidem, sed nec sollemnia verba
5   nec laetōs vultūs nec fēlīx attulit ōmen;
6   fax quoque, quam tenuit, lacrimōsō strīdula fūmō
7   ūsque fuit nūllōsque invēnit mōtibus ignēs.
8   Exitus auspiciō gravior. Nam nūpta per herbās
9   dum nova, Nāiadum turbā comitāta, vagātur,

Discussion Questions

1. How is the positioning of **immēnsum . . . / aethera** (1–2) appropriate to the scene described?

2. How does meter reinforce meaning in verses 2–3? What is especially effective in the shift of rhythm in 3?

3. Comment on the wordplay in **vōce vocātur** (3).

4. What are the multiple effects of the meter, the polysyndeton, and the positioning of the adjectives in 4–5?

5. How does the ominous scene conjured up by **lacrimōsō . . . fūmō** (6) foreshadow the events that follow?

6. Notice that Eurydice is at first (like Orpheus) not named, but only referred to as **nūpta . . . nova** (8–9); knowing that Ovid's audience was already well familiar with the story, what do you see as the effect?

---

*auspicium, -ī, n., *omen, augury*.
Nam . . . vagātur (9): there are some striking sound effects, including alliteration of **n** and **t**, the assonance of **per/her-**, **dum/-dum**, and the series of **ā**'s, especially in **comitāta vagātur**.
nūpta, -ae, f., *married woman, wife*; with **nova**, *bride*.
9   dum: as often, the conjunction (which we should expect to precede **nūpta**) is delayed; cf. the position of **postquam** (11).
Nāias, Nāiadis, f., *Naiad (a river nymph)*.
vagor, -ārī, -ātus sum, *to wander, roam*.

10   occidō, occidere, occidī, occāsūrus, *to fall, collapse; to die.*
        tālus, -ī, m., *ankle-bone, ankle.*
            in tālum . . . receptō: lit., *with a snake's tooth received into her ankle;* even in Latin the circumlocution is rather odd, as are other aspects of the narrative.
        dēns, dentis, m., *tooth, fang.*

11   Quam: = Eam, object of dēflēvit (12); Eurydice, like Orpheus, is still not named (their names are delayed to verses 31 and 64, respectively). Note the internal rhyme Quam . . . -rās (at the caesura) -quam . . . -rās.
        satis: a curious modifier (did Orpheus mourn Eurydice merely "enough"?), one of several elements in the narrative which Ovid deliberately introduces to undercut, and even burlesque, Orpheus' heroic image.
        *superus, -a, -um, *above, upper.*
            ad superās . . . aurās: freely, *in the air above,* i.e., *in the upper world;* the alliteration of s in this verse (seven times) may onomatopoetically suggest the swirling of the winds on earth, in opposition to the stillness of the Underworld.
        *Rhodopēius, -a, -um, *of Mt. Rhodope* (in Thrace, Orpheus' homeland).
            Rhodopēius . . . vātēs (12): for the epic circumlocution, cf. 3 above.

12   *dēfleō, dēflēre, dēflēvī, dēflētus, *to weep for, mourn.*
        *vātēs, vātis, m., *prophet; bard, poet.*
            The word suggests divine inspiration, aptly of Orpheus, whose songs had mystical effect; cf. *Am.* III.15.1 below.
        nē nōn temptāret: *that he might not fail to try;* a slightly odd double negative formulation.
        et: = etiam, with umbrās, the antithesis of aurās (11).

13   Styx, Stygis, acc., Styga, f., *the Styx* (principal river of the Underworld) or, by metonymy, *the Underworld.*
        Taenarius, -a, -um, *of Taenarus* (a promontory in the southern Peloponnese, legendary site of a cave leading into Hades).
            Taenariā . . . portā: abl. of route (common with words like porta, terra, and via).

14   levēs populōs: here, *thin* or even *weightless tribes,* i.e., ghosts.
        *simulācrum, -ī, n., *likeness; image, statue; phantom, ghost.*
            simulācra . . . fūncta sepulcrō: *phantoms of the dead* (lit., *ghosts that have suffered burial*).
        *fungor, fungī, fūnctus sum + abl., *to perform; to experience, suffer* (with morte and sepulcro, *to die*).

15   Persephonē, Persephonēs, acc., Persephonēn, f., *Persephone* or *Proserpina* (daughter of Zeus and Demeter, wife of Pluto, and queen of the Underworld).
        adiīt: the second i, normally short, is here lengthened under the ictus and before the caesura (diastole).
        inamoenus, -a, -um, *unpleasant, unlovely.*
            inamoenaque . . . dominum (16): an epic periphrasis for Pluto, lord of the dead.

10   occidit in tālum serpentis dente receptō.
11   Quam satis ad superās postquam Rhodopēius aurās
12   dēflēvit vātēs, nē nōn temptāret et umbrās,
13   ad Styga Taenariā est ausus dēscendere portā,
14   perque levēs populōs simulācraque fūncta sepulcrō
15   Persephonēn adiīt inamoenaque rēgna tenentem
16   umbrārum dominum, pulsīsque ad carmina nervīs

Discussion Questions

1.   What effect does Ovid achieve through the enjambement of **occidit** (10) and the shift of meter following? Comment too on the line's striking **c/d/t** alliteration; are these sounds appropriate to the context?

2.   What is your response to Ovid's quick narration of Eurydice's death and Orpheus' mourning before descending into the underworld (10–12)? Is the narrative too abbreviated and the transition in 11 deliberately abrupt, and, if so, what is the poet's intent?

3.   How might the negative phrasing of the purpose clause in 12 serve to undercut Orpheus' heroic image?

4.   How is the meter in 12 suited to the scene shift from 11? Comment on other sound effects in the line.

5.   By comparison with Aeneas' descent into Hades in *Aeneid* VI, Orpheus' journey seems to have been accomplished with lightning-fast speed; how does the meter in 14–15 help convey this impression?

---

16   **umbrārum dominum**: a highly effective enjambement, punctuated by caesura and intensified by the roaring **r**'s and the foreboding assonance of **um-/-um/-um** (under the ictus in each of the first three feet).
    *pellō, pellere, pepulī, pulsus, *to beat against, strike; to drive away, banish, expel.*
        pulsīsque ad carmina nervīs: *with the strings* (of his lyre) *strummed to accompany his song*; Orpheus does not merely address the prince of darkness and his bride, but tries to charm them through the magic of his lyrics.

17   **sīc ait**: the enjambement and diaeresis effectively introduce Orpheus' lengthy song.

     nūmina: voc., with the gen. phrase **positī . . . mundī**; note the soundplay with **carmina** (identically positioned in 16) and **mundī**.

     mundus, -ī, m., *world, universe.*

18   **reccidō, reccidere, reccidī, reccāsūrus**, *to fall back, sink back.*

     *****quisquis, quidquid**, indefinite rel. pron., *any who, whoever, whatever.*

       quidquid . . . creāmur: "we," the subject of **reccidimus**, is the antecedent; the n. sing. pron. is used here for a generalizing effect, *whichever of us are created mortal.*

     mortālis, -is, -e, *subject to death, mortal.*

     creō, -āre, -āvī, -ātus, *to beget, create.*

19   **sī licet et . . . sinitis** (20): the protasis of a simple fact condition, with **dēscendī** (21) the verb of the apodosis.

     *****falsus, -a, -um**, *untrue, false; misleading, deceptive.*

       falsī . . . ōris: the beguiling singer here promises to utter only the truth (whether he does or not is a matter of interpretation).

     positīs: = **dēpositīs**, *set aside*; the implication is that he sometimes does, or at least can, speak evasively or obscurely.

     ambāgēs, ambāgum, f. pl., *a circuitous path; long-winded/obscure/evasive speech.*

20   *****opācus, -a, -um**, *shaded; shadowy, dark, dim.*

21   **Tartara, -ōrum**, n. pl., *Tartarus* (the Underworld).

     utī: = **ut**.

     villōsus, -a, -um, *shaggy, hairy.*

     colubra, -ae, f., *serpent, snake* (used especially of the "hair" of monsters, as here with **villōsa**, *bristling with serpents*).

22   **ternī, -ae, -a**, pl. adj., *three (each), three at a time, three in succession.*

     Medūsaeus, -a, -um, *of Medusa* (the Gorgon whose hair consisted of living serpents); (here) *resembling Medusa, Medusa-like.*

       Medūsaeī . . . mōnstrī: Cerberus, the three-headed watchdog of the Underworld, was born of the snake-demon Echidna, a sister of Medusa; like Medusa, he had snaky locks and was so hideous that a single glance at him could turn a man to stone.

     vinciō, vincīre, vīnxī, vīnctus, *to bind, tie up.*

     guttur, gutturis, n., *throat.*

     mōnstrum, -ī, n., *omen, portent; monster.*

       villōsa . . . / terna . . . guttura (22): note the elaborate interlocked word order, producing with **Medūsaeī . . . mōnstrī** a brilliant golden line.

23   **causa . . . coniūnx**: an abrupt formulation; note the harsh alliteration of **c**, continued in **calcāta**.

     calcō, -āre, -āvī, -ātus, *to trample; to tread, step on.*

     venēnum, -ī, n., *potent herb; poison, venom.*

24   **vīpera, -ae**, f., *viper, serpent.*

17   sīc ait: "Ō positī sub terrā nūmina mundī,

18   in quem reccidimus, quidquid mortāle creāmur,

19   sī licet et falsī positīs ambāgibus ōris

20   vēra loquī sinitis, nōn hūc, ut opāca vidērem

21   Tartara, dēscendī, nec utī villōsa colubrīs

22   terna Medūsaeī vincīrem guttura mōnstrī;

23   causa viae est coniūnx, in quam calcāta venēnum

24   vīpera diffūdit crēscentēsque abstulit annōs.

25   Posse patī voluī nec mē temptāsse negābō;

Discussion Questions

1.   In what respects does the expression **falsī positīs ambāgibus ōris / vēra loquī** (19–20) seem redundant? What might Ovid's purpose be in having Orpheus speak this way?

2.   What is the point of having Orpheus mention two purposes that did *not* motivate his descent into the Underworld (20–22)?

3.   How is the intricate interweaving of the three adjectives and three nouns in 21–22 (**villōsa . . . mōnstrī**) neatly suited to Ovid's depiction of the hellhound Cerberus?

---

diffundō, diffundere, diffūdī, diffūsus, *to pour widely; to pour into, diffuse.*

crēscentēs annōs: *her budding years* (we might say, *in the bloom of youth*).

25   **Posse . . . temptāsse**: note the striking p/t alliteration and the assonance of -osse/-āsse.

patī: *to endure* (i.e., his loss), complementary infin. with **posse**.

nec mē temptāsse negābō: *nor shall I deny that I tried* (to endure). Both the verb (**temptāsse = temptāvisse**) and the curious double negative recall **nē nōn temptāret et umbrās** (12); each clause follows a reference to the serpent's strike and Orpheus' mourning.

26   **vīcit Amor**: supply **mē**; asyndeton (we expect **sed** or **autem**) and the very brevity of the sentence underscore Orpheus' point (cf. the expanded **vōs quoque iūnxit Amor** 29).

    Superā . . . ōrā: cf. **superās . . . aurās** (11).

27   **an sit**: supply **bene nōtus**; the series of monosyllables, and the consequent jerkiness of the dactylic rhythm, both preceding and following **dubitō**, help suggest Orpheus' initial hesitancy (or the hesitancy he feigns).

    et: = **etiam**; the anaphora of **et hīc** strengthens the equation Orpheus makes between Love's two victories in 26 and 29.

    auguror, -ārī, -ātus sum, *to foretell by augury; to intuit, sense, surmise.*

    esse: i.e., **eum (Amōrem) esse nōtum**, indirect statement with **auguror**.

28   ***fāma, -ae**, f., *news, report; tradition, story.*

    rapīna, -ae, f., *plunder; kidnapping.*

        veteris . . . rapīnae: i.e., Pluto's rape of Persephone (which Ovid himself had included in *Met.* V, in a tale narrated by Orpheus' own mother, the Muse Calliope).

    mentior, mentīrī, mentītus sum, *to lie; to invent, fabricate.*

29   **Per**: with oaths, *by.*

        Per . . . loca . . . / per Chaos (30): anaphora and asyndeton lend intensity to Orpheus' oath, as do the strong epithets (**plēna timōris, ingēns, vāstī**—these last two effectively juxtaposed). Cf. **in loca plēna metūs** (IV.111 above).

    ego: in prose this word (subject of **ōrō** 31) would either precede or follow the prepositional phrases; but in oaths Ovid favors this arrangement, which emphasizes the subject.

30   **Chaos, -ī**, n., *Chaos* (the formless state of the universe before creation); *the Underworld.*

    vāstus, -a, -um, *desolate, lifeless; huge, immense.*

    silentia: poetic pl.; cf. 53 below.

31   ***Eurydicē, Eurydicēs**, acc., **Eurydicēn**, f., *Eurydice* (a Thracian nymph, wife of Orpheus).

        For the delay of her name to this late point in the narrative, see above on **quam** 11, and for the Greek case endings cf. **Daphnē** and **Thisbē**.

    properāta . . . fāta: *premature death*; note the assonance of the entire phrase.

    retexō, retexere, retexuī, retextus, *to unweave.*

        Ovid has in mind the myth of the Fates, or Parcae, weaving the tapestry of a person's life from birth to death.

    *fātum, -ī, n., *prophecy; destiny, fate; Fate* (as a deity); *doom, death* (often pl. for sing.).

34   **Tendimus . . . vōsque**: note the **hūc/haec** anaphora, the parallel placement of **omnēs** and **ultima**, and the emphatic **vōsque** (and cf. **vōs** 29, **vōbīs** 32, **vestrī** 37).

35   **longissima rēgna**: poetic pl., *the most enduring dominion over* (with the objective gen. **generis**).

26 vīcit Amor. Superā deus hic bene nōtus in ōrā est;
27 an sit et hīc, dubitō. Sed et hīc tamen auguror esse,
28 fāmaque sī veteris nōn est mentīta rapīnae,
29 vōs quoque iūnxit Amor. Per ego haec loca plēna timōris,
30 per Chaos hoc ingēns vāstīque silentia rēgnī,
31 Eurydicēs, ōrō, properāta retexite fāta!
32 Omnia dēbentur vōbīs, paulumque morātī
33 sērius aut citius sēdem properāmus ad ūnam.
34 Tendimus hūc omnēs, haec est domus ultima, vōsque
35 hūmānī generis longissima rēgna tenētis.
36 Haec quoque, cum iūstōs mātūra perēgerit annōs,

Discussion Questions

1. In view of its context, what do you suppose is the intended effect of the poetic plural **silentia** (30)?

2. Some readers take **properāta retexite fāta** (31) to mean *reweave Eurydice's destiny, too swiftly ended* rather than *unweave her premature death*; which makes better sense in this context and why?

3. Comment on the placement of **omnia** and **ūnam** (32–33); what is the intended effect and how is the idea continued in the next verse?

---

tenētis: note the wordplay with this verb at the end of the sentence and the assonant **tendimus** at the beginning.
36 **Haec**: i.e., Eurydice, but the word continues the anaphora with **hūc** and **haec** in 34.
* **iūstus, -a, -um,** *lawful, legitimate; rightful, proper, deserved.*
* **mātūrus, -a, -um,** *ripe; advanced in age.*
* **peragō, peragere, perēgī, perāctus,** *to chase; to complete; to go through* (space or time); *to live out, complete* (a period of time).

37   **iūris . . . vestrī**: *under your authority* (a variety of possessive gen.).

     *__mūnus, mūneris__, n., *a required task; tribute, offering* (to a deity); *gift; favor, service.*

     *__ūsus, -ūs__, m., *use, employment; the right to use/enjoy* (especially with reference to property owned by another); *potential for use, utility; marriage* (one type of Roman civil marriage, which became binding following a full year of cohabitation).

38   **Quod**: here, *But.*

     *__venia, -ae__, f., *favor, kindness, blessing* (especially in a religious sense); *forgiveness, pardon; reprieve, remission.*

     certum est / . . . **mihī** (39): *I am determined* (lit., *it is a certainty for me*) + infin.; **mihī** is delayed to balance **coniuge.**

39   **nōlle**: essentially equivalent to **nōn** here, but with greater force.

     lētō gaudēte duōrum: the **t/d** alliteration, the assonance of **lēt-/-dēt-**, the accented **ō**'s, and the abrupt imperative add a harsh, melancholy tone to the song's close.

40   **Tālia . . . moventem**: this line corresponds precisely to **pulsīsque . . . / sīc ait** (16–17) and with it provides a chiastic frame for Orpheus' song; the internal rhyme in **dīcentem . . . moventem** adds an aptly musical effect. With the participles supply **Orpheum**, object of **flēbant** (41).

41   **exsanguis, -is, -e**, *bloodless; pale; lifeless.*

     *__fleō, flēre, flēvī, flētus__, *to weep, cry; to weep for, lament.*

     Tantalus, -ī, m., *Tantalus* (a Lydian king, son of Zeus and father of Pelops).

42   **refugus, -a, -um**, *fleeting; receding.*

     Tantalus . . . refugam (42): like the others named in the next few lines (and described by Ovid earlier in *Met.* IV), Tantalus had committed a crime that earned him eternal torment in Hades. Since Tantalus' offense was culinary (he had butchered his son and served him to the gods in a stew to test their omniscience), he was cursed with perpetual hunger and thirst, standing beneath a tree whose fruits remained just beyond his reach and in a stream whose waters receded from his lips whenever he sought to drink. Here, stunned by Orpheus' song, each shade momentarily ceases from its labors.

     stupuitque Ixīonis orbis: *and Ixion's wheel, in amazement, ceased to turn*; Orpheus' song was powerful enough to mesmerize not only men and beasts (like the **volucrēs** in 43), but even inanimate objects.

     Ixīōn, Ixīonis, m., *Ixion* (king of the Lapiths, who was tied to a perpetually turning wheel in Hades as punishment for his attempt to seduce Juno).

43   *__carpō, carpere, carpsī, carptus__, *to pluck, gather; to tear at; to travel, pursue* (a path).

     carpsēre . . . volucrēs: the allusion is to the giant Tityus, who, for his attempted rape of Leto, was tied down to several acres of ground in the Underworld and exposed to vultures that tore constantly at his liver (the organ thought to be the source of the libido and other passions).

     carpsēre: = **carpsērunt.**

    iecur, iecoris, n., *the liver.*

37 iūris erit vestrī—prō mūnere poscimus ūsum.

38 Quod sī Fāta negant veniam prō coniuge, certum est

39 nōlle redīre mihī; lētō gaudēte duōrum."

40 Tālia dīcentem nervōsque ad verba moventem

41 exsanguēs flēbant animae; nec Tantalus undam

42 captāvit refugam, stupuitque Ixīonis orbis,

43 nec carpsēre iecur volucrēs, urnīsque vacārunt

Discussion Questions

1. What rhetorical effect does Ovid hope to achieve by his repeated use of the second person pronoun in 29–37?

2. One argument for releasing Eurydice (25–29) precedes Orpheus' oath and entreaty in 29–31, and another (32–37) follows; what are the arguments and which is stronger? How economically is the second point made, and how does this economy (or the lack of it) coincide with Orpheus' promise in **positīs ambāgibus** (19)? At what point earlier in Orpheus' speech is the second argument anticipated?

3. What tone is established through the use of the words **iūstōs, iūris,** and **poscimus ūsum** (36–37)? What impression of Orpheus' attitude toward his spouse may this language be intended to convey?

4. How does Ovid carefully position his words to accentuate the internal rhyme in 40?

---

*volucris, volucris, f., *winged creature, bird.*

urnīs . . . / Bēlides (44): 49 of the 50 Danaids (daughters of the Libyan king Danaus, son of king Belus), in obedience to their father, murdered their bridegroom-cousins on their wedding night and were punished in Hades by having to fill with water urns that perpetually leaked.

*vacō, -āre, -āvī, -ātūrus, *to be empty, unfilled; to be free from, take a rest from.*

 vacārunt: = vacāvērunt.

44   **Bēlis, Bēlidos**, nom. pl. **Bēlides**, f., *descendants of Belus* (the **-is**, **-idos** endings are a common patronymic formation), *the Danaids*.

        Sīsyphus, -ī, m., *Sisyphus* (this king of Corinth had offended both Zeus and Pluto and was condemned in Hades to push a huge stone up a hill, only to have it roll back down again each time he neared the top; the apostrophe here enlivens the narrative).

        *__saxum, -ī__, n., *stone, rock, boulder*.

45   **Tunc . . . genās** (46): the clause is an indirect statement dependent on **fāma est**, *there is a story that* or *it is said that*; the prose word order would be **Fāma est genās Eumenidum, carmine victārum, tunc prīmum lacrimīs maduisse.**

46   **Eumenis, Eumenidos**, gen. pl., **Eumenidum**, f., usually pl., *one of the Eumenides/Furies* (goddesses of vengeance, who were generally severe and implacable).

        *__madēscō, madēscere, maduī__, *to become wet*.

        *__gena, -ae__, f., *the side of the face, cheek*; pl., *the area around the eyes, the eyes*.

        rēgius, -a, -um, *of the king, royal*.

47   **ōrantī**: supply **Orpheō**, indirect object with **negāre**, *to say no to* (complementary infin. with **sustinet**).

        quī regit īma: i.e., Pluto, subject (with **rēgia coniūnx** = Persephone) of **sustinet**.

49   **inter . . . tardō**: the anastrophe and enjambement of **inter** (which in prose would precede its object **umbrās**), with the off-beat caesura and **et** following, the three spondees and conflict of ictus and accent in **incessit passū**, and the harsh alliteration of **t**, all sound out the slow, limping cadence of Eurydice's gait.

        incessit: this verb is often used of the slow, orderly movement of a person of stately, even majestic bearing; there is perhaps that nuance here: Eurydice steps slowly, serenely, not just because of her wound, but also as befits the ghostly spectre of a river nymph.

        dē vulnere: Eurydice still feels the effects of the snakebite because she is among the recently deceased (**umbrās . . . recentēs** 48).

        tardō: with **passū** (not **vulnere**), abl. of manner.

50   **Hanc . . . et lēgem . . . accipit**: **hanc** = Eurydice; the zeugma (Orpheus *received* his wife and *accepted* the condition that Pluto and Persephone imposed) is perhaps meant as a further depersonalizing effect.

        lēgem: the *restriction* is explained in the following jussive noun clause (an indirect command).

        Rhodopēius . . . hērōs: some manuscripts have **Orpheus** instead of **hērōs**, but with the epithet **Rhodopēius** the name is a redundancy and the reading adopted here is comparable with **Rhodopēius . . . vātēs** (11–12 above) and **Paphius . . . hērōs** (X.290 below).

        *__hērōs, hērōos__, m., *hero* (another Greek formation).

51   **retrō**: i.e., back down into the Underworld; this condition may recall for readers the biblical story of Lot in Sodom and Gomorrah.

44   Bēlides, inque tuō sēdistī, Sīsyphe, saxō.
45   Tunc prīmum lacrimīs victārum carmine fāma est
46   Eumenidum maduisse genās; nec rēgia coniūnx
47   sustinet ōrantī nec quī regit īma negāre,
48   Eurydicēnque vocant. Umbrās erat illa recentēs
49   inter, et incessit passū dē vulnere tardō.
50   Hanc simul et lēgem Rhodopēius accipit hērōs,
51   nē flectat retrō sua lūmina, dōnec Avernās
52   exierit vallēs, aut irrita dōna futūra.
53   [Carpitur acclīvis per mūta silentia trāmes,

Discussion Questions

1.   What seem to you the most striking sound effects in 43–44?

2.   What is your reaction to the picture of Sisyphus presented in 44? How does this color your interpretation of the narrative's overall tone and purpose?

3.   What consonant sound predominates in Ovid's description of the Furies (45–46) and what is the effect?

4.   Comment on the word-picture in **Umbrās . . . illa recentēs** (48).

---

    *lūmen, lūminis, n., *light; eye* (especially pl.); *vision, gaze, glance* (sing. or pl.).

    dōnec, conj., *until.*

    Avernus, -a, -um, *of the Underworld, infernal.*

52   **vallēs, vallis,** f., *valley*; with reference to Hades, *the abyss.*

    irritus, -a, -um, *nullified, void.*

        irrita dōna futūra: = **dōna futūra esse irrita,** indirect statement after the implied speech word in **lēgem.**

    dōna: pl. for sing., i.e., the gift of Eurydice's resurrection from the dead.

53   **acclīvis, -is, -e,** *inclined, sloping upwards.*

        acclīvis . . . opācā (54): the numerous epithets and asyndeton counterbalance the brevity of Ovid's narration of the trek to upper earth.

    mūtus, -a, -um, *mute, soundless, speechless.*

    trāmes, trāmitis, m., *footpath, trail.*

        Carpitur . . . trāmes: English would use an active construction, *they pressed their way along the upward sloping path.*

54   **cālīgō, cālīginis**, f., *darkness; gloom.*

      *****dēnsus, -a, -um**, *thick, dense; frequent.*

55   *****margō, marginis**, m., *wall; border, edge; margin.*

56   **dēficiō, dēficere, dēfēcī, dēfectus**, *to fail; to lose strength, collapse, faint.*

      nē dēficeret: the understood subject of the (positive) fear clause is
         Eurydice.

      nē dēficeret metuēns avidusque videndī: note the effective chiasmus
         and the soundplay in **avidus . . . videndī**; both epithets modify the
         subject **amāns** (57), *the lover* (i.e., Orpheus).

      *****metuō, metuere, metuī, metūtus**, *to fear, be afraid of.*

      avidus, -a, -um, *greedy; desirous* (of), *eager* (for) + gen.

      videndī: supply **eam**, i.e., Eurydice.

57   **flexit amāns . . . illa relāpsa est**: chiasmus, with the verbs framing the line.

      relābor, relābī, relāpsus sum, *to fall/slip backward.*

58   **bracchiaque . . . certāns**: the cacophonous alliteration of **r**, **c/q**, and **t/d**, the
         series of spondees, elisions, and conflict of ictus and accent following the
         opening dactyl, the anaphora and assonance in the four verbals (each
         describing intense or violent action), and the division of the verse by the
         carefully positioned participles (the first at the caesura, the second at line's
         end), all contribute to the "soundtrack," as Eurydice starts to slip backward
         into the abyss and desperately thrashes out her arms toward Orpheus.

      intendō, intendere, intendī, intentus, *to stretch; to stretch forth, hold out.*

      *****prēndō, prēndere, prēndī, prēnsus**, *to grasp, seize, take hold of; to catch,*
         capture.

      certō, -āre, -āvī, -ātūrus, *to contend, strive, struggle.*

      intendēns . . . certāns: these participles are taken by most editors to
         describe Orpheus, since he is assumed to be the subject in the next
         verse (see on **cēdentēs . . . aurās**), but 58–59 more likely refer to
         Eurydice for several reasons: the clauses immediately preceding and
         following both refer to Eurydice; the actions in 58, especially the
         priority given to the passive **prēndī**, and the violent **arripit** in 59,
         seem more naturally attributed to her as she slips and falls; **īnfēlīx** (59)
         is deliberately repeated in **īnfēlīx Lēthaea** (70), a reference to
         Eurydice's counterpart, not Orpheus', in the simile of 68–71; and
         finally, the contrast between Eurydice's valiant struggle and her
         husband's relative ineptitude further diminishes the hero's image, in
         keeping with Ovid's parodic intentions.

59   **cēdentēs . . . aurās**: *the retreating air* (of the world of the living); for **aurae**
         in this fairly common sense, cf. *Met.* IV.478. As Eurydice reaches out for
         Orpheus, she catches hold of nothing but the longed-for air of upper earth,
         which they had very nearly reached (55) but which now retreats from her
         outstretched arms as she falls backward. Most readers, comparing (among
         other examples) the scene in *Aen.* II.791–94, where Aeneas grasps only a
         wisp of air as he tries to embrace Creusa's ghost, refer **īnfēlīx arripit** to
         Orpheus and **aurās** to Eurydice's shade (a possible interpretation, but see

54   arduus, obscūrus, cālīgine dēnsus opācā.
55   Nec procul āfuerant tellūris margine summae;
56   hīc, nē dēficeret metuēns avidusque videndī,
57   flexit amāns oculōs. Et prōtinus illa relāpsa est,
58   bracchiaque intendēns, prēndīque et prēndere certāns,
59   nīl nisi cēdentēs īnfēlīx arripit aurās;
60   iamque iterum moriēns, nōn est dē coniuge quicquam
61   questa suō (quid enim nisi sē quererētur amātam?),
62   suprēmumque "Valē," quod iam vīx auribus ille

Discussion Questions

1. What is the intended effect of the chiasmus in 56?

2. How are the meter, the elision, and the chiasmus in 57 especially appropriate to the sense?

---

       above on 58 and note also that in *Aen*. II.772 Creusa, not Aeneas, is
       described as **īnfēlīx**).
       arripiō, arripere, arripuī, arreptus, *to grasp, take hold of, embrace.*
60   **est . . . / questa** (61): Eurydice is subject.
       quicquam, adv., *in any respect, at all.*
61   **quid . . . amātam: sē . . . amātam (esse)** is an indirect statement dependent
       on the potential subjn. **quererētur**, *for what could she complain of except
       that. . . .*
62   **suprēmum**: n. acc., modifying the word **Valē**, which as Eurydice's final
       utterance is object of **dīxit** (63). Only that last fleeting word falls into a
       quick dactyl—the rest of the line, with the series of monosyllables, is in an
       aptly halting, spondaic rhythm.

63   **acciperet**: subjn. in a rel. clause of characteristic, perhaps with the force of result (her cry was so quick and faint that Orpheus could barely hear it).

    revolvō, revolvere, revoluī, revolūtus, *to roll back, return*; pass., *to fall back again* (cf. **relāpsa est** 57—there she first slips and now she tumbles quickly backward).

    eōdem, adv., *to/into the same place* (the redundancy in re- and the adverbs **rūrsus** and **eōdem** are deliberately emphatic—and cf. **iterum** 60 and **geminā** 64).

64   **Nōn aliter stupuit . . . / quam . . . quī** (65) . . . / **quam quī** . . . (68) . . . **tūque** (69): momentarily the hero *was paralyzed* with horror; the quick dactyls in 64–65 suggest how suddenly this happened. In his inability to act or speak, Orpheus is compared in this double simile with characters who were turned to stone in two otherwise unattested transformation tales; for **nōn aliter quam**, cf. IV.122 above.

    geminā nece: abl. of cause; cf. **iterum moriēns** (60) and **geminī . . . cruōris** (IV.161 above).

    Orpheus, -ī, m., *Orpheus* (the hero is at last named; -eu- in the nom. case here is a diphthong).

65   **tria . . . / colla canis** (66): the tale's second reference to Cerberus (cf. **terna . . . guttura mōnstrī** 22).

    quī timidus: with **vīdit**; in prose the words would follow **quam**. The character (whose name is unknown) apparently gazed upon Cerberus as Hercules was leading him on a chain leash to king Eurystheus and, paralyzed by fear, was turned to stone.

    mediō: supply **collō**.

    catēna, -ae, f., *chain*; pl., *chains, fetters*.

66   **quem . . . prior** (67): the full expression here would be **quem pavor nōn relīquit, antequam nātūra prior relīquit**; in English we would say, *who did not lose his fear until he lost his original nature* (i.e., as a human being)—but what is the lit. translation?

    pavor, pavōris, m., *sudden fear, terror*.

    antequam or by tmesis **ante . . . quam**, conj., *before*.

67   **oborior, oborīrī, obortus sum**, *to rise up, spring up*.

68   **quam quī . . . / Ōlenos** (69): i.e., **aut quam Ōlenos, quī . . . trāxit**; most manuscripts read **quīque**, but (as Anderson notes) **quam quī** more clearly introduces the second simile in parallel with the first (cf. **quam . . . quī** 65). We can only deduce from the context, and roughly comparable tales, that Lethaea had offended some deity, apparently in boasting of her own beauty, and when her lover (or spouse) Olenos attempted to accept both the blame and the punishment in her place, the two were transformed to stone.

69   **Ōlenos, -ī**, m., *Olenos*.

        The character is otherwise unknown, but there are several Greek towns with this name—and Herodotus 4.35 mentions an early Greek named Olen who, like Orpheus, was a minstrel and composer of hymns.

    nocēns: here, *guilty*.

    tūque: with **quam** (68), i.e., *than Olenos . . . and you, oh Lethaea*; for the

63   acciperet, dīxit, revolūtaque rūrsus eōdem est.
64   Nōn aliter stupuit geminā nece coniugis Orpheus,
65   quam tria quī timidus, mediō portante catēnās,
66   colla canis vīdit, quem nōn pavor ante relīquit,
67   quam nātūra prior, saxō per corpus obortō;
68   quam quī in sē crīmen trāxit voluitque vidērī
69   Ōlenos esse nocēns, tūque, ō cōnfīsa figūrae
70   īnfēlīx Lēthaea tuae, iūnctissima quondam
71   pectora, nunc lapidēs, quōs ūmida sustinet Īdē.

Discussion Questions

1. Contrast the meter of 63 with that of 62; in what way is the shift appropriate?

2. What are the several points of correspondence between the circumstances of Orpheus and Eurydice and those of the characters in the two similes (64–71)? Are the similes an effective part of the narrative, or do you find them unduly digressive?—defend your response.

---

    dramatic apostrophe, cf. **Sīsyphe** (44).
cōnfīdō, cōnfīdere, cōnfīsus sum + dat., *to trust in, have confidence in, be sure of.*
    cōnfīsa figūrae . . . tuae: freely, *so self-assured in your beauty.*

70 **īnfēlīx Lēthaea:** enjambement underscores the epithet and draws our attention back to **īnfēlīx** (Eurydice) in 59; both women were young (presumably) and beautiful, and had lovers who hoped to rescue them from death.
    Lēthaea, -ae, f., *Lethaea.*
    The character is not otherwise known, but the name, like the adj.
        Lēthaeus, -a, -um, is doubtless meant to recall Lethe, the River of Forgetfulness in the Underworld, and all of its dark associations.
    *****quondam,** adv., *once, formerly.*
        iūnctissima quondam / pectora, nunc lapidēs (71): both phrases, linked by the antithetical *then/now* adverbs (and the **iūnc-/nunc** assonance), are in apposition with **Ōlenos** and **Lēthaea.**

71 **ūmidus, -a, -um,** *wet, moist; rainy.*
    sustinet: here, simply *holds* (i.e., the rocks, boulders perhaps, were situated on the mountain).
    Īdē, Īdēs, f., *Mt. Ida.*
        There were mountains of this name in both Crete and Troy—probably Ovid means the latter, site of the judgment of Paris and described by Horace, *Carmina* III.20.16, as **aquōsa.**

72 **Ōrantem . . . volentem**: supply **eum** (Orpheus); the participles, both objects of **arcuerat** (73) and both to be taken with the adv. **frūstrā**, effectively frame the line.

73 **portitor, portitōris**, m., *tollkeeper* (one who collects import or export taxes); as applied to Charon (who collected pennies from the tongues of the dead before allowing them to cross over the Styx into Hades), *ferryman.*
arceō, arcēre, arcuī, *to contain, restrain; to keep away, drive back.*
Septem . . . diēbus: abl. of duration of time, instead of the much commoner acc. construction.

74 **squālidus, -a, -um**, *rough; filthy, unbathed, unkempt.*
rīpa, -ae, f., *bank* (of a river, here the Styx).
***Cerēs, Cereris**, f., *Ceres* (goddess of grain, identified with the Greek Demeter, mother of Persephone/Proserpina).
    Cereris sine mūnere: Orpheus is *without Ceres' gift* (of grain), first because he refuses to eat (just as he refuses to bathe) and also perhaps because Ceres, as Persephone's mother, will not aid in his further assault on her daughter's realm.

75 **alimentum, -ī**, n., *food*; pl., *nourishment, sustenance.*
    alimenta: predicate nom. with **fuēre = fuērunt**.

76 **Esse . . . crūdēlēs**: the prose order would be **deōs Erebī esse crūdēlēs**, an indirect statement dependent on **questus** (*complaining that*).
Erebus, -ī, m., *Erebus* (son of Chaos, father of Charon, and god of darkness); *the Underworld.*

77 **Rhodopē, Rhodopēs**, acc. **Rhodopēn**, f., *Mt. Rhodope* (see on **Rhodopēius** 11).
aquilō, aquilōnis, m., *north wind.*
Haemus, -ī, m., *Haemus* (a mountain in northern Thrace).
    Rhodopēn pulsumque aquilōnibus Haemum: the harsh **p/q** alliteration, the booming assonance of **-um** (under the ictus in **pulsum**), and the hissing **s**'s are perhaps intended to suggest the storming of the wild north winds as Orpheus retreats from Hades, and indeed from civilization itself, here at the close of the tale.

And then he struck from forth the strings a sound
Of deep and fearful melody. Alas!
In times long past, when fair Eurydice
With her bright eyes sat listening by his side,
He gently sang of high and heavenly themes.

From "Orpheus," Percy Bysshe Shelley, 1820

72	Ōrantem frūstrāque iterum trānsīre volentem
73	portitor arcuerat. Septem tamen ille diēbus
74	squālidus in rīpā Cereris sine mūnere sēdit;
75	cūra dolorque animī lacrimaeque alimenta fuēre.
76	Esse deōs Erebī crūdēlēs questus, in altam
77	sē recipit Rhodopēn pulsumque aquilōnibus Haemum.

Discussion Questions

1. Comment on the combined effects of sound, meter, and polysyndeton in 75.

2. Orpheus' actions at the very end of the tale (76–77) do not coincide with what he had pledged he would do in the end of his song to Pluto and Persephone. What do you make of the discrepancy? Compare Pyramus' pledge and his actions in IV.108–21 and Thisbe's words and deeds in 151–63 with Orpheus' actions here. In view of the burlesque elements that appear at least occasionally in the story, what overall response to the tale do you suppose Ovid expected of his readers? What is your own response?

Hermes, Eurydice, and Orpheus, 5th century B.C. relief
Museo Archeologico Nazionale, Naples, Italy

PYGMALION

Metamorphoses X.238–97

From the beginning of time it would seem, at least from the male perspective, man has quested for, and even sought to create, the perfect woman. Robotics produced *The Stepford Wives*, Frankenstein stitched together a bride for his monster, and Professor Henry Higgins fashioned his "Fair Lady" from the raggedy flower girl, Liza Doolittle, in Lerner and Loewe's delightful musical, an adaptation from George Bernard Shaw's *Pygmalion*. But Ovid, Shaw's own ultimate inspiration and our principal ancient literary source for the tale, has provided us with a far more miraculous transformation. Offended by the profligacy of the daughters of Propoetus (who, for their impiety, were transformed by Venus into prostitutes and then hardened into stone), the Cypriote sculptor Pygmalion withdrew from all contact with women, living the life of a celibate and dedicating himself wholly to his art. Eventually he sculpted an ivory statue of a maiden more beautiful than any ever born, and then promptly fell in love with his own creation. The central panel of Ovid's narrative focuses in detail on the artist's elegiac (and to some extent ritualistic) courtship of his ivory maiden and then, when the festival of Venus had arrived, on his prayer to the goddess that his own wife might be, if not the statue itself, then at least a woman in her likeness. In return for his piety, Venus grants Pygmalion's wish, reversing both the process by which she had transformed the impious Propoetides and the usual (human to sub-human) direction of metamorphosis in Ovid's poem: as the sculptor kisses his "Sleeping Beauty," her skin grows warm and soft, her veins begin to pulse, a blush comes to her face (unlike the bloodless, shameless Propoetides), and she raises up her eyes to glimpse at once the light of heaven and her lover's gaze. Despite the unnatural inception of their affair, and under the benign guidance of Venus, the two are wed and soon have a daughter, Paphos, who (in an etiological aspect of the myth) gave her name to a city of Cyprus famous for its cult of the goddess.

It is little wonder that a story with these fairy-tale qualities, so sensuous and sentimental, and so focused on artistic creation, should have inspired, not only the talents of George Bernard Shaw, and Lerner and Loewe, but such artists (among many, many others) as Falconet, Rodin, and Gerome, whose own creations are pictured in the pages that follow. "Fellow-artists," one ought to say—for it was very much Ovid's point that we should see Pygmalion, not merely as a man, but as a creative genius. In this role, Pygmalion shares certain qualities with Orpheus, which the reader is invited to explore, even as his ivory maiden has much in common with Ovid's Eurydice. To note only an obvious point or two, both men attempt to use their artistic talents to control their women: the one fails, despite the magical charm of his music, to restore his spouse to life; the other succeeds, through piety and the power of art, in bringing his ideal woman to life. The wives themselves are one-dimensional, manipulated: Eurydice's role is but to die, and die again, uttering only an uncomplaining "farewell"; the ivory maiden, who speaks not even a single word and has no name (though in postclassical adaptations she is called Galatea), is shaped, and handled, and, when brought to life, gazes heavenward at her creator as at a god.

With these points in mind, along with the condemning attitudes about the virtue and beauty of "real" women that are expressed early in the narrative, some readers view Pygmalion in a negative light, as an eccentric misogynist and a manipulator. But the story's misogyny is perhaps better attributed to the persona of its narrator, Orpheus himself, who in mourning the death of Eurydice has gone on to reject all other women and is here singing (hence the quotation marks enclosing the text below) one of a series of ballads protesting their vile and illicit loves. Pygmalion's religious devotion to Venus is remarkable, as can be seen from her extraordinary intervention on his behalf, and, in the intensity of his reverence for his beloved, he is certainly nearer to Pyramus than to Ovid's Apollo or even to Orpheus: in the end, it may be that the poet expects us to fault Pygmalion for nothing more than the extremity of his idealism.

In his role as artist in fact, and in particular as an artist of the erotic, Pygmalion has much in common with Ovid himself. Both the poet and Pygmalion (who is at once a creator and the poet's own creation) revere love, and beauty, and the illusion of reality. It has been observed that Ovid's comment on the realism of Pygmalion's statue—*ars adeo latet arte sua* ("so utterly was his artifice concealed by his art")—might well serve as a prime tenet of the poet's own philosophy of art.

"Pygmalion and Galatea"
Auguste Rodin, 1889
Metropolitan Museum of Art
New York

238 **Sunt . . . ausae**: the opening line is neatly symmetrical, with **Venerem** at the
axis, surrounded by **obscēnae . . . Prōpoetides**, and verbals framing the
whole; the sentence's prose order would be **Tamen Prōpoetides obscēnae
ausae sunt negāre Venerem esse deam.**

tamen: i.e., ignoring the fate of their compatriots, the Cerastae, whom
Venus had transformed into bulls for butchering their guests—a story told
by Ovid in the preceding passage.

obscēnus, -a, -um, *ill-omened; filthy, loathsome; lewd.*

> **obscēnae . . . ausae**: Ovid likes to arrange pairs of end-rhyming and
> grammatically connected words such as these two by setting one at the
> caesura, with the last syllable under the ictus, and the other at line's
> end; the effect is to accentuate both the connection and the assonance
> (cf. I.460 above).

Prōpoetides, Prōpoetidum, f. pl., *the Propoetides* (daughters of Propoetus
of Cyprus, who were, according to this legend, the first prostitutes).

239 **prō quō**: i.e., *for this offense.*

sua . . . / corpora cum fōrmā (240): a kind of hendiadys; we would say
simply *their beautiful bodies.*

īrā: abl. of cause.

240 **prīmae . . . feruntur**: supply **esse**, *they are said to be the first.*

vulgō, -āre, -āvī, -ātus, *to make available to the masses; to prostitute.*

> **vulgāsse**: = **vulgāvisse.**

241 *__pudor, pudōris__, m., *sense of shame; decency, chastity.*

sanguisque indūruit ōris: Ovid imaginatively blends the physiological with
the psychological—when we are ashamed, blood rushes to our faces and we
blush, but when we cease to feel shame and to blush, it is because the
blood has hardened in our veins.

indūrēscō, indūrēscere, indūruī, *to grow hard, harden, set.*

242 **rigidus, -a, -um**, *rigid, stiff; unyielding.*

parvō . . . discrīmine: *with little noticeable change*, i.e., from their former
nature as "hardened" prostitutes; abl. of attendant circumstance.

*__silex, silicis__, m., *hard stone, flint* (often used of the absence of emotions, or
"hard-heartedness," in persons—cf. *Am.* I.11.9 below).

versae: supply **sunt.**

243 **Quās**: = **Eās** (with **agentīs** = **agentēs**).

quia, conj., *since, because.*

*__Pygmaliōn, Pygmaliōnis__, m., *Pygmalion* (legendary king of Cyprus, though
here seen only as a sculptor).

*__aevum, -ī__, n., *time, age.*

> **aevum agere**: idiom, *to spend one's life, live.*

per crīmen: here, *in wickedness, viciously.*

244 **offēnsus, -a, -um**, *offended, shocked.*

vitiīs, quae plūrima: English would take the adjective with the noun rather
than the pron., *the countless vices which . . . .*

245 **sine coniuge caelebs / vīvēbat . . . cōnsorte carēbat** (246): the second
clause intensifies the first; note the harsh **c** alliteration at the end of both

238	"Sunt tamen obscēnae Venerem Prōpoetides ausae
239	esse negāre deam; prō quō sua, nūminis īrā,
240	corpora cum fōrmā prīmae vulgāsse feruntur,
241	utque pudor cessit sanguisque indūruit ōris,
242	in rigidum parvō silicem discrīmine versae.
243	"Quās quia Pygmaliōn aevum per crīmen agentīs
244	vīderat, offēnsus vitiīs, quae plūrima mentī
245	fēmineae nātūra dedit, sine coniuge caelebs
246	vīvēbat thalamīque diū cōnsorte carēbat.
247	Intereā niveum mīrā fēlīciter arte
248	sculpsit ebur fōrmamque dedit, quā fēmina nāscī

Discussion Questions

1. In 241–42 Ovid wants his readers to visualize the actual metamorphosis of the Propoetides, but how might the incident and the transformation also be viewed metaphorically?

2. Comment on the word order, and its effect, in 242.

3. What is your response to Pygmalion's actions, and his motivations, in 243–46? Is the characterization of woman's nature (244–45) Pygmalion's, the narrator's (i.e., Orpheus'), or Ovid's?

---

verses, and the framing of 246 with the assonant imperfect tense verbs.

caelebs, caelibis, *unmarried, celibate.*

246   **thalamus, -ī,** m., *inner chamber; bedroom.*

  cōnsors, cōnsortis, m./f., *one who shares with another; partner, consort, companion.*

  careō, carēre, caruī, caritūrus + abl., *to lack, be without.*

247   **niveum mīrā fēlīciter arte / . . . ebur** (248): the ABCBA arrangement—with the epithets first, and the nouns suspensefully delayed—is as "felicitously artful" as the sculpture Ovid describes. The full significance of **mīrā** becomes apparent as the tale unfolds (cf. **mīrātur** 252).

248   **sculpō, sculpere, sculpsī, sculptus,** *to carve, sculpt.*

    sculpsit ebur, fōrmamque dedit: another chiasmus.

  quā: *(beauty) with which,* abl. of description.

  quā fēmina nāscī / nūlla (249): the alliteration and assonance add a delicate sound effect.

249 **operis . . . suī**: objective gen. with **amōrem** (cf. **simulātī corporis ignēs** 253).

    ***concipiō, concipere, concēpī, conceptus**, *to receive; to conceive, develop; to express, compose* (in words); *to pronoune solemnly* (a prayer, oath).

250 **quam**: subject of both **vīvere** and **velle** in the indirect statement after **crēdās**, *which you would think was alive and wanted to move*; the 2nd-pers. verb serves to involve the audience.

251 **reverentia, -ae**, f., *reverence; modesty, shyness* (the statue's imagined modesty is quite appropriate, since she is, of course, still nude—see 263).

    movērī: the passive, while essentially equivalent to the English intransitive *to move*, is especially suited to the description of a statue which has the will, but not the power, *to move itself* (a reflexive usage comparable to the Greek middle voice).

252 **ars . . . suā**: a brilliant, oxymoronic **sententia**, and certainly a prime tenet in Ovid's own philosophy of art.

    haurit / . . . ignēs (253): **ignēs**, used here, as often, of the fires of love, = *a passion for*, with **simulātī corporis**.

    pectore: supply **in**.

253 **simulātī**: a deliberate contrast with **vērae** (250).

254 **operī**: dat. with the compound **admovet**.

    temptantēs: the participle modifies **manūs** and introduces the indirect question **an . . . ebur** (255) and so should be translated at the end of the main clause, *testing (to see) whether it is flesh or ivory*. The halting monosyllables at line's end suspensefully anticipate the question.

255 **corpus . . . fatētur**: the anaphora and the breathless series of dactyls and one- and two-syllable words are perhaps meant to suggest Pygmalion's excitement as his hands move over the statue's body, an effect continued in the alliteration and polysyndeton of the next verse.

256 **dat . . . putat**: Ovid accentuates the internal rhyme by carefully setting the rhyming syllables under the ictus.

257 **tāctīs . . . membrīs**: dat. with the compound **īnsīdere**; the separation of participle from noun, and in fact the entire structure of the line, is precisely paralleled in the next verse.

    īnsīdō, īnsīdere, īnsēdī, īnsessus, *to settle upon; to sink into*.

258 **et . . . artūs**: the prose arrangement would be **et metuit nē līvor in artūs pressōs veniat**, and again (as with **tāctīs** 257) English would use a relative clause rather than a participle—*and he fears that a bruise may appear on the limbs he has pressed*.

    līvor, līvōris, m., *bluish discoloration, bruise*.

259 **adhibeō, adhibēre, adhibuī, adhibitus**, *to hold out; to make use of, employ; to offer*.

    puellīs: dat. with **grāta**.

260 **mūnera**: like the elegiac lover, Pygmalion showers his beloved with gifts.

    ***concha, -ae**, f., *shellfish* (especially the murex, the ancients' principal source for purple dye); *shell, pearl*.

    teres, teretis, *smooth, rounded*.

249 *no* *worked and* *conceived* *loved*
nūlla potest, operisque suī concēpit amōrem.
250 Virginis est vērae faciēs, quam vīvere crēdās
251 et, sī nōn obstet reverentia, velle movērī—
252 ars adeō latet arte suā. Mīrātur et haurit
253 pectore Pygmaliōn simulātī corporis ignēs.
254   "Saepe manūs operī temptantēs admovet an sit
255 corpus an illud ebur, nec adhūc ebur esse fatētur.
256 Ōscula dat reddīque putat, loquiturque tenetque,
257 et crēdit tāctīs digitōs īnsīdere membrīs,
258 et metuit pressōs veniat nē līvor in artūs.
259 Et modo blanditiās adhibet, modo grāta puellīs
260 mūnera fert illī: conchās teretēsque lapillōs
261 et parvās volucrēs et flōrēs mīlle colōrum
262 līliaquē pictāsque pilās et ab arbore lāpsās

Discussion Questions

1. Comment on the very striking sound effects in 250–51. How are the halting monosyllables in 251 appropriate to the context?

2. Several elements in the narrative at 247–53 purposely recall the opening tale of the Propoetides (cf., for example, **fōrmam** 248 and **fōrma** 240; **reverentia** 251 and **pudor** 241; **simulātī corporis** 253 and **corpora** 240). Explore the several connections between the description of Pygmalion's statue and the character and transformation of the Propoetides. Why does Ovid link the two stories as he does? How is Pygmalion's reaction to the statue in 252–53 ironic in view of his earlier response to the Propoetides?

3. What do the verbs **putat**, **crēdit**, and **metuit** (256–58) tell us about Pygmalion's emotional state?

---

lapillus, -ī, m., *small stone, pebble; gem.*
261 **mīlle colōrum:** gen. of description; note the assonance with **flōrēs.**
262 **līlium, -ī,** n., *lily.*
    līliaquē: lengthening of a short vowel (diastole) is not uncommon in poetry, especially (as here with **-quē**) when the syllable is under the ictus and precedes a caesura.
pictus, -a, -um, *painted, colored.*

263 **Hēliades, Hēliadum**, f. pl., *the Heliades* (daughters of the sun god Helios, who, as they lamented the death of their brother Phaëthon, were transformed into poplar trees that "wept" tears of amber—Ovid tells the story in *Met.* II).

lacrimās: here, *amber beads*.

264 *__gemma, -ae__*, f., *jewel, gem*.

monīle, monīlis, n., *necklace, ornamental collar; jewelry*.

265 **aure . . . pectore**: prose would include the prepositions **dē** and **in**, respectively.

__baca, -ae__, f., *berry, nut; pearl, bead*.

redimīculum, -ī, n., *decorative band, garland*.

266 **Nec . . . minus . . . vidētur**: litotes; Pygmalion not only dressed his statue, it seems, but also undressed her—for bed!

__fōrmōsus, -a, -um__, *beautiful, lovely* (a common epithet in elegy).

267 **collocō, -āre, -āvī, -ātus**, *to set up, arrange*.

hanc: supply **statuam**.

__strātum, -ī__, n., *bedding, coverlet*; often in pl., *bed*.

Sīdōnis, Sīdōnidis, *of Sidon, Sidonian*.

    The town of Sidon, on the coast of Phoenicia, was famous for its production and export of purple dye from the murex—see on **concha** 260).

268 **appellō, -āre, -āvī, -ātus**, *to speak to; to call* (someone) *by a particular name*.

socia, -ae, f., *female associate, partner*.

    appellatque . . . sociam: supply **hanc** (from 267)—*and he calls her* (or *it!*) *the companion of his bed* (cf. **thalamī . . . cōnsorte** 246). The alliteration of **l**/**ll** in this passage adds an elegant sound effect to the scene's close (note especially the soundplay in **collō/collocat/colla** 264–68, and cf. 280 and 285).

acclīnō, -āre, -āvī, -ātus, *to lay down, rest (on)*.

    acclīnāta colla / . . . repōnit (269): *he lays its head to rest*.

269 *__plūma, -ae__*, f., *feather; feather cushion, pillow*.

__tamquam__, conj., *just as, as if, as though*.

    tamquam sēnsūra: supply **eās** (i.e., the pillows); freely, *just as though it could feel them*.

repōnō, repōnere, reposuī, repositus, *to put back; to put down, lay down* (in a position of rest).

270 *__fēstus, -a, -um__*, *festive*; with **diēs** (and often pl.), *holiday, festival*.

    The festival of Venus, goddess of sensual love, aptly, and suspensefully, interrupts the bedroom scene of 266–69.

diēs: often f., as here, when reference is to a specific day.

tōtā . . . Cyprō: supply **in**.

Cyprus, -ī, f., *the island of Cyprus*.

271 **pandus, -a, -um**, *curving, bowed*.

inductae: here, with **aurum** as a "retained acc." object and **pandīs . . . cornibus** (dat. with compounds), the participle has a middle force, lit.,

263   Hēliadum lacrimās. Ōrnat quoque vestibus artūs,
264   dat digitīs gemmās, dat longa monīlia collō;
265   aure levēs bācae, redimīcula pectore pendent—
266   cūncta decent. Nec nūda minus fōrmōsa vidētur:
267   collocat hanc strātīs conchā Sīdōnide tīnctīs,
268   appellatque torī sociam, acclīnātaque colla
269   mollibus in plūmīs tamquam sēnsūra repōnit.
270   "Fēsta diēs Veneris tōtā celeberrima Cyprō
271   vēnerat, et pandīs inductae cornibus aurum
272   conciderant ictae niveā cervīce iuvencae,
273   tūraque fūmābant, cum mūnere fūnctus ad ārās
274   cōnstitit et timidē, 'Sī, dī, dare cūncta potestis,

Discussion Questions

1.   What is the intended effect of the polysyndeton in 260-63?

2.   Comment on the word order, and its effect, in 264–65.

3.   How is the progression of Pygmalion's actions in 254-69 like a courtship? How is it different?

4.   Comment on the alliteration in 272. Is the effect onomatopoetic? How do the sound effects of 273 differ?

---

    having applied gold to their arching horns, but more freely, *with their arching horns gilded*; the entire phrase modifies **iuvencae** (272).

272   *****īciō, īcere, īcī, ictus**, *to strike* (with a weapon—here a sacrificial knife or ax).

    niveā cervīce: abl. of respect with **ictae**.

    iuvenca, -ae, f., *young cow, heifer*.

    Appropriately, a female animal is sacrificed to the female deity.

273   **tūs, tūris**, n., *frankincense* (often pl. for the incense used in religious rites).

    fūmō, -āre, -āvī, *to fume, (emit) smoke*.

    mūnere: with **fūnctus** (not **cum**, which here is a conj.).

274   **timidē**: with **dīxit** (276); Pygmalion addresses the goddess with all due reverence.

275 **coniūnx**: with **mea** (276). The prose arrangement would be '**Sī, dī, cūncta dare potestis, coniūnx mea sit, optō, similis eburnae**,' **Pygmaliōn timidē dīxit** (**nōn ausus dīcere** '**eburnea virgō**'); in his modesty, Pymalion did not dare ask that he marry the statue itself but only some maiden with the statue's beauty. The disjointedness of Pygmalion's language here is perhaps meant to mirror his hesitancy in making the request.

    optō: used here (as often) parenthetically.

    eburneus, -a, -um, *(made of) ivory.*

276 **eburnus, -a, -um**, *(made of) ivory.*

        eburnae: supply **statuae**.

277 **Sēnsit**: **Venus** is subject of this verb (cf. 293) as of **aderat**.

    fēstīs: supply **diēbus**, dat. with the compound **aderat** (cf. 295).

278 **vōta . . . velint**: indirect question with **sēnsit**; in prose **quid** would introduce the clause. Despite the indirection of Pygmalion's prayer, Venus understands what he truly wants.

    amīcī . . . ōmen: the phrase (*as an omen . . .*) is in apposition with the signs described in 279.

279 **flamma**: i.e., from the incense burning on the altar.

    ter, adv., *three times* (here, as often, a mystical number).

    *__accendō, accendere, accendī, accēnsus__, *to kindle, ignite; to make hotter, intensify.*

    apex, apicis, m., *top/point of something*; here, *tip* (of a flame).

280 **rediit**: **ille** (Pygmalion) is subject; his return home from the festival and his rush to find the statue are described entirely in quick dactyls.

    simulācra: the word, an emphatic pl., perhaps deliberately recalls **similis** (276); there Pygmalion prays for a wife *like his ivory statue*, while here his statue is *the likeness of his very own girl*. **Suae** is likewise emphatic, as is **petit**, a verb connoting intentional action; and, in anticipation of the transformation to come, Ovid describes the statue here for the first time with the noun **puella**, a word straight out of the vocabulary of Latin elegy (cf. Catullus' frequent, and insistent, **mea puella**). The **ll** alliteration (a favorite Catullan sound effect) in **ille puellae** adds a further elegiac touch (see on 268).

281 **dedit ōscula**: a deliberate echo of **ōscula dat** (256), just as **Admovet . . . manibus . . . temptat** in the next verse looks back to **manūs . . . temptantēs admovet** (254), and **subsīdit digitīs** (284) recalls **digitōs īnsīdere** (257)—the earlier seduction resumes, but now under Venus' inspiration.

    vīsa tepēre est: supply **statua** or **puella**; the ivory maiden grew warm with life and with passion. The preceding diaeresis and the very brevity of the clause itself (cf. **Corpus erat** 289) focus our attention on this first sign of the statue's animation; Pygmalion here plays the handsome prince to his Sleeping Beauty, as his kiss brings her to life.

282 **Admovet . . . temptat**: the seduction proceeds again from kiss to caress (cf. 256–58); chiasmus intensifies the eroticism by bringing **ōs**, **manibus**, and **pectora** together, with the verbs framing the scene. The root meaning of

275   sit coniūnx, optō' (nōn ausus 'eburnea virgō'
276   dīcere), Pygmaliōn, 'similis mea,' dīxit, 'eburnae.'
277   Sēnsit, ut ipsa suīs aderat Venus aurea fēstīs,
278   vōta quid illa velint, et, amīcī nūminis ōmen,
279   flamma ter accēnsa est apicemque per āera dūxit.
280   "Ut rediit, simulācra suae petit ille puellae,
281   incumbēnsque torō dedit ōscula; vīsa tepēre est.
282   Admovet ōs iterum, manibus quoque pectora temptat;
283   temptātum mollēscit ebur, positōque rigōre
284   subsīdit digitīs cēditque, ut Hymettia sōle

Discussion Question

The references to Venus and her **nūmen** in 270–79 again recall the
narrative's opening lines. In what ways do the Propoetides' treatment of
Venus and her response compare with Pygmalion's attitude toward the
goddess and her response to him? Consider again how the fate of the
Propoetides compares with the fate of Pygmalion's statue.

---

    temptāre, *to feel*, is the correct sense here (and with **vēnae** 289, where
Pygmalion tests his beauty's pulse), but the word's repetition in this context
(at 282, 283, 289, and cf. 254) strongly suggests its common metaphorical
sense of *making a sexual advance* upon a woman.

    temptat; / temptātum (283): the immediate (and alliterative) repetition
underscores the rapidity of the transformation.

283   **mollēscō, mollēscere**, *to become soft/yielding*.

    positō: = **dēpositō**; use of the simple form of a verb in place of an expected
compound form is common in verse.

    rigōre: cf. the Propoetides' transformation to **rigidum . . . silicem** (242).

284   **subsīdō, subsīdere, subsēdī**, *to crouch down*; + dat., *to yield, give way to*
(some outside force).

       subsīdit digitīs: the sense of the verb here is clarified by the following
simile; Pygmalion's fingers leave their imprint on the statue's flesh in
fact, just as he had fantasized they might in 257.

    Hymettius, -a, -um, *from Mt. Hymettus* (a mountain near Athens noted for
its honey and so also, as here, for its beeswax).

285   ***cēra, -ae**, f., *beeswax, wax* (in any of its various uses, including, as here, modeling); *writing tablet* (of the common type which was coated with wax, on which notes could be easily incised and erased).
    remollēscō, remollēscere, *to become soft again* (cf. **mollēscit** 283).
    *tractō, -āre, -āvī, -ātus, *to keep pulling, dragging; to handle, rub, stroke.*
    *pollex, pollicis, m., *thumb.*
        remollēscit . . . pollice: for the alliteration see on 268.
        tractātaque pollice: wax used for modelling or other purposes was left in the sun and then worked with the fingers to make it softer and thus more readily shaped.
    multās: with **faciēs** (286), here *shapes* or *forms.*

286   **flectitur . . . ūsū**: sound effects are added by the alliteration of **f** and the aptly soft assonance of **ū** at the end of the verse (where there is also some etymologizing wordplay in **ūtilis ūsū**).
    fit ūtilis ūsū: the more it is used, or rather handled, the more easily worked and usable the wax becomes.

287   **dubiē**, adv., *hesitatingly, with hesitation.*
    fallīque verētur: supply **sē**, acc. subject of the infin. in indirect statement.

288   **vōta**: here, not *prayers*, but *the object of his prayers.*
    retractō, -āre, -āvī, -ātus, *to draw back; to handle/feel again/repeatedly.*
    retractat: cf. **tractāta** (285).

289   **Corpus erat**: the brevity of the clause and its placement at the beginning of the verse underscore Pygmalion's astonishment.
    saliō, salīre, saluī, saltus, *to jump, leap; to move suddenly, pulse.*
    *vēna, -ae, f., *blood-vessel, vein; vein, streak* (of some stone or mineral).

290   **Paphius, -a, -um**, *of Paphos* (a city in southwest Cyprus).
        Paphius . . . hērōs: cf. **Rhodopēius . . . hērōs**, of Orpheus (X.50 above); and note the interlocking word order in **Paphius . . . / verba** (291). The use of the epithet here anticipates the naming of the city after Pygmalion's child, referred to in 297.
    plēnissima: here, *most abundant* or *generous.*

291   **grātēs, grātium**, f. pl., *thanks, thanksgiving*; with **agere**, *to give thanks.*
    agit: some mss. have **agat**, and editors accepting that reading view the clause as a rel. clause of purpose. But, given Pygmalion's piety in 270–79, the indicative seems preferable—in gratitude he offers a prayer of thanks to the goddess at the very moment of his dream's fulfillment.
    ōra . . . falsa (292): the use of pl. for sing. is common with **ōs**, but may be intentionally emphatic here; note too the effect of the framing order, the suspenseful delay of **nōn falsa**, the wordplay with **ōra/ōre/ōscula**, and the repeated **ō**'s in 292 that perhaps suggest the lovers' passion.

293   **sēnsit**: the same verb is used of both Venus herself (277) and the lover she has brought to life for Pygmalion; both are sensitive and sensual.
    ērubēscō, ērubēscere, ērubuī, *to blush with shame, feel shame.*
        ērubuit: Pygmalion's creation had the sense of shame and modesty which the Propoetides lacked (cf. **pudor cessit** 241).
    timidum: a trait the girl shares with Pygmalion (cf. **timidē** 274).

285   cēra remollēscit tractātaque pollice multās
286   flectitur in faciēs ipsōque fit ūtilis ūsū.
287   Dum stupet et dubiē gaudet fallīque verētur,
288   rūrsus amāns rūrsusque manū sua vōta retractat.
289   Corpus erat: saliunt temptātae pollice vēnae!
290   "Tum vērō Paphius plēnissima concipit hērōs
291   verba, quibus Venerī grātēs agit, ōraque tandem
292   ōre suō nōn falsa premit, dataque ōscula virgō
293   sēnsit et ērubuit, timidumque ad lūmina lūmen
294   attollēns pariter cum caelō vīdit amantem.

Discussion Questions

1. Discuss the effectiveness and appropriateness of the simile in 284–86. Notice how the words **remollēscit tractātaque pollice** (285) are connected to identical or closely related words in the surrounding narrative; consider the imagery and the implications of these interconnections.

2. In what respects do diction and sound effects lend intensity to the scene described in 288?

3. How does Ovid's manipulation of verb tenses enliven the narrative in 280–89?

4. Comment on the sound effects in 293.

---

      lūmina lūmen: the juxtaposition neatly suits the action, as the statue, now alive, raises *her timid gaze up to his*, and the lovers' eyes meet for the very first time.

294   ***pariter**, adv., *together; at the same time.*

        pariter . . . vīdit: freely, *at the very same time she saw both her lover and the light of her first day*—but what is the lit. translation? With **cum caelō** there is a play on the double sense of **lūmen** as both *eye(s)* and *light*, and the resulting imagery is brilliant—as Pygmalion's creation opens her eyes, she raises them upward like a newborn child into the light of day and then, in the very same instant, like a blushing maiden, she gazes into the eyes of her lover.

295 **coniugium, -ī**, n., *marriage*.
  coniugiō: dat. with the compound **adest**—cf. 277.
  quod fēcit: i.e., through her response to Pygmalion's prayer.
  coāctīs / . . . orbem (296): an epic circumlocution for the passage of nine months, the length of a pregnancy; interlocking word order and the **n/m** alliteration add to the solemn tone.
296 **cornibus**: the points of the crescent moon were thought to resemble horns.
  noviēns, adv., *nine times*.
  lūnāris, -is, -e, *of the moon*.
297 **illa**: Pygmalion's bride, who remains nameless to the very end of the tale (though later writers call her Galatea).
  Paphos, -ī, acc. **Paphon**, f. (or m., as some texts read **dē quō** for **dē quā** in this line), *Paphos* (child of Pygmalion).
  gignō, gignere, genuī, genitus, *to create, give birth to*.
  dē quā tenet īnsula nōmen: Cyprus, or rather its town of Paphos (see on **Paphius** 290), is said to be named for Pygmalion's daughter.

"Pygmalion and Galatea," Jean-Léon Gérôme, 1890
Metropolitan Museum of Art, New York

295   "Coniugiō, quod fēcit, adest dea, iamque coāctīs
296   cornibus in plēnum noviēns lūnāribus orbem
297   illa Paphon genuit, dē quā tenet īnsula nōmen."

Discussion Questions

1.   On the surface level of this narrative, Pygmalion may seem to be some kind
      of pervert with a bizarre fetish for his female statue, but in the end, as the
      statue is miraculously brought to life, we realize that we have been drawn out
      of the real world and into the world of magic and metamorphosis. With this
      in mind, how might you interpret in metaphorical terms Pygmalion's
      withdrawal from society and his surrender to art? Discuss the themes of art,
      its effects, and its relationship to reality as they are developed through the
      symbolism of the entire narrative.

2.   Comment on the function of the statue as a character in the story and
      especially on the paradox that, while central to the tale, she remains utterly
      passive. How are Pygmalion and Ovid alike in their relation to the character?
      What other correspondences do you detect between the poet and the sculptor?

"Pygmalion and Galatea"
Étienne-Maurice Falconet, 1763
Musée des Arts Décoratifs
Paris, France

DAEDALUS AND ICARUS

Metamorphoses VIII.183–235

The ability to fly like a bird must have been among man's earliest imaginings; and from Ovid to Leonardo da Vinci to the Wright brothers, the invention of a flying machine, whether real or surreal, has been one of his most impassioned quests. At the same time, however, we seem always to associate flight with peril. As commonplace as the sight of a jetliner soaring overhead may be, scenes of malfunction, falling, crashing are—thanks to the wonders of video—equally familiar; we may fly, and dream of flying, but visions of the shuttle Challenger, of TWA Flight 800, of loved ones plummeting from the sky are ever lurking in our subconscious. In the ancient mythic imagination the ascension of man like a bird into the heavens was likewise conceived of as both liberating and fraught with peril—even more so, perhaps, as ancient man was in reality firmly bound to the earth, viewing the heavens as the proper sphere of the gods alone.

Ovid was fascinated with the notion of man's flight, its dangers, and its symbolic potential. In *Metamorphoses* Book II, he tells at length the story of Apollo's son Phaethon, who insisted on driving the chariot of the sun to prove at once his divine origin and his manhood; ignoring his father's warnings, Phaethon impetuously seized the reins and steered the sun wildly through the heavens, ultimately losing control, plunging dangerously close to earth, and nearly destroying the entire planet with the sun's scorching flames, before Jupiter finally struck him dead with a thunderbolt. In the end, while we may feel some sympathy for Phaethon, one senses that he has justly paid the price for his arrogance, for usurping divine privilege, and for disobeying his father.

Like Phaethon, Icarus in the story next presented in our text takes flight and ultimately loses his life because of his failure to heed his father's advice, but there are important differences in the two stories. Icarus' father Daedalus is not a god, but a mortal, an Athenian citizen and inventor exiled to Crete for murdering his nephew in a fit of jealousy over the young man's talents. While on Crete Daedalus served as architect and engineer for king Minos, but eventually angered him by constructing for his wife Pasiphae a hollow cow in which she hid in order to mate with a bull; outraged, Minos compelled Daedalus to build the labyrinth as a prison for the half-man, half-bull Minotaur born to Pasiphae from her bestial adultery. When, years later, Daedalus assisted the king's daughter Ariadne and the Athenian hero Theseus in overcoming the Minotaur, Minos imprisoned Daedalus and Icarus in the same labyrinth.

Escape from the labyrinth would be difficult in itself, but, as Minos' navy controlled the seas surrounding Crete, escape from the island might have seemed nearly impossible. Not so, however, for Daedalus, who in Greco-Roman myth

90

is the archetype for the ingenious inventor and master craftsman. As our narrative opens, Daedalus moves quickly and expertly to craft wings of feathers and wax for both himself and his son, to engineer their flight. Realizing the potential risk, Daedalus cautions Icarus, as Apollo had Phaethon, to steer a middle course, neither flying too high in the heavens nor too low. But in the end, and inevitably it seems, Icarus fails to heed his father's advice and flies too close to the sun; the sun's heat melts the wax, destroying Icarus' wings and plunging him into the sea below, near an island, both of which ever after bore his name. In the story's closing moment, Icarus' face is seen in the waters below, shouting out his father's name just before he is submerged, while Daedalus himself soars overhead, pathetically calling his son's name in turn and cursing his own powers of invention for their destructive consequences.

There is a poignancy and a universality in the relationship between the impetuous youth and his talented father which is genuinely sympathetic. At the same time, particularly if we reflect upon Daedalus' earlier transgressions, we can see in him a touch of the "mad scientist" type familiar from both fiction and film—brilliant, highly capable, but obsessed with science, and not mindful enough of the risks involved in "plying unknown arts and reinventing nature" (lines 188–89). The story (told also by Ovid in his *Ars Amatoria*) has been prized both for its pathos and for its fantasy of human flight, and over the centuries has inspired countless writers, artists, and composers, among them Chaucer, Ben Jonson, and James Joyce (whose hero in *A Portrait of the Artist as a Young Man* is an Ovidian Stephen Dedalus), Rodin and Salvador Dali, and even choreographer John Butler, whose ice ballet *Icarus* was first performed in London in 1977.

*"Daedalus Attaching
    the Wings of Icarus"
Joseph Marie Vien, 1754
École des Beaux-Arts
Paris, France*

183 **Daedalus, -ī, m.,** *Daedalus* (mythic Athenian hero and craftsman who built the labyrinth of king Minos on the island of Crete).

  Crētē, Crētēs, f., *Crete* (island in the Aegean sea, famous for the myth of the Minotaur).

   For the Greek case endings, see above on **Daphnē** (*Met.* I.452).

  perōdī, perōdisse, perōsus, *to hate greatly, detest.*

   perōsus: here, as often, the perf. participle has the force of the pres. and is act. in meaning.

184 **exilium, -ī, n.,** *exile.*

   longum . . . exilium: Daedalus had been exiled to Crete for killing his nephew in a jealous rage over his superior artistic skills.

185 **pelagus, -ī, n.,** *sea, ocean.*

   clausus erat pelagō: according to legend, Minos headed a vast thalassocracy, controlling all the nearby seas with his fleet.

  licet: here, with the adversative subjn. **obstruat,** *although.*

186 **obstruō, obstruere, obstrūxī, obstrūctus,** *to erect as a barrier; to bar access to, block off.*

   obstruat: Minos is understood as the subject.

  illāc, adv., *by that route.*

187 ***possideō, possidēre, possēdī, possessus,** *to have in one's control; to take control of, seize.*

   possideat: supply **licet** from 185.

  Mīnōs, Mīnōis, m., *Minos* (legendary king of Crete).

188 ***ignōtus, -a, -um,** *unknown, unfamiliar.*

   ignōtās . . . artēs: James Joyce applies this phrase to the emerging artist Stephen Dedalus, hero of his *Portrait of the Artist as a Young Man.*

189 **novō, -āre, -āvī, -ātus,** *to make new, renew; to give a new form to, alter.*

   nātūramque novat: enjambement and alliteration underscore the startling image.

  *ōrdō, ōrdinis, m., *row, line; social status, class; order, arrangement.*

190 ***coepī, coepisse, coeptus,** *to begin.*

   ā minimā coeptās: supply **pennā;** we would say *beginning with . . . ,* but what is the lit. translation?

  longam breviōre sequentī: supply **pennā.** Some readers, taking this phrase to mean that Daedalus started with longer feathers and then continued with progressively shorter ones, sense a contradiction with **ā minimā coeptās** and suppose there is some corruption in the text; but what we are perhaps meant to imagine is that Daedalus started with very short feathers at the tip of the wing and then added increasingly longer ones, *with a somewhat shorter (feather) following (each) long one,* giving the wing's edge a serrated appearance (a notion reinforced by the images in 191–92).

191 ***clīvus, -ī, m.,** *sloping ground, slope; hillside; inclined surface.*

   ut . . . putēs: i.e., **ut pennās in clīvō crēvisse putēs;** this result clause invites us to compare Daedalus' arrangement of the wing's feathers to trees growing up on the side of a hill.

  rūsticus, -a, -um, *of the country, rural, rustic.*

183   Daedalus intereā Crētēn longumque perōsus
184 exilium, tactusque locī nātālis amōre,
185 clausus erat pelagō. "Terrās licet," inquit, "et undās
186 obstruat, at caelūm certē patet; ībimus illāc!
187 Omnia possideat, nōn possidet āera Mīnōs."
188 Dīxit et ignōtās animum dīmittit in artēs,
189 nātūramque novat. Nam pōnit in ōrdine pennās
190 ā minimā coeptās, longam breviōre sequentī,
191 ut clīvō crēvisse putēs (sīc rūstica quondam
192 fistula disparibus paulātim surgit avēnīs);

Discussion Questions

1. Explain how **Crētēn longumque . . . exilium** (183–84) might be construed as a hendiadys.

2. How do meter and other sound effects enhance the meaning in 186?

3. In what way is the word order of 187 especially effective?

4. How is the simile of 191–92 appropriate to both the immediate context and the larger context of the poem?

Villa Albani, Rome

quondam: with **rūstica**, the sense here is *from ancient times/old-fashioned*.
192 **dispār, disparis,** *unequal*.
avēna, -ae, f., *oat; stem, (hollow) stalk*.
        fistula . . . avēnīs: the ancient shepherd's pipe, known as the Pan-pipe or syrinx, was made of several hollow reeds of increasing length, connected in a row and rising or tapering to a point.

193   **līnum, -ī**, n., *flax plant; thread, string.*
       mediās et . . . īmās: supply **pennās**
       alligō, -āre, -āvī, -ātus, *to tie, bind, fasten.*
194   **curvāmen, curvāminis**, n., *curvature, arc.*
195   **imitor, -ārī, -ātus sum**, *to copy, imitate (the actions of); to resemble.*
       *****Īcarus, -ī**, m., *Icarus* (the son of Daedalus).
196   **sē tractāre**: indirect statement dependent on **ignārus**.
       perīcla: a common syncope (contraction) for **perīcula**; pl. here (of the
           wings), where English might use the sing. *imperilment.*
197   **renīdeō, renīdēre**, *to shine, gleam; to smile (with pleasure), beam.*
       quās: as is common in Latin verse, the antecedent follows.
       vagus, -a, -um, *freely moving, wandering; shifting.*
       modo . . . modo (198): the correlatives connect **captābat** (198) and **mollībat**
           (199).
198   *****flāvus, -a, -um**, *yellow, golden; fair-haired, blonde.*
199   *****molliō, -īre, -īvī/-iī, mollītus**, *to make soft, soften; to weaken, make*
           effeminate.
              mollībat: a common alternate for **molliēbat**.
       lūsus, -ūs, m., *playing, sport.*
200   **Postquam . . . imposita est** (201): i.e., after the finishing touches had been
           applied.
       coeptō: English would prefer a relative clause, *to what he. . . .*
201   **opifex, opificis**, m., *craftsman, artisan.*
       librō, -āre, -āvī, -ātus, *to hold suspended, balance, poise.*
       *****āla, -ae**, f., *wing.*
              in ālās: the acc. is used rather than the abl. to imply a more forceful
                  action.
202   **mōtā**: as Daedalus miraculously rises from the ground, the air is stirred by
           his flapping wings.
203   *****īnstruō, īnstruere, īnstrūxī, īnstrūctus**, *to build, construct*; + abl., *to*
           equip, furnish (with); *to instruct, teach.*
       et: = **etiam**.
       līmes, līmitis, m., *boundary; course, route.*
              Mediō . . . līmite: the "abl. of route" is regularly used without a
                  preposition.
204   **ait**: as usual, Ovid delays the speech verb, which in English would precede
           the direct quotation.
       dēmissior: we would say *too low*, but what is the lit. sense?
205   **gravō, -āre, -āvī, -ātus**, *to make heavy, weigh down.*
       celsus, -a, -um, *high, lofty.*
       adūrō, adūrere, adūssī, adūstus, *to damage by burning, scorch, burn.*
206   *****volō, -āre, -āvī, -ātus**, *to fly.*
       Boōtēs, Boōtae, acc., **Boōtēn**, m., *the constellation Boötes* (also known as
           Arctophylax, the "Bear-keeper").
207   **Helicē, Helicēs**, acc., **Helicēn**, f., *the constellation Ursa Major* (the "Great
           Bear").

193	tum līnō mediās et cērīs alligat īmās
194	atque ita compositās parvō curvāmine flectit,
195	ut vērās imitētur avēs.

               Puer Īcarus ūnā

196	stābat et, ignārus sua sē tractāre perīcla,
197	ōre renīdentī modo, quās vaga mōverat aura,
198	captābat plūmās, flāvam modo pollice cēram
199	mollībat, lūsūque suō mīrābile patris
200	impediēbat opus. Postquam manus ultima coeptō
201	imposita est, geminās opifex lībrāvit in ālās
202	ipse suum corpus mōtāque pependit in aurā;
203	īnstruit et nātum, "Mediō"que, "ut līmite currās,
204	Īcare," ait, "moneō, nē, sī dēmissior ībis,
205	unda gravet pennās, sī celsior, ignis adūrat:
206	inter utrumque volā. Nec tē spectāre Boōtēn
207	aut Helicēn iubeō strīctumque Ōrīonis ēnsem:

Discussion Questions

1. Comment on the aptness of word order to meaning in 193.

2. What contrast is underscored in the chiasmus **lūsū . . . opus** (199–200)?

3. Describe the word-picture in 201.

4. What do you suppose are the intended effects of the juxtapositions **sua sē** (196) and **ipse suum** (202)?

Ōrīōn, Ōrīonis, m., *Orion* (a giant hunter turned into a constellation).
    Boōtēn . . . Ōrīonis: Boōtes and Ursa Major are especially conspicuous in the northern hemisphere, while Orion is most prominent in the south, so Daedalus' order here essentially rephrases the warning of 204–05 to keep to the middle course; these constellations were regularly used for navigation.

208 **praeceptum, -ī,** n., *advice, precept; instruction, order; principle, rule.*

209 **trādit et ignōtās . . . ālās:** cf. **Dīxit et ignōtās . . . artēs** (188); each line serves as a kind of refrain, punctuating the close of Daedalus' two brief speeches and equating his **artēs** with the mystical **ālās.**

    accommodō, -āre, -āvī, -ātus, *to fit, fasten on, attach.*

210 **monitus, -ūs,** m., *advice, warning.*

    *senīlis, -is, -e, *of an old man, old man's; in old age, aged.*

211 **patrius, -a, -um,* *of a father, father's.*

    nātō . . . suō (212): indirect object with **dedit ōscula,** but perhaps secondarily dat. of agent with **repetenda**—the father's kisses will never be repeated, nor ever sought again; the delayed reflexive, with the abrupt caesura following, adds poignancy to the scene.

212 **levō, -āre, -āvī, -ātus,* *to lift, raise up.*

213 **āles, ālitis,** m./f., *large bird, fowl.*

214 **quae:** since he might have opted for the masculine pronoun (**āles** is common gender), Ovid may be comparing Daedalus specifically to a mother bird.

    *tener, tenera, tenerum, *soft, tender; immature, young.*

    prōlēs, prōlis, f., *offspring.*

    *prōdūcō, prōdūcere, prōdūxī, prōductus, *to bring forth, lead out, produce.*

    nīdus, -ī, m., *nest.*

215 **sequī:** supply **nātum** as subject.

    damnōsus, -a, -um, *destructive, ruinous.*

        damnōsās: the adjective, like **perīcla** (196) and the admonitions in 203–08, suspensefully anticipate the episode's grim conclusion.

    ērudiō, -īre, -īvī/-iī, -ītus, *to teach* (a person and/or a skill).

216 **ipse suās:** for the juxtaposition, cf. **ipse suum** (202).

217 **Hōs:** object of both **vīdit** and **obstipuit** (219), antecedent of **quī** (219), and subject of **esse** (220).

    tremulus, -a, -um, *trembling, shaking.*

        tremulā . . . harundine: the fisherman's slender pole is quivering either because he has a fish on his line or because he is himself trembling in amazement at the sight of Daedalus and Icarus.

    piscis, piscis, m., *fish.*

218 **stīva, -ae,** f., *plow-handle.*

    arātor, arātōris, m., *plowman; farmer.*

        pāstor . . . arātor: chiasmus, with **innīxus** modifying both nouns and governing both **baculō** and **stīvā.**

219 **obstipēscō, obstipēscere, obstipuī,* *to be stunned, dazed, awestruck.*

    carpere: cf. **carpe** (208); here, *press on through.*

    possent: subjn. in a rel. causal clause within the indirect statement **crēdidit (hōs) esse** (220).

220 **Iūnōnius, -a, -um,** *of Juno, sacred to Juno.*

    laevus, -a, -um, *left, on the left.*

208   mē duce, carpe viam!" Pariter praecepta volandī
209   trādit et ignōtās umerīs accommodat ālās.
210   Inter opus monitūsque genae maduēre senīlēs,
211   et patriae tremuēre manūs; dedit ōscula nātō
212   nōn iterum repetenda suō, pennīsque levātus
213   ante volat comitīque timet, velut āles ab altō
214   quae teneram prōlem prōdūxit in āera nīdō,
215   hortāturque sequī, damnōsāsque ērudit artēs,
216   et movet ipse suās et nātī respicit ālās.
217   Hōs aliquis, tremulā dum captat harundine piscēs,
218   aut pāstor baculō stīvāve innīxus arātor
219   vīdit et obstipuit, quīque aethera carpere possent,
220   crēdidit esse deōs. Et iam Iūnōnia laevā

Discussion Questions

1. Comment on the word order and sound effects in **genae . . . manūs** (210–11).

2. Compare the context of **patriae cecidēre manūs** in Vergil *Aeneid* VI.33 with **patriae tremuēre manūs** in verse 211 here. Explain why the Ovidian phrase is likely a deliberate echo of Vergil.

3. What is most striking in the rhythm of lines 210–13, and how is this appropriate to the actions described?

4. Why does Ovid position **altō** (213) and **nīdō** (214) as he does?

"The Fall of Icarus"
Carlo Saraceni, ca. 1608
Galleria di Capodimonte
Naples, Italy

221 **Samos, Samī,** f., *Samos* (an island off the coast of Asia Minor, near Ephesus and northeast of Crete).

> **Iūnōnia . . .** (220) / **. . . Samos:** the importance to Juno of her shrine on Samos is attested, for example, at Vergil *Aeneid* I.16.
>
> **laevā** (220) / **parte Samos:** supply **erat** from 222; the abl. of place **(in) laevā parte** parallels the predicate nom. **dextra** in 222. Daedalus and Icarus have flown northward from Crete, past the islands of Delos and Paros, then northeast toward Samos, which at this moment must be just to their north, with Lebinthos and Calymne to the south. They are off course, if the intention was to fly straight home to Athens, but quite near (what was to become) the Icarian Sea.

fuerant . . . relictae: a common alternate form for the pluperf., = **relictae erant.**

Dēlos, Dēlī, f., *Delos* (an Aegean island, one of the Cyclades, north of Crete).

Paros, Parī, f., *Paros* (another of the Cyclades islands).

222 **Lebinthos, Lebinthī,** f., *Lebinthos* (one of the Sporades islands off the coast of Asia Minor).

fēcundus, -a, -um, *fertile; productive* (of), *rich* (in).

*****mel, mellis,** n., *honey.*

> **melle:** abl. of respect.

Calymnē, Calymnēs, f., *Calymne* (another of the Sporades).

> **fēcunda . . . Calymnē:** Calymne was famous for its honey, according to the Greek geographer Strabo (10.5.19).

223 **audācī:** a transferred epithet, applying more logically to the **puer** himself; note the deliberate assonance with **gaudēre.**

volātus, -ūs, m., *the act of flying, flight.*

224 *****dēserō, dēserere, dēseruī, dēsertus,** *to leave, desert.*

caelī: i.e., even greater heights.

cupīdō, cupīdinis, f., *passionate desire, longing.*

225 **rapidus, -a, -um,** *swiftly flowing, quick; consuming, scorching.*

226 **odōrātus, -a, -um,** *sweet-smelling, fragrant.*

> **odōrātās . . . cērās:** the adj. is proleptic, as the wax becomes aromatic only after beginning to melt.

*****vinculum, -ī,** n., *chain;* usually pl., *shackles.*

227 **tābēscō, tābēscere, tābuī,** *to waste/dwindle away; to melt away.*

nūdōs: i.e., stripped of their wings.

quatiō, quatere, (no perf.), **quassus,** *to move vigorously, shake.*

228 **rēmigium, -ī,** n., *array of oars, oarage; (set of) wings.*

percipiō, percipere, percēpī, perceptus, *to take, acquire; to catch hold of.*

229 **ōra . . . aquā** (230): the intricately interlocked ABCACB arrangement well suits the image of the youth's drowning. Poignantly, the last we see and hear of the boy, after his flailing arms in 227, is his **ōra . . . clamantia,** which in an instant is submerged in the sea, **excipiuntur aquā** (230).

caeruleus, -a, -um, *sky-blue.*

221	parte Samos (fuerant Dēlosque Parosque relictae),
222	dextra Lebinthos erat fēcundaque melle Calymnē,
223	cum puer audācī coepit gaudēre volātū
224	dēseruitque ducem caelīque cupīdine tractus
225	altius ēgit iter. Rapidī vīcīnia sōlis
226	mollit odōrātās, pennārum vincula, cērās.
227	Tābuerant cērae: nūdōs quatit ille lacertōs,
228	rēmigiōque carēns nōn ūllās percipit aurās,
229	ōraque caeruleā patrium clāmantia nōmen
230	excipiuntur aquā, quae nōmen trāxit ab illō.

Discussion Questions

1. Comment on the multiple sound effects in 224–25; how is the meter appropriate to the emotions and actions described?

2. Describe the word-picture in 226.

caeruleā . . . / excipiuntur aquā (230): a brilliant wordplay with **percipit aurās**—Icarus can no longer catch hold of the air, as he had with his wings, but is instead caught hold of himself by the water below, the color of which is ironically compared to the very **caelum** he had so recklessly longed for (**caelī . . . cupīdine** 224). The notion is anticipated in 228, when Ovid purposely refers to the boy's lost wings as oars, which are more suited to traversing the seas than the sky.

230 **quae nōmen trāxit ab illō**: the profound importance to this tale of Icarus' name and its survival in the names of the Icarian Sea and the island of Icaria (**tellūs ā nōmine dicta** 235) is accentuated through the two triple repetitions, **nōmen** (229) / **nōmen** (230) / **nōmine** (235) and **Īcare** / **Īcare** / **Īcare** (231–33), as well as the repeated forms of **dīcō** (four times in 231–35) and the anaphora **patrium** (229) / **pater . . . pater** (231).

232 **regiō, regiōnis**, f., *direction; district, region.*

233 ***aspiciō, aspicere, aspexī, aspectus**, *to look at, observe; to consider, think about.*

234 **dēvoveō, dēvovēre, dēvōvī, dēvōtus**, *to vow as an offering/sacrifice; to devote, dedicate; to devote to the infernal gods, curse.*

    dēvōvit . . . suās artēs: the reflexive here is particularly emphatic, and Daedalus' curse evokes lines 215–16, especially **damnōsās . . . artēs**.

    corpusque sepulcrō / condidit (235): harsh alliteration and the abrupt caesura underscore both the finality of Daedalus' act and the conclusion of the story's action.

235 **dicta**: supply **est**; the last clause is a postscript to the tale, explaining the origin of the name of the island Icaria, just as line 230 had provided an etiology for the name of the Icarian Sea.

    sepultī: echoing **sepulcrō** at the end of the preceding line, this final reference to Icarus, or rather his corpse, effectively punctuates the narrative.

"Daedalus and Icarus"
Antonio Canova, 1779
Museo Civico Correr
Venice, Italy

231   At pater īnfēlīx, nec iam pater, "Īcare," dīxit;
232   "Īcare," dīxit, "ubi es? Quā tē regiōne requīram?"
233   "Īcare," dīcēbat. Pennās aspexit in undīs,
234   dēvōvitque suās artēs, corpusque sepulcrō
235   condidit; et tellūs ā nōmine dicta sepultī.

Discussion Questions

1.   Discuss the effect of the repetition of **"Īcare," dīxit** in 231–32 and of the shift to the imperfect tense in 233.

2.   How is the relationship between Daedalus and his son comparable to that of ordinary fathers and sons? In what way is the story allegorical or philosophical?

3.   Compare Daedalus' invention with that of Pygmalion. How do both artisans manipulate nature? Why does one succeed and the other fail?

"Landscape with the Fall of Icarus," Pieter Brueghel the Elder, 1555–56
Musées Royaux des Beaux-Arts, Brussels, Belgium

BAUCIS AND PHILEMON
Metamorphoses VIII.616–724

Analogous in some respects to the biblical stories of Noah and the Great Flood and Sodom and Gomorrah, and replete with other religious motifs, Ovid's highly sympathetic tale of the old couple Baucis and Philemon, their gracious hospitality when visited in their humble cottage by Jupiter and Mercury, and the rewards they receive from Jupiter for their extraordinary piety, has delighted countless readers over the years and proven to be one of the most beloved of the *Metamorphoses* episodes. Allegorizing interpretations which viewed Jupiter and Mercury as representations of God and Christ helped to popularize the story in Europe, where it appears in numerous works of art from the 16th century onward; Bramantino's painting and the drawing by Ingres reproduced in this book are typical, and other artists who depicted scenes from the story include Peter Paul Rubens, Jacob Jordaens (one of a series of paintings on the theme is in the North Carolina Museum of Art in Raleigh), and Rembrandt (his painting from 1658 can be seen in the National Gallery). Dryden retold the story and Jonathan Swift parodied it (a treatment invited by the little drama's comic moments); Nathaniel Hawthorne's "The Miraculous Pitcher," in his moralizing *Wonderbook for Boys and Girls*, focuses on the couple's wine crater, which mystically replenished itself through the agency of their divine guests; and the tale inspired operas by Gluck, Haydn, and Gounod. The 1984 painting by David Ligare, reproduced at the end of this unit, depicts the temple Baucis and Philemon were given charge of by Jupiter and the intertwined oak and linden trees into which they were simultaneously transformed. The *Metamorphoses* is the only extant classical text preserving the story, which probably originated as a folktale in Asia Minor (where the action is set) and was elaborated by Ovid out of his own imagination and through allusion to Callimachus and other writers.

Much of the story's charm lies in its simplicity. Disguised as humans, Jupiter and Mercury visit the earth to test mankind's morality and, having been turned away from a thousand homes, they are at last offered rest and dinner at the tiny hut of Baucis and Philemon. The poor and aged couple spare no effort in making their unknown guests comfortable and preparing for them a meal that, while modest indeed, was the very best they had and most generously offered. The hustle and bustle of Baucis' preparations and Ovid's detailed descriptions of the home's ramshackle furnishings and of the smoked pork and vegetables that are served (which are meant to recall the poor cuisine of Italian peasants) make for some humorous scenes, and, in an abrupt shift from realism to fantasy, the couple's astonishment at the sight of their wine-bowl magically refilling itself— another biblical motif—provides a powerful sense of the miraculous.

But the real miracle comes next, as the gods reveal their true identity and Jupiter, after condemning all the region's inhabitants for their impiety, leads the old couple to the top of a nearby hill. From here Baucis and Philemon behold the entire countryside overwhelmed by flood and then, turning their gaze toward their own cottage, they see it marvelously transformed into a resplendent temple, its thatched roof turned to gold, its earthen floor to marble. Deliberate verbal repetitions from earlier scenes within the couple's hut make clear the narrator's point that the temple's most splendid features had already been present, conceptually at least, in the wonderful cheer and piety of Baucis and Philemon's humble dwelling; their cottage had been in spirit a temple, and now was a temple in fact. Besides sparing them, like Noah, from the devastation of the flood, Jupiter also granted their two modest wishes, first making them guardians of the holy shrine that had been their hut and then, since they had prayed to die, not alone, but together, transforming them at the moment of their deaths into the two trees we see in eternal embrace in the painting of Paul Ligare, to be forever venerated, like saints, for their exemplary goodness.

The entire story, it should be noted, is narrated in the cave of the mystical river god Achelous—in the midst of a flood—by a heroic guest named Lelex, who recounts the tale as proof of the omnipotent power of the gods and of the reward that can come to those who worship them with true devotion. And indeed, the story of Baucis and Philemon, whose devotion to the gods was equalled only by their loving devotion to one another, is a more satisfying illustration than any other episode in Ovid's poem of the moral goodness potential in man and the spiritual rewards that come from a virtuous life.

"Philemon and Baucis Hosting Jupiter," Jean Auguste Dominique Ingres
1780–1867, Musée Crozatier, Le Puy-en-Velay, France

616   ***probō, -āre, -āvī, -ātus,** *to approve, commend*; with acc. + infin., *to consider it proper* (for someone to do something).

       Obstipuēre . . . probārunt: the setting is the cave of the river-god Achelous; following his narration of several transformation tales, when one guest expresses disbelief in the power of the gods to work such miracles, the others present reject his cynicism. **Obstipuēre omnēs** is a stock epic formula for connecting two speeches, and the line makes a neat chiasmus; cf. **Conticuēre omnēs** at Vergil *Aeneid* 2.1 (also chiastic), which links Dido's request for the story of Troy's fall with Aeneas' telling of the tale.

617   **Lelex, Lelegis,** m., *Lelex* (a Greek from Locri who participated in the hunt for the Calydonian boar).

618   **potentia:** though delayed, the word is subject of **est** as well as of **habet.**

   caelī: metonymy for **deōrum.**

620   **Quōque:** = **Quō** + **-que**; with **minus dubitēs,** a rel. clause of purpose.

   tilia, -ae, f., *linden tree.*

621   **est:** with **quercus** and **circumdata** in the predicate, *there is an oak. . . .*

   Phrygius, -a, -um, *Phrygian, of Phrygia* (a country in western Asia Minor).

   modicus, -a, -um, *moderate in size, small; ordinary.*

       modicō . . . mūrō: a typical Ovidian word-picture.

622   **Pelopēius, -a, -um,** *of Pelops* (son of the Lydian king Tantalus and father of Atreus and Thyestes).

       Pelopēia . . . arva (623): i.e., Asia Minor, Pelops' homeland before his flight to Greece.

   Pittheus, -ī, m., *Pittheus* (a son of Pelops and grandfather of the Greek hero Theseus).

623   **mīsit:** the purpose of Lelex' mission is unknown.

   suō . . . parentī: dat. of agent with **rēgnāta.**

624   **stāgnum, -ī,** n., *pool, lagoon, swamp.*

   habitābilis, -is, -e, *fit to live in, inhabitable.*

625   **mergus, -ī,** m., *sea-bird, gull.*

   fulica, -ae, f., *water-fowl, coot.*

  *palūster, palūstris, palūstre, *marshy; of/living in marshes.*

   undae: metonymy for **aqua** or **lacus** (*lake, pond*).

626   **speciēs, -ēī,** f., *spectacle, sight; appearance, form; guise.*

627   **Atlantiadēs, -ae,** m., *the grandson of Atlas, Mercury* (son of Jupiter, appearing here in his role as protector of travelers).

   positīs: = **dēpositīs** (the simple verb form in place of a compound is common in Latin verse).

   cādūcifer, cādūciferī, m., *the staff-bearer* (i.e., Mercury).

       positīs cādūcifer ālīs: Mercury was regularly depicted with winged hat and sandals and carrying the caduceus, a herald's staff, but in this story he sets aside his winged accoutrements in order to pass for a mortal.

628   **locum requiemque:** hendiadys.

629   **sera, -ae,** f., *bar* (to latch a door).

616	Obstipuēre omnēs nec tālia dicta probārunt,
617	ante omnēsque Lelex, animō matūrus et aevō,
618	sīc ait: "Immēnsa est fīnemque potentia caelī
619	nōn habet et, quidquid superī voluēre, perāctum est.
620	Quōque minus dubitēs, tiliae contermina quercus
621	collibus est Phrygiīs modicō circumdata mūrō;
622	ipse locum vīdī, nam mē Pelopēia Pittheus
623	mīsit in arva suō quondam rēgnāta parentī.
624	Haud procul hinc stāgnum est, tellūs habitābilis ōlim,
625	nunc celebrēs mergīs fulicīsque palūstribus undae;
626	Iuppiter hūc speciē mortālī cumque parente
627	vēnit Atlantiadēs, positīs cādūcifer ālīs.
628	Mīlle domōs adiēre locum requiemque petentēs,
629	mīlle domōs clausēre serae. Tamen ūna recēpit,
630	parva quidem, stipulīs et cannā tēcta palūstrī,

Discussion Questions

1. How does the language in 620–23 add a touch of epic grandeur to what would otherwise be a simple rustic vista?

2. Comment on the several special effects achieved through word order in 623–25.

3. What several features are most striking in Ovid's use and placement of adjectives of number and size in 628–30, and what is their purpose?

630   **canna, -ae**, f., *small reed*.
          cannā . . . palūstrī: sing. for pl.

631   *Baucis, Baucidis, acc., Baucida, f., *Baucis* (the aged wife of Philemon).
     parilis, -is, -e, *equal, similar.*
   *aetās, aetātis, f., *age, time of life.*
     parilī . . . aetāte: abl. of description.
   *Philēmōn, Philēmonis, acc., Philēmona, m., *Philemon* (a poor Phrygian
     farmer, husband of Baucis).
   sed pia: some editors do not punctuate here, taking pia with Baucis; but
     more logically the epithet applies to the couple's domus, contrasting its
     poverty (parva quidem 630) with its piety.

632   illā . . . illā: supply in and take both demonstratives with casā (633); the two
     demonstratives frame the line in a way that deftly marks the transition from
     the couple's early years of marriage to their old age.

633   cōnsenēscō, cōnsenēscere, cōnsenuī, *to reach old age, grow old.*
   paupertās, paupertātis, f., *poverty.*
     paupertātem: object of both gerunds as well as of effēcēre (634).

634   efficiō, efficere, effēcī, effectus, *to manufacture, make; to make* (something)
     become (something else).
   inīquus, -a, -um, *uneven, rough; not equable, resentful, discontented.*
     nec inīquā: = et aequā; litotes.

635   rēfert, rēferre, rētulit, impers., *it makes a difference, is important, matters*
     (whether).
   illīc, adv., *there, in that place.*
   famulus, -ī, m., *servant, attendant; slave.*
     dominōs . . . famulōsne: a common poetic alternative for dominōsne
     . . . an famulōs, *whether . . . or. . . .*; the internal rhyme of -ōs,
     under the ictus, helps underscore the contrast.
   requīrās: subjn. in indirect question; use of 2nd pers. involves the audience.

637   *ergō (with final -ō often shortened in verse), conj., *therefore.*
   caelicola, -ae, m./f., *heaven-dweller, god/goddess.*
   Penātēs, Penātium, m. pl., *the Penates* (tutelary gods of the Roman house
     and its food supply); lower case, *home, dwelling.*

638   submissō . . . postēs: the golden line, following the epic caelicolae (637),
     adds majesty to the gods' entrance.
   intrārunt: = intrāvērunt, a common perf. tense contraction.
   vertex, verticis, m., *whirlpool, eddy; top of the head.*

639   relevō, relevāre, relevāvī, relevātus, *to reduce the load of, lighten; to ease,*
     rest.
   sedīle, sedīlis, n., *seat, bench, chair.*

640   quō: abl., in place of the dat. expected with the compound verb.
   superiniciō, superinicere, superiniēcī, superiniectus, *to throw/scatter*
     (something, acc.) *on over the top of* (something, usually dat.).
   textum, -ī, n., *woven fabric, cloth.*
   rudis, -is, -e, *roughly fashioned, coarse.*
   *sēdulus, -a, -um, *attentive, painstaking, sedulous.*

641   *focus, -ī, m., *hearth, fireplace.*

631 sed pia; Baucis anus parilīque aetāte Philēmōn
632 illā sunt annīs iūnctī iuvenālibus, illā
633 cōnsenuēre casā paupertātemque fatendō
634 effēcēre levem nec inīquā mente ferendō.
635 Nec rēfert, dominōs illīc famulōsne requīrās:
636 tōta domus duo sunt—īdem pārentque iubentque.
637   "Ergo ubi caelicolae parvōs tetigēre penātēs
638 submissōque humilēs intrārunt vertice postēs,
639 membra senex positō iussit relevāre sedīlī;
640 quō superiniēcit textum rude sēdula Baucis,
641 inque focō tepidum cinerem dīmōvit, et ignēs
642 suscitat hesternōs foliīsque et cortice siccō
643 nūtrit et ad flammās animā prōdūcit anīlī,
644 multifidāsque facēs rāmāliaque ārida tēctō

Discussion Questions

1. How is word order appropriate to sense in 631 and again in 632?

2. What remarkable sound effects are heard in 633–34?

3. How again in 636 do sound effects contribute to the principal notion Ovid means to convey?

---

tepidus, -a, -um, *warm.*
dīmoveō, dīmovēre, dīmōvī, dīmōtus, *to move apart, move aside.*
642 **suscitō, -āre, -āvī, -ātus,** *to cause to move upward; to stir up.*
hesternus, -a, -um, *of yesterday, yesterday's.*
  ignēs (641) / . . . **hesternōs:** the hearth still contained a smoldering log or two from the previous day.
folium, -ī, n., *leaf* (of a plant).
643 **anīlis, -is, -e,** *of an old woman, old woman's.*
  animā . . . anīlī: i.e., she blew on the kindling to reignite the flames.
644 **multifidus, -a, -um,** *split into many pieces, splintered.*
facēs: here, *firewood.*
rāmāle, rāmālis, n., usually pl., *branches, twigs* (of a tree).
āridus, -a, -um, *dry.*
***tēctum, -ī,** n., *roof, ceiling; house, dwelling.*
  tēctō: supply **dē;** the couple kept firewood and kindling hanging from the rafters of their hut to dry.

645   **dēferō, dēferre, dētulī, dēlātus,** *to bring down.*

      aēnum, -ī, n., *bronze vessel; pot, cauldron.*

646   **quod: holus** (647) is antecedent.

      riguus, -a, -um, *irrigating; irrigated, well-watered.*

    ***colligō, colligere, collēgī, collēctus,** *to gather (together); to arrange.*

647   **truncō, -āre, -āvī, -ātus,** *to cut;* + abl., *to strip* (something) *of* (branches, foliage, etc.).

      holus: here, as often, collective sing.

    ***furca, -ae,** f., *forked stick, fork.*

      bicornis, -is, -e, *two-horned, two-pronged.*

648   **sordida:** here, *coarse* or perhaps *discolored;* the slab of smoked or salted pork is not a prime cut, but part of a poor man's humble cuisine.

      sūs, suis, m., *pig.*

      tignum, -ī, n., *beam, plank* (of wood).

        nigrō . . . tignō: supply **dē;** the beam is blackened from the smoky hut.

649   **resecō, resecāre, resecuī, resectus,** *to trim, cut off.*

      tergus, tergoris, n., *back* (of an animal).

650   **secō, secāre, secuī, sectus,** *to sever, cut, slice.*

        partem (649) **/ . . . sectam:** i.e., *the slice;* note Ovid's interweaving of his verses through the echoes **terga** (648) **/ tergore** (649) and **resecat** (649) **/ sectam** (650).

    ***domō, domāre, domuī, domitus,** *to subdue, tame; to conquer.*

        domat: a bit of Ovidian humor—as the long preserved pork was a bit "gamy," its taste needed "taming" by a chef.

      undīs: an apt, albeit dramatized, metaphor for boiling water.

651   **mediās:** *intervening,* i.e., throughout the preparations for the meal that have already been described and as they wait for the food to cook; lines 652-54 are generally regarded as a scribal interpolation and are omitted here.

655   **concutiō, concutere, concussī, concussus,** *to cause to vibrate, shake.*

      torum: here, *bedding* (i.e., cushions); with **impositum lectō** (656).

      ulva, -ae, f., *aquatic grass, sedge.*

        dē . . . ulvā: i.e., *made of. . . .*

656   **sponda, -ae,** f., *bed-frame.*

    ***salignus, -a, -um,** *made of willow-wood.*

      spondā . . . salignīs: abl. of description.

657   **Vestibus:** here, *blankets* or *spreads.*

      vēlō, -āre, -āvī, -ātus, *to cover, veil.*

658   **cōnsuēscō, cōnsuēscere, cōnsuēvī, cōnsuētus,** *to be accustomed* (to).

      cōnsuērant: = **cōnsuēverant**

    ***vīlis, -is, -e,** *cheap, worthless; contemptible, of inferior rank.*

659   **indignor, -ārī, -ātus sum,** *to regard with indignation, regard as unworthy, take offense at.*

        lectō nōn indignanda salignō: the dat. of agent with **indignanda** produces, with **pedibus** (656) and **vetus** (658), a lively personification—bed and bedding, like Baucis and Philemon, may be

645 dētulit et minuit parvōque admōvit aēnō,
646 quodque suus coniūnx riguō collēgerat hortō,
647 truncat holus foliīs. Furcā levat ille bicornī
648 sordida terga suis nigrō pendentia tignō
649 servātōque diū resecat dē tergore partem
650 exiguam sectamque domat ferventibus undīs.
651   Intereā mediās fallunt sermōnibus hōrās
655 concutiuntque torum dē mollī flūminis ulvā
656 impositum lectō spondā pedibusque salignīs.
657 Vestibus hunc vēlant, quās nōn nisi tempore fēstō
658 sternere cōnsuērant, sed et haec vīlisque vetusque
659 vestis erat, lectō nōn indignanda salignō;
660 adcubuēre deī. Mēnsam succīncta tremēnsque

Discussion Questions

1. Some manuscripts (and editors) read **illa** in 647, others have **ille**; which variant seems more likely what Ovid wrote, and why?

2. What is the emotional effect of the phrase **servātō . . . diū . . . tergore** in 649?

3. Why are there so many verbs, and the actions so detailed, in 639–50?

4. Which words in 645–50 are calculated to evoke the very humble character of Baucis and Philemon's home?

5. Comment on the several devices of diction, word order, and sound effect that Ovid employs to impress on us his description of the couple's couch in 657–59; what, by contrast with the details of 655–59, is especially effective in the following clause, **adcubuēre deī** (660)?

---

      old, poor, and decrepit (willow not being the sturdiest wood for a bed), but they are a perfect match and get along just fine.

660   **adcumbō, adcumbere, adcubuī, adcubitūrus,** *to lie down, recline (at table).*

    Mēnsam . . . / pōnere (661): cf. our idiom "to set the table"; only the two gods recline, while the elderly couple scurry around to serve them.

    succīnctus, -a, -um, *with one's clothes gathered up* (by a belt, etc., usually in preparation for vigorous activity).

661   **impār, imparis**, *unequal in size/length; uneven.*

       pēs . . . impār: Roman tables regularly had three legs, not four; this one is "lame" and therefore, like Baucis herself (**tremēns** 660), a bit shaky (for the likelihood that Ovid intendes the personification, see above on **lectō . . . salignō** 659).

662   **testa, -ae**, f., *roof-tile; potsherd.*

    subditus, -a, -um, *(having been) situated beneath, set under.*

    quae postquam . . . / sustulit (663): *after this* (the tile). . . .

663   **sufferō, sufferre, sustulī, sublātus**, *to hold up, raise up.*

    aequātus, -a, -um, *leveled.*

       aequātam: supply **mēnsam.**

    menta, -ae, f., *mint, mint-leaf.*

    vireō, virēre, viruī, *to show green growth, be green; to be full of youthful vigor.*

       mentae . . . virentēs: with **mentae** as subject of **tersēre** (= **tersērunt**), the personification continues; the mint-leaves used (instead of the usual cloth) to wipe the table are not just *green* but *in the flower of youth*, as Baucis is not, and hence the leaves themselves, not Baucis, perform the task. Once again Ovid animates, not just his human characters, but their surroundings as well, so that the entire household of Baucis and Philemon seems alive. The mint-leaves are a rustic touch, but their fragrance must add a charming elegance to the table.

664   **bicolor, bicolōris**, *of two colors.*

       bicolor . . . bāca: sing. for pl. (like several of the other menu items enumerated below), i.e., olives, which are black when ripe, green when not; these may be half-ripe, or perhaps both ripe and unripe varieties are served. Interlocked word order here, in the next verse, and again in 667–69 embellishes Ovid's description of what is in fact a very humble first course.

    sincērus, -a, -um, *unblemished, pure.*

    *****Minerva, -ae**, f., *Minerva* (virginal goddess of wisdom and warfare, the Roman counterpart to the Greek's Athena).

       sincērae . . . Minervae: the olive tree was sacred to Minerva.

665   **condita**: here, *preserved* or *pickled.*

    liquidus, -a, -um, *liquid, fluid.*

    cornum, -ī, n., *cornelian cherry, cornel-berry.*

    autumnālis, -is, -e, *(of/in) autumn, autumnal.*

    faex, faecis, f., *solid matter/impurities suspended in wine, dregs.*

       condita . . . faece: the berries, harvested in the fall, were thriftily preserved in wine dregs, after the wine had been poured off and consumed; though fastidiously served, all these appetizers (what the Romans called the **gustātiō**) are low-budget items and some of them less than appetizing.

666   **intibum, -ī**, n., *chickory, endive.*

    rādīx, rādīcis, f., *root* (of a plant, tree, etc.); *radish.*

    lac, lactis, n., *milk.*

661 pōnit anus, mēnsae sed erat pēs tertius impār:
662 testa parem fēcit; quae postquam subdita clīvum
663 sustulit, aequātam mentae tersēre virentēs.
664 Pōnitur hīc bicolor sincērae bāca Minervae
665 conditaque in liquidā corna autumnālia faece
666 intibaque et rādīx et lactis māssa coāctī
667 ōvaque nōn ācrī leviter versāta favillā,

"Jupiter Visiting Philemon and Baucis," Bramantino (Bartolomeo Suardi), ca. 1500
Wallraf-Richartz-Museum, Cologne, Germany

---

lactis . . . coāctī: i.e., *cheese.*
māssa, -ae, f., *lump, mass.*
667 **ōva**: eggs are naturally included in this first course, as Roman meals
       conventionally progressed, not "from soup to nuts," but "from egg to
       apples" (**ab ōvō ad māla**—the apples turn up in 675); and, though Baucis
       and Philemon are not Roman, Ovid's audience is.
nōn ācrī: i.e., warm, not hot.
leviter, adv., *lightly, gently.*
favilla, -ae, f., *ashes* (of a fire).

668   **fictile, -is**, n., *earthenware vessel, dish, plate.*

       fictilibus: supply **in**; the dinnerware, like the dinner, is quite modest. Enjambement and the strong caesura aptly conclude the list of hors d'oeuvres.

  *****caelō, -āre, -āvī, -ātus**, *to engrave, emboss.*

669   **sistō, sistere, stetī, status**, *to cause* (something, someone) *to stand; to set up; to place, set down.*

       sistitur: sing. to agree with the nearer of its two subjects, **crātēr** and **pōcula** (670).

    argentum, -ī, n., *silver.*

       eōdem (668) / . . . **argentō**: abl. of description; the narrator is jesting, of course, since the couple's "silverware" is really clay (though not an exact analogy with Ovid's purpose here, those of us who can't afford silver at today's prices still call our knives and forks "silverware"—at least we do in our house!).

  *****crātēr, crātēris**, acc., **crātēra**, m., *mixing-bowl* (usually for wine).

       caelātus (668) . . . **crātēr**: the "golden" arrangement (adj. A/adj. B/verb/noun A/noun B, intensifies the joke by delaying the "silver" crockpot to the end.

    fabricō, -āre, -āvī, -ātus, *to fashion, forge, make.*

    fāgus, -ī, f., *beech-tree, beech-wood.*

       fāgō: abl. of material, often without a prep. in verse; the alliteration in **fabricātaque fāgō** and the noun's emphatic position underscore the truth of this description vs. the humorous lie in the one before.

670   **quā**, adv., *in which part, where.*

    cavus, -a, -um, *having a hole on the surface, hollow; full of holes, porous.*

  *****flāvēns, flāventis**, *golden, yellow.*

    inlinō, inlinere, inlēvī, inlitus, *to apply by smearing, smear; to coat* (with).

       quā . . . cērīs: the beech-wood cups are smeared with yellow wax, that much is clear; but is it *where they are hollow*, i.e., on the inside, or *where they are porous* or *full of holes*, and are they coated with the wax as a sealant, "to make them impermeable," as Hollis suggests (probably) or to patch holes or cracks in the aging wood (so Anderson). Certainly the color of the wax is emphasized as a counterpoint to **argentō** in the preceding verse (as Hill too tentatively suggests); the old couple may not have any real silver or gold, only crockery and wood, but there is a resplendent, golden aura about their table.

671   **focī mīsēre**: poetic pl. for sing., and another personification.

    caleō, calēre, caluī, *to be hot, warm.*

       calentēs: with **epulās** more likely than **focī**, though both of course are hot; we have at last the main course, the pork and vegetables described earlier, now served up from the hearth.

672   **rūrsus referuntur**: the alliterative redundancy underscores the narrator's point—the same wine set out before the main course is served up again afterwards, most inelegant by Roman standards!

    vīna: pl. for sing. to suggest the separate goblets.

668	omnia fictilibus. Post haec caelātus eōdem
669	sistitur argentō crātēr fabricātaque fāgō
670	pōcula, quā cava sunt, flāventibus inlita cērīs.
671	Parva mora est, epulāsque focī mīsēre calentēs,
672	nec longae rūrsus referuntur vīna senectae
673	dantque locum mēnsīs paulum sēducta secundīs:

Discussion Question

Why do you suppose the main course is mentioned with such remarkable brevity in 671, by contrast with the details of its preparation earlier in the story?

senecta, -ae, f., *old age.*
nec longae . . . senectae: the litotes (nec longae = et nōn longae = brevis) and hyperbaton (wide separation of adj. and noun) build comic suspense; this second round of wine is not only left over from before dinner but is of recent vintage, not aged. In the traditional cēna poem, multiple varieties of well-aged wine are served, and named; this nameless vintage is clearly last week's basement-brew.

673 paulus, -a, -um, *little, small.*
paulum: possibly the adv., with sēducta, but more likely construed as an adj. with locum, producing another interlocked line like the several above (see on bicolor 664).
sēdūcō, sēdūcere, sēdūxī, sēductus, *to draw aside; to separate off, set aside.*
dantque locum . . . sēducta: supply vīna. No sooner are the after-dinner drinks served than they are set aside to make room for the dessert; the narrative is rushed, perhaps to suggest that these last courses were too. The deliberate soundplay in senectae (672) / sēducta secundīs is followed immediately by the delightful hīc nux, hīc mixta (674).

674   **rūgōsus, -a, -um**, *wrinkled, shriveled.*

      cārica, -ae, f., *fig* (a type of fig from Caria, in Asia Minor).

      palma, -ae, f., *palm* (of the hand); *palm-tree*; usually pl., *fruit of the date-palm, date.*

         rūgōsīs . . . palmīs: rūgōsīs, because they were dried.

675   **prūnum, -ī,** n., *plum.*

      patulus, -a, -um, *wide-open, gaping; broad.*

      redoleō, redolēre, *to give off a smell, be fragrant.*

      canistrum, -ī, n., *basket.*

         prūnaque . . . canistrīs: in contrast with the emphatic spondees of 674, this line's rapid, alliterative dactyls seem appropriate to its image of broad, spreading baskets of fruit, pouring forth their rich aromas.

676   *****vītis, vītis,** f., *grapevine.*

         purpureīs . . . vītibus: the effect of the transferred epithet (which applies logically, of course, to **ūvae**) is enhanced through interlocked word order.

677   **favus, -ī,** m., *honeycomb.*

678   **accēdō, accēdere, accessī, accessus,** *to come to, approach.*

         accessēre: = **accessērunt;** supply **ad mēnsam.**

      bonī: here, *happy* or *pleasant.*

      nec: = **et nōn,** with both **iners** (i.e., *lively/animated*) and **pauper;** litotes.

      voluntās, voluntātis, f., *disposition to choose, will; approval; goodwill.*

         vultūs (677) / **. . . voluntās:** the assonance in **iners pauperque** and especially **vultūs / voluntās** sonorously closes the scene.

679   **totiēns,** adv., *as often as, whenever.*

         totiēns haustum: English would use a clause rather than a participial phrase, *as often as it. . . .*

      repleō, replēre, replēvī, replētus, *to refill, replenish.*

680   **(spōns), spontis,** f., used only in gen. and abl. sing., *will, volition;* **sponte suā, meā,** etc., *of (one's) own will, spontaneously.*

      suā per sēque: = **suā et per sē;** the reflexives refer, not to the subjects of **vident** (Baucis and Philemon), but to the subjects of the indirect statements it governs, which are arranged in a chiasmus that cleverly suggests the depletion and refilling of the wine vessels, **haustum crātēra replērī** (679) / **. . . succrēscere vīna.** The alliteration of s is doubtless also a deliberate effect, perhaps intoning the spectators' amazement (**attonitī** 681) at the miracle (which parallels a number of biblical miracles).

      succrēscō, succrēscere, succrēvī, *to rise up (from below).*

681   **novitās, novitātis,** f., *newness, novelty; strange/unusual phenomenon.*

      paveō, pavēre, *to be frightened, terrified.*

      supīnus, -a, -um, *lying face upward; turned palm upwards* (of the raised hands of a suppliant).

683   **daps, dapis,** f., *sacrificial meal; feast, meal, banquet.*

         dapibus: this word, rather than **cēnae** or some other, is perhaps deliberately chosen for its ritual connotations.

674	hīc nux, hīc mixta est rūgōsīs cārica palmīs
675	prūnaque et in patulīs redolentia māla canistrīs
676	et dē purpureīs collēctae vītibus ūvae,
677	candidus in mediō favus est. Super omnia vultūs
678	accessēre bonī nec iners pauperque voluntās.
679	"Intereā totiēns haustum crātēra replērī
680	sponte suā per sēque vident succrēscere vīna:
681	attonitī novitāte pavent, manibusque supīnīs
682	concipiunt Baucisque precēs timidusque Philēmōn,
683	et veniam dapibus nūllīsque parātibus ōrant.
684	Ūnicus ānser erat, minimae custōdia vīllae,

Discussion Questions

1. In what several ways does word order enhance meaning in 674–77?

2. Comment on the thematic effectiveness of the litotes in 678.

3. What do **ūnicus** and **minimae** in 684 have in common and what point do they add to the story?

---

parātus, -ūs, m., *preparation; proper appointments/service* (of the dinner-
table, including food, dinnerware, etc.).
    nūllīs . . . parātibus: i.e., *lack of. . . .*
684   ūnicus, -a, -um, *one and only, sole, single.*
    ānser, ānseris, m., *goose.*
    custōdia, -ae, f., *protection, defense, guard; guardian.*
        ānser . . . custōdia: geese, sacred to Juno, were credited with saving
           Rome from attack by the Gauls in 390 B.C. and were venerated as
           protectors of home and hearth.

685   **mactō, -āre, -āvī, -ātus,** *to honor; to offer sacrificially* (to a god).
       parābant: an intentional echo of **parātibus** (683); the promptness of the
          couple's actions, once they recognize their guests as gods, compensates
          for what they perceive as their earlier shortcomings.
686   **fatīgō, -āre, -āvī, -ātus,** *to weary, tire out.*
       ille . . . fatīgat: a moment of comic relief.
687   **ēlūdō, ēlūdere, ēlūdī, ēlūsus,** *to deceive, fool; to escape from, elude.*
       ad ipsōs / . . . deōs (688): the intensive adj. is emphatically placed, and the
          noun enjambed, to heighten suspense over the portent.
688   **vetuēre:** = **vetuērunt;** supply **ānserem.**
689   **meritus, -a, -um,** *deserved, merited.*
       luō, luere, luī, *to suffer* (a punishment, by way of expiation).
       impia: emphatically enjambed, and deliberately contrasted with **immūnibus.**
690   **immūnis, -is, -e,** *exempt from tribute/taxation;* + gen., *having no part* (in),
       free/immune (from).
          immūnibus: in the predicate, agreeing with **vōbīs** after **esse,** *it will be*
            granted to you to be. . . .
692   **vestra relinquite tēcta** (691) / **ac nostrōs comitāte gradūs:** having fully
       balanced the couple's piety against their neighbors' impiety, the gods'
       retribution is swift (689–90), their clemency to Baucis and Philemon
       unambiguous (690–91), and their commands emphatic (**īte simul** 693) and
       orderly, as this ABCDABC arrangement helps to suggest.
       ardua: a substantive here, producing an effective hendiadys with **montis.**
693   **levātī:** here, *supported.*
694   **nītor, nītī, nīxus sum,** *to lean on;* + infin., *to strain, struggle* (to
       accomplish a task).
       vēstīgia pōnere: i.e., to walk or climb, but the word choice here aptly
          suggests a more strenuous effort, as do (Anderson observes) the line's slow
          initial spondees.
695   **tantum . . . quantum,** correlative adv., *so much . . . as, so far . . . as.*
       summō: here used as a substantive, *the highest (point),* i.e., *the summit.*
       semel . . . / missa (696): i.e., in a single shot.
696   **mergō, mergere, mersī, mersus,** *to dip, immerse; to flood, inundate.*
       palūs, palūdis, f., *flood-water, swamp.*
          mersa palūde / cētera (697): the countryside has now become the
            stagnum Lelex described in 624–25.
697   **prōspiciō, prōspicere, prōspexī, prōspectus,** *to see before oneself* (that), *see*
       in front.
       tantum . . . manēre: indirect statement dependent on **prōspiciunt.**
698   **dum . . . suōrum:** a highly musical line, whose assonance, alliteration, and
       anaphora all dramatize the aged couple's bewilderment and evoke our
       anticipation of the metamorphosis that is to occur next.
       suōrum: i.e., their neighbors.
699   **illa . . . duōbus:** interlocked order; take **illa vetus** with **casa parva,** and
       etiam with **dominīs duōbus,** dat. with **parva.** The hut was tiny even for
       its poor inhabitants.
700   **Furcās:** here, *forked supports;* but Ovid means us to recall and contrast with

685 quem dīs hospitibus dominī mactāre parābant;
686 ille celer pennā tardōs aetāte fatīgat
687 ēlūditque diū tandemque est vīsus ad ipsōs
688 cōnfūgisse deōs. Superī vetuēre necārī,
689 'Dī'que, 'sumus, meritāsque luet vīcīnia poenās
690 impia,' dīxērunt; 'vōbīs immūnibus huius
691 esse malī dabitur. Modo vestra relinquite tēcta
692 ac nostrōs comitāte gradūs et in ardua montis
693 īte simul!' Pārent ambō baculīsque levātī
694 nītuntur longō vēstīgia pōnere clīvō.
695 Tantum aberant summō, quantum semel īre sagitta
696 missa potest: flexēre oculōs et mersa palūde
697 cētera prōspiciunt—tantum sua tēcta manēre—
698 dumque ea mīrantur, dum dēflent fāta suōrum,
699 illa vetus dominīs etiam casa parva duōbus
700 vertitur in templum. Furcās subiēre columnae,
701 strāmina flāvēscunt aurātaque tēcta videntur,

Discussion Question

How are diction, word order, and meter appropriate to meaning in 686?

this temple earlier scenes within the hut through his deliberate repetitions of **Furcā** (647) / **Furcās** (700—in the same metrical position and each at the beginning of a sentence), **caelātus** (668) / **caelātae** (702), **flāventibus** (670) / **flāvēscunt** (701), and even the analogous **argentō** (669) / **aurāta** (701).

*subeō, subīre, subiī, subitus, *to go underneath; to replace; to come upon* (someone) *stealthily, sneak up on* (someone).

columna, -ae, f., *column, pillar.*

701 strāmen, strāminis, n., often pl., *straw, thatching.*

flāvēscō, flāvēscere, *to turn yellow, become golden.*

tēcta: pl. for sing., and subject, along with forēs and tellūs, of videntur; a number of temples in Rome had gilded roofs, so the image would be familiar to Ovid's audience.

702   **adopertus, -a, -um**, *covered.*

    marmor, marmoris, n., *marble.*

    tellūs: i.e., the cottage's earthen floor.

703   **Tālia . . . ōre**: another musical verse, suited to the transition.

    placidus, -a, -um, *kindly, pleasant; calm, serene.*

    Sāturnius, -a, -um, *of Saturn* (an ancient Roman god); *son of Saturn* (Jupiter).

    ***ēdō, ēdere, ēdidī, ēditus**, *to give forth, emit; to utter sollemnly; to narrate, publish.*

706   **iūdicium, -ī**, n., *judgment, decision.*

707   **sacerdōs, sacerdōtis**, m./f., *priest, priestess.*

    dēlūbrum, -ī, n., *temple, shrine.*

        dēlūbra: pl. for sing., i.e., the temple into which their hut has been transformed.

708   **concors, concordis**, *agreeing, like-minded; harmonious, in harmony.*

710   **tumulō, -āre, -āvī, -ātus**, *to cover with a burial mound, bury.*

    illā: abl. of agent instead of the dat. usual with the pass. periphrastic.

711   **fidēs**: here, as often, the word means *the fulfillment of (their) wish.*

    tūtēla, -ae, f., *guardianship; protection, defense.*

712   ***solūtus, -a, -um**, *unbound, loosened; opened; weakened.*

713   ***sacer, sacra, sacrum**, *sacred, religious.*

        gradūs sacrōs: the steps leading up to the temple.

714   ***frondeō, frondēre**, *to sprout leaves.*

    frondēre Philēmona . . . / Baucida . . . frondēre (715): indirect statements dependent on **cōnspexit**; chiasmus and asyndeton emphasize the simultaneity of the transformations (and cf. **dīxēre simul, simul . . . tēxit** 718).

716   **cacūmine**: i.e., of each of the two trees. One can almost hear the rustling of leaves, or the branches crackling, in the striking alliteration **crēscente cacūmine**, as the couple are metamorphosed into the oak and linden trees which Lelex had told of in 620; the onomatopoeia is continued in the x/s alliteration of 718-19, where the two whisper their last farewell.

717   **mūtua . . . reddēbant dicta**: i.e., they spoke to each other in turn.

718   **abditus, -a, -um**, *hidden from sight, concealed.*

        abdita: proleptic.

719   **frutex, fruticis**, f., *shrub, bush; shoot, stem, stalk,* (plant) *growth.*

    Thȳnēius, -a, -um, *Bithynian, of Bithynia* (a district of Asia Minor north of Phrygia).

        Thȳnēius . . . / incola (720): a farmer living in the vicinity; he is either an immigrant from Bithynia, or Ovid generalizes the name Bithynia to include Phrygia, where the story takes place (621).

720   **truncus, -ī**, m., *body of a man, trunk, torso; tree-trunk.*

        geminō . . . truncōs: the interlocked order produces a poignant word-picture—the trees are so close that they seem to grow from a single trunk.

702 caelātaeque forēs adopertaque marmore tellūs.
703 "Tālia tum placidō Sāturnius ēdidit ōre:
704 'Dīcite, iūste senex et fēmina coniuge iūstō
705 digna, quid optētis.' Cum Baucide pauca locūtus,
706 iūdicium superīs aperit commūne Philēmōn:
707 'Esse sacerdōtēs dēlūbraque vestra tuērī
708 poscimus, et quoniam concordēs ēgimus annōs,
709 auferat hōra duōs eadem, nec coniugis umquam
710 busta meae videam, neu sim tumulandus ab illā.'
711 Vōta fidēs sequitur: templī tūtēla fuēre,
712 dōnec vīta data est. Annīs aevōque solūtī,
713 ante gradūs sacrōs cum stārent forte locīque
714 narrārent cāsūs, frondēre Philēmona Baucis,
715 Baucida cōnspēxit senior frondēre Philēmōn.
716 Iamque super geminōs crēscente cacūmine vultūs,
717 mūtua, dum licuit, reddēbant dicta, 'Valē'que,
718 'ō coniūnx,' dīxēre simul, simul abdita tēxit
719 ōra frutex. Ostendit adhūc Thȳnēius illīc
720 incola dē geminō vīcīnōs corpore truncōs.
721 Haec mihi nōn vānī (neque erat cūr fallere vellent)

Discussion Question

Comment on the effect of the chiasmus in 704 and the enjambement of **digna** in 705.

---

721   **vānus, -a, -um,** *empty, insubstantial; unreliable, foolish.*
    nōn vānī: i.e., wise or truthful; litotes.
    cūr: here, *(any reason) why.*
    vellent: deliberative subjn.

723 **serta, -ōrum**, n. pl., *chains of flowers, garlands.*
    serta: with **recentia** as well as **pendentia**; local worshippers, and Lelex himself, had venerated the spirits of Baucis and Philemon by placing ritual garlands on the branches of the two trees.

724 **Cūra deum**: *(Those who have been) the care of the gods* (**deum** = **deōrum**), i.e., those who have been of concern or importance to the gods; some readers take **deum** as objective gen., rather than subjective, in the sense of *(Those who have taken) care of the gods*, so that the idea in **Cūra . . . sint** more nearly parallels that in **quī . . . colantur**, but Ovid's usage seems rather like Vergil's description of Anchises as **cūra deum**, *beloved of the gods*, at *Aeneid* III.476 (and cf. *Am.* I.3.16 below).

722   nārrāvēre senēs; equidem pendentia vīdī
723   serta super rāmōs pōnēnsque recentia dīxī,
724   'Cūra deum dī sint, et, quī coluēre, colantur.'"

Discussion Questions

1. Comment on the multiple sound effects accompanying the story's conclusion in 722–24.

2. Compare the relationship of Baucis and Philemon with that of Pyramus and Thisbe. What are the most striking correspondences and differences? How would Roman audiences react to the two couples?

3. Compare in detail Pyramus' prayer at IV.154–61 with Philemon's here, as well as the final outcomes of both tales. Which story is more tragic?

4. How do the stories of these two couples differ from the other four *Metamorphoses* selections in this book?

"Landscape for Philemon and Baucis," David Ligare, 1984
Wadsworth Atheneum, Hartford, Connecticut

THE *AMORES*

In the seven selections from the *Amores* that close out this volume, we cross over the boundary from the epic world into the elegiac, and yet as noted in the introduction (which readers may wish to review at this point), that boundary is seldom in Ovid very clearly defined; gods and heroes like Apollo and Orpheus are transformed, so to speak, and cross over the *limen*, while the elegiac lover joins Cupid's army, brandishes his weapons, and wages his own wars in the boudoir. A brief overview of the individual poems may tempt the reader likewise to escape for a moment into Ovid's Fantasyland, where Cupid reigns triumphant, where real wars and violence are bid farewell, and where Good Sense is held prisoner by Love.

The prefatory I.1 announces the poet's intention to write romantic verse—not, alas, his original plan, but savage Cupid had chuckled, sneaked out a foot from his epic's every second verse, and turned his song from weaponry to love. Transfixed by one of those surefire arrows that would later (in the *Metamorphoses*) inflame Apollo's passion for Daphne, Ovid bids farewell to "iron war" and invokes a Muse he will measure out in the eleven unheroically limping feet of elegy's couplets.

The sequel in I.2, like some 1950s rock-and-roll tune, opens dramatically with poor Ovid, blankets thrown to the floor, "tossing and turning all night." Clearly Love's arrows have taken effect, and the time to surrender is at hand. The poet invites Cupid to celebrate his conquest in triumphal procession, just like a victorious Roman general, except that his chariot will be golden and drawn by doves, his lieutenants will be "Sweet-talk, Miscalculation, and Madness," and his prisoners-of-war will include not only all the world's young lovers but also, bound in chains, "Good Sense and Chastity." In the poem's closing lines, Cupid is first likened to Bacchus (a kindred spirit who similarly exults in passion) and then implored to follow the example of his "kinsman Caesar" and bestow mercy on those he has conquered, the poet among them—a curious allusion to an emperor who in the end would show Ovid himself very little of the much vaunted Caesarian *clementia*.

Just as the poet closes *Amores* I.2 begging Cupid for mercy, so he opens I.3 with an entreaty to Venus for justice, praying that the girl who has taken him captive (a metaphor also resumed from the preceding piece) either love him, or in some way show her affection, or at least allow herself to be loved. Ovid then invokes the girl herself, arguing that, if his own lineage is not sufficiently noble to merit her esteem, at least the gods—Apollo, and Bacchus, and Cupid—are on his side, as is his sterling character. The whole piece is very much tongue-in-cheek, not least Ovid's repeated pledge of fidelity (in verses 6, 13, and 16), which is immediately undercut when he promises the girl that his love for her will be celebrated in song, as was Jupiter's love for Io, and for Leda, and for Europa—just three of that god's innumerable adulterous trysts. In the end Ovid's *puella* remains nameless and his poem seems more a proclamation of poetic purpose (forms of *carmen* occur three times in lines 19–21 and *cantabimur* is the key verb in the closing couplet) than a profession of true love.

Poem I.9 is a clever tour de force arguing the thesis that "every lover is truly a soldier, and Commander Cupid has his own camp," an elaboration of the military imagery seen in the previous selections and a variant on a stock rhetorical exercise, which Ovid had doubtless encountered in his own schooling, comparing the soldier's life with the lawyer's. Lovers and soldiers alike must be youthful, vigorous, and brave, prepared for long marches, spy missions, breaking down doors (their mistresses' or their foes'), and launching night attacks. In the tradition of the great heroes at Troy and even of Mars himself—who performed double-duty as both god of war and Venus' lover—Ovid is a true man of action, never the slacker, ever prepared to raise up his sword and wage Cupid's battles in the night.

Poems I.11 and 12 describe a diptych, a Roman writing tablet consisting of two wax-covered boards hinged to fold over at the center, and at the same time form one. Page one, I.11, focuses initially on Nape, Ovid's veteran maidservant and go-between, whom he praises for her loyalty, her ingenuity, and her past successes in coaxing Corinna, the poet's mistress, to visit him in the night. Now, brusquely ordering Nape to deliver a love-letter to Corinna, the poet fantasizes that the tablet itself, inscribed with his own charming words, will accomplish the mission; this most faithful of servants will return with just the right message from Corinna— "Come!"—and be garlanded with laurel for the victory. Page two, I.12, a lamentation: Nape had stubbed her toe at the door when setting out (a BAD SIGN!) and the (now fully personified) Diptych itself has come home, sad-faced, with the miserable message, "Can't!" Through the rest of the poem Ovid rewards the unfortunate Tablet and its "notes that say 'No'," not with a garland, but with a gleeful curse on its blood-red wax and its gallows-wood frame for their ill-omened, loveless "duplicity."

Finally, just as I.1 had been a farewell to arms, as it were, our last selection, *Amores* III.15, bids farewell to Venus and Cupid and to the poet's "warless elegies" (*imbelles elegi*). But with his own characteristic duplicity, Ovid infuses the poem with a series of military images, announcing in the end that he will steer his war horses next across an even greater field, the *Metamorphoses* and the *Fasti*, he means, which he was soon to commence. In the poem's (and the book's) closing couplet, he expresses his hope that the *Amores* might survive beyond his own death—a well-founded hope, we must surely concede, as we venture forth into the territory of his Cupid poems some two thousand years after their publication.

1   **Arma**: Ovid aptly begins his prefatory, anti-epic elegy with the same
     dramatic word (and the same metonymy for *violence* or *war*) that opens
     Vergil's *Aeneid*; the somber tone is temporarily continued in **gravī numerō
     violentaque bella**, so that by the end of this first verse a listening audience
     might suppose that it is about to hear an epic recited. In a later poem (*Am.*
     II.1.11–16) Ovid tells us (again doubtless in jest) that the epic he had
     started to write was about the battle between the gods and the hundred-
     handed giants.

     gravī numerō: here, *in solemn meter*; this reference to dactylic hexameter as
     the proper form for epic is, through ring composition, taken up again in
     the poem's penultimate couplet (cf. **numerō violentaque bella** and **modīs**,
     1–2, with **numerīs** and **ferrea cum vestrīs bella . . . modīs**, 27–28).
     Aptly, the rhythm of this opening line, and the first half of the next, is
     entirely dactylic.

     violentus, -a, -um, *violent, savage, aggressive*.

2   *****māteria, -ae**, or **māteriēs, -ēī**, f., *wood* (as a building material); *material,
     subject-matter*.

     modīs: here (and in 28, and cf. **ēmodulanda** 30), *rhythms*; dat. with the
     compound **conveniente**.

3   **pār, paris**, *equal* (in measure or magnitude).

         Pār . . . versus: in the dactylic hexameter, of course, every verse has
         six feet.

     inferior, inferior, inferius, gen., **inferiōris**, *lower; following, subsequent*
     (here referring to the second verse of a poem or couplet, specifically the
     elegiac couplet in which this poem is written).

     rīsisse . . . surripuisse (4): assonance and similar line positioning help link
     the two infinitives and underscore the point that Cupid's larceny was to
     him a wonderful practical joke.

4   **dīcitur**: by the poet's friends? his audience? his detractors?—the passive is
     deliberately ambiguous.

     surripuisse: the verb comically implies a sneaky, surreptitious theft.

     pedem: here (and cf. 30), of course, a metrical *foot*, or rather the two half-
     feet which the elegiac's pentameter lacked.

5   **Quis . . . iūris**: for the complaining question, and the provocative epithet
     applied to Cupid, cf. *Met.* I.456 above; and for the god's **saevitia**, cf.
     saeva Cupīdinis īra (*Met.* I.453). The speaker in 5–20 is the poet himself,
     in an earlier moment when he was still contemplating writing epic; **questus
     eram** closes out his harangue in 21.

     Quis . . . Quid (7) **. . . Quis** (9) **. . . quis** (11): the series of interrogative
     pronouns, the first three placed at the beginning of a couplet, and the
     barrage of rhetorical questions in 5–16 underscore the poet's indignation.

     hoc: here (as often with both **hoc** and **hic**), the word is scanned long though
     the vowel is short (see on **hic** *Met.* IV.150 above).

     in carmina: *over poetry* (**in** often has this meaning with **iūs**).

     iūris: partitive gen. with **hoc**, *this authority*.

6   **Pīeris, Pīeridos**, gen. pl., **Pīeridum**, f., *daughter of Pierus, a Muse* (a

AMORES I.1

"A Farewell to Arms"

1 Ārma gravī numerō violentaque bella parābam
2   ēdere, māteriā conveniente modis. *3rd & 5th feet are always long*
3 Pār erat īnferior versus; rīsisse Cupīdo
4   dīcitur atque ūnum surripuisse pedem.
5 "Quis tibi, saeve puer, dedit hoc in carmina iūris?
6   Pīeridum vātēs, nōn tua, turba sumus!
7 Quid, sī praeripiat flāvae Venus arma Minervae,

Discussion Question

Compare the poet's complaint to Cupid in 1–6 with Apollo's complaint in *Met*. I.456–62 above. Who prevailed in the earlier narrative? Who do you suppose will prevail here? What is the point of these correspondences in the characterization of Cupid?

Cupid 2x
epic w/ love poems and Cupid
Cupid to both w/c, get rid of / place in an epic

---

common patronymic form—Pierus, King of Emathia in Macedonia, was in some accounts father of the Muses).

Pīeridum: with **turba,** the predicate noun.

vātēs: Ovid uses this solemn term for poets as *inspired bards* with mock solemnity; here subject of **sumus,** *we bards.*

7   **Quid:** i.e., *What would we think*; the two clauses following constitute the protasis to this understood apodosis.

praeripiō, praeripere, praeripuī, praereptus, *to seize first, snatch away.*
   praeripiat: the verb recalls **surripuisse** (4) and makes a distinction—Venus' imagined theft is brazen and violent, while her son's is surreptitious.

flāvae: a frequent epithet of Minerva.

arma: the poem's opening word is deliberately recalled; and in the neat juxtaposition **Venus arma,** Venus' imagined usurpation of Minerva's weapons of war parallels her son Cupid's obstruction of the poet's desire to write poems of war rather than love.

8 **ventilō, -āre, -āvī, -ātus**, *to fan*.

  accēnsās . . . facēs: i.e., the flames of passion kindled by Venus; note the chiasmus, with **flāva Minerva** at the center, and cf. the deliberately opposite arrangement in 7.

9 **silvīs . . . iugōsīs**: forests were properly the domain of Diana, not of Ceres.

 ***rēgnō, -āre, -āvī, -ātus**, *to rule, govern, reign*.

  iugōsus, -a, -um, *hilly, mountainous*.

10 **lēge**: the word picks up the notion in **rēgnāre** in the preceding verse; within his or her proper sphere, each deity governs by divine law.

  pharetrātus, -a, -um, *quiver-bearing*.

   pharetrātae virginis: bow and arrows were Diana's emblem, as they were her brother Apollo's—cf. *Met.* I.456–65 above).

  arva colī: an acc. + infin. phrase dependent on **probet**, paralleling **Cererem rēgnāre** in 9.

11 **Crīnibus**: abl. of respect, with **īnsignem**; Apollo was commonly depicted with long curly locks.

  īnsignis, -is, -e, *conspicuous, remarkable* (in appearance).

12 **Āonius, -a, -um**, *of Aonia, Boeotian*.

   Aonia was that region of the Greek district of Boeotia where Mt. Helicon was located—a precinct sacred to the Muses and Apollo.

 ***Mars, Martis**, m., *Mars* (Roman god of agriculture and especially of war).

   The deity is humorously imagined here strumming Apollo's lyre rather than brandishing a spear, which was his usual attribute.

 ***lyra, -ae**, f., *lyre* (a stringed instrument sacred to Apollo and a symbol of lyric poetry).

   īnsignem . . . acūtā cuspide Phoebum / . . . Āoniam Marte movente lyram (12): note the reverse chiastic arrangement of these two phrases (adj. A / adj. B / noun-emblem B / noun-deity A, line 11; adj. A / noun-deity B / adj. B / noun-emblem A, line 12), and cf. 7–8; the word order suits the imagined role reversals.

13 **tibi**: dat. of possession.

  magna . . . rēgna: the wide separation of adj. and noun suggests the expansiveness of Cupid's realm; cf. **rēgnat Amor** (26).

  puer: cf. line 5; after the three couplets (7–12) each describing role reversals between a pair of gods, the poet again addresses Cupid directly and accusingly.

14 **affectō, -āre, -āvī, -ātus**, *to attempt; to strive for, aspire to*.

  ambitiōsus, -a, -um, *self-seeking, ambitious*.

15 **An . . . est**: the full expression would be **An id quod ubīque tuum est**.

  ubīque, adv., *anywhere, everywhere*.

  Helicōnius, -a, -um, *of Helicon* (a mountain in Boeotia sacred, not to Cupid, but to Apollo and the Muses).

  tempē, Greek n. pl. (but sing. in meaning), *valley* (a generalized term taken from Tempe, the valley of the Peneus river in Thessaly—see on **Pēnēius**, *Met.* I.452 above).

16 **Vix . . . est**: the notion of this line deliberately evokes the image in 11–12.

8 ventilet accēnsās flāva Minerva facēs?
9 Quis probet in silvīs Cererem rēgnāre iugōsīs,
10 lēge pharetrātae virginis arva colī?
11 Crīnibus īnsignem quis acūtā cuspide Phoebum
12 īnstruat, Āoniam Marte movente lyram?⌉
13 Sunt tibi magna, puer, nimiumque potentia rēgna—
14 cur opus affectās, ambitiōse, novum?
15 An quod ubīque tuum est? Tua sunt Helicōnia tempē?
16 Vix etiam Phoebō iam lyra tūta sua est?

Discussion Questions

1. How is the word order in 7–8 appropriate to the hypothetical circumstances the poet describes?

2. Discuss in detail the three pairs of examples in 7–12. What is the significance of each pair? How are the visual images incongruous? What are the interconnections among the three pairs? How is the progression from Venus/Minerva to Apollo/Mars especially effective, and what do those two couplets have in common in their conception and imagery? How is the comparison in 11–12 especially suited to the overall subject of the poem?

3. What is the tone of the short, rapid-fire questions in 15–16?

17   **Cum . . . surrēxit**: a **cum** temporal clause. The verb **surgere**, lit., *to rise to one's feet*, along with **attenuat nervōs** (*weakens my muscles*) in the next line, plays on the metaphor of the metrical *foot* in **pedem** (4)/**pedēs** (30), *When my brand-new page had gotten off on just the right foot with the first verse*. This image of the poet's work coming to life is continued with **surgat** and **resīdat** in 27, and in both passages there seems to be a deliberate sexual double entendre (**nervus**, **opus**, and **surgere** are all commonly used of the male sexual apparatus, as are metaphorical allusions to both the bow and the lyre with their strings which are alternately stretched taut and then relaxed).

       pāgina, -ae, f., *page*.

18   **attenuō, -āre, -āvī, -ātus**, *to make thin; to weaken*.

       nervōs . . . meōs: notice the internal rhyme, with adj. and noun set at the caesura and line's end; the same device appears in 20, 22, and 28.

       proximus, -a, -um, *nearest; next, immediately following*.

             proximus ille: possibly Ovid means Cupid (*then that fellow immediately . . .*), thus repeating the image of the god's theft of a metrical foot in 3–4 (and cf. the assonant **prōtinus ille** 21 and **puer ille** 25, both referring to Cupid). But it is perhaps more likely that the poet is still in 17–18 addressing Cupid directly, as he was in 5–16, and that by **proximus ille** he refers to *the very next (verse)* itself, i.e., the **īnferior versus** of line 3; that pentameter verse, missing a foot, is lame, so to speak, and thus diminishes the poet's strength. A similar personification is certainly intended in 27–28.

19   **mihi**: dat. of possession.

       māteria . . . apta: cf. **māteriā . . . modīs** (2).

       numerīs leviōribus: i.e., the elegiac couplet; dat. with **apta**.

20   **aut puer aut . . . puella**: the poet has neither a boyfriend nor a girlfriend to inspire elegiac verse; the flippant homosexual reference is a convention of the genre.

       longās . . . comās: acc. of respect with **cōmpta**, freely, *with her long tresses beautifully arranged*.

21   **Questus eram . . . cum prōtinus**: supply **sīc**, *I had complained in just this way, when suddenly . . .* ; the **cum** temporal clause has **ille** (Cupid) as subject of the three verbs, **lēgit** (22), **lūnāvit** (23), and **dīxit** (24).

       pharetrā . . . solūtā: supply **ex**.

22   ***legō, legere, lēgī, lēctus**, *to gather, collect, select; to read*.

       exitium, -ī, n., *death, destruction*.

             in exitium . . . meum: acc. of purpose, *for my destruction*.

       spīculum, -ī, n., *sharp point; pointed weapon, arrow*.

23   **lūnō, -āre, -āvī, -ātus**, *to make crescent-shaped, bend back*.

       genū, -ūs, n., *knee*.

             genū: supply **in**.

       sinuōsus, -a, -um, *bent, curved*.

24   **"Quod"que . . . "opus"**: the prose order would be **dīxitque, "Vātēs, accipe opus quod canās"**; Cupid sarcastically calls Ovid by the elevated

17 Cum bene surrēxit versū nova pāgina prīmō,
18   attenuat nervōs proximus ille meōs.
19 Nec mihi māteria est numerīs leviōribus apta,
20   aut puer aut longās cōmpta puella comās."
21 Questus eram, pharetrā cum prōtinus ille solūtā
22   lēgit in exitium spīcula facta meum,
23 lūnāvitque genū sinuōsum fortiter arcum,
24   "Quod"que, "canās, vātēs, accipe," dīxit, "opus."
25 Mē miserum! Certās habuit puer ille sagittās:
26   ūror, et in vacuō pectore rēgnat Amor.

Discussion Questions

1. In what several respects do 17–20, the last four lines of the poet's complaint to Cupid, recall 1–4, the poem's opening lines?

2. How is the description of Cupid's actions in 21–26 connected with the *war → 1st word in 1st verse* imagery of the poem's first verse? What is the purpose of this connection?
   Ovid shot w/ a war weapon   connecting god of love w/ war

3. Comment on the several correspondences between Apollo's complaint over Cupid's power in *Met.* I.519–20 above and the poet's outcry here in 25–26.
   love conquers all → Cupid doesn't miss

---

   term he had used of himself in 6, *Oh Holy Bard, here's a genre for you to chant!* So saying, the love god shoots the poor poet with a passion-dart, thus providing him with the inspiration for writing elegy, which he had claimed to lack in 19–20. The rel. clause indicates purpose, hence the subjn. mood.

   opus: here, and in 27, the word is used of a literary *genre* (and with a possible sexual allusion as well—see on 17).

25 **Mē miserum**: acc. of exclamation.

   Certās . . . sagittās: for the power of Cupid's arrows, cf. *Met.* I.456–73 above.

26 **ūror . . . Amor**: cf. **pectore tōtō / ūritur** of Cupid's effect on Apollo in *Met.* I.495–96 above; assonance interconnects the line's key words, **ūror**, **pectore**, and **Amor**.

   vacuō pectore: the reason for the poet's *empty heart* is given in 19–20; and cf. *Met.* I.520 above.

   rēgnat Amor: Ovid deliberately recalls the images evoked in **Cererem rēgnāre** (9) and **magna . . . rēgna** (13).

27 **surgat . . . resīdat**: not just a prosaic *rise* and *fall*, but *stand up* and *sit down*; Ovid not only continues the imagery of 17–18 (the line with six feet can stand while the lame pentameter cannot) but also has in mind the fact that epic poets would generally rise to recite their verse, whereas more mundane works would often be read sitting down. The subject **opus** and the phrase **in (sex or quīnque) numerīs** should be taken with both verbs.

numerīs . . . / ferrea cum vestrīs bella . . . modīs (28): for the ring composition, evoking the poem's opening lines, see on **gravī numerō** (1). Note also the interlocked order of adjectives and nouns in 28.

resīdō, resīdere, resēdī, *to sit down.*

28 **ferreus, -a, -um,** *made of iron; cruel, violent* (suggesting, by a common synecdoche, the weapons of war).

valēte: the personification of genre, form, and subject is continued with this verb of farewell; cf. the farewell to genre and Muse in Ovid's final elegy, *Am.* III.15.19–20 below.

29 **Cingere**: pass. imper. with reflexive force (sometimes called the middle voice); with **flāventia tempora**, *bind your golden tresses.*

lītoreus, -a, -um, *of/from the seashore.*

lītoreā . . . myrtō: the sea-myrtle (here f. gender) was sacred to Cupid's mother Venus, who was herself born from the sea, and hence a garland of its leaves is appropriately worn by Ovid's lyric Muse; cf. *Am.* I.2.23 below.

tempus, temporis, n., *the side of the forehead, temple* (with **flāventia** here of the hair flowing down the Muse's head).

30 **Mūsa, -ae,** f., *Muse* (one of the nine goddesses of the arts, associated with Apollo—of the nine, Erato in particular was associated with lyric verse and was usually depicted wearing a garland of myrtle).

Ovid's invocation of his Muse, which might otherwise be expected nearer the beginning of the poem, comes aptly here in the closing couplet, since this piece serves as preface to the entire first book of the *Amores*.

per . . . pedēs: as often is the case, English would likelier use a relative clause than the participial phrase, *who will have to be measured out eleven feet at a time!* This final comic reference to the 11 feet of elegy—and its limping Muse—deliberately recalls the poem's second couplet, with **ūndēnōs . . . pedēs** in particular echoing **ūnum . . . pedem** (4).

ūndēnī, -ae, -a, pl., *eleven each, eleven at a time.*

ēmodulor, -ārī, *to measure out, regulate; to put into meter* (as the poem's penultimate word, **ēmodulanda** plays on the root word **modīs** in 2 and 28—the Muse will be both *measured out* and melodiously *set to rhythm*).

The closing line's interlocked word order suits the image and neatly balances the arrangement in 28, the one verse a farewell to epic and its meter, the other a welcome to the Muse and metric of elegy.

27 Sex mihi surgat opus numerīs, in quīnque resīdat;
28   ferrea cum vestrīs bella, valēte, modīs.
29 Cingere(lītoreā flāventia tempora)myrtō,
30   Mūsa per ūndēnōs ēmodulanda pedēs!

Discussion Questions

1. Comment on the word-picture in verse 29. *myrtle binding*
    temples

2. Discuss in detail the several ways in which lines 25–30 provide an effective
    conclusion to the poem. *now he has reason to write elegy*
    shot w/ Cupid's arrow → burns w/ love
    bids farewell to epic → invokes Muse & welcomes elegy

3. An overarching image of the poem is that of reversal (of the poet's
    intentions, of genres, of the roles played by various gods). How is this
    imagery reinforced through the poem's ring composition and through the
    word order of individual lines (how many verses can you find with an ABBA
    arrangement)?

4. What is the overall purpose of the poem? How is it at once both serious and
    flippant? Why does Ovid make such a point of his original intention to write
    epic rather than elegy? *intro to the rest of the Amores*
    really wanted to write epic
    tongue in cheek or defense if didn't like it

"Sappho and Alcaeus," Sir Lawrence Alma-Tadema, 1881
Walters Art Gallery, Baltimore

1 **Esse . . . quod**: the verb is deliberative subjn.; freely, *What can I say the reason is that . . .* ; the question introduces a series of four complaints in 1–4. The line's halting one- and two-syllable words and the harsh dentals and q/c sounds are meant to suggest the poet's agitated state of mind.

    ***dūrus, -a, -um**, *hard, firm; harsh.*

2 **pallium, -ī**, n., *cloak; bedspread, blanket.*

    nostra: = **mea** (1st pers. pl. for sing.—cf. **cēdimus** 9, **porrigimus** 20).

    sedent: here, *stay in place.*

3 ***somnus, -ī**, m., *sleep.*

        somnō: abl. with **vacuus**, i.e., *sleepless.*

    quam longa: supply **fuit nox**.

4 **lassus, -a, -um**, *tired, weary.*

        lassaque versātī corporis ossa: Ovid likes this sort of chiastic arrangement, with the adjectives first, then the nouns (adj. A—adj. B—noun B—noun A).

    versātī: not just *turned*, but *which has tossed and turned.*

5 **puto**: although parenthetical (*I would know it—I think*), the word is important, as it anticipates the quick concession in 7–8; the final -o is shortened (systole), as it often is in poetry when not under the ictus (i.e., in an unaccented position in the verse).

    quō . . . amōre: after **sī**, **quō** is indefinite, *by some romantic passion.*

7 **Sīc erit**: the consideration in 6 leads to this sudden, dramatic realization, which is punctuated by the strong diaeresis.

8 **possessa ferus pectora . . . Amor**: the interlocking order with adjectives first, nouns following, is another favorite Ovidian arrangement (see on **lassaque . . . ossa** 4); cf. 28, 30, 39, 46, 51. For **possessa . . . versat** (which deliberately recalls **versātī** 4) English would use two verbs, *takes possession of and tortures.* With **ferus . . . Amor**, cf. **saeve puer** (*Am.* I.1.5).

    Amor: the indefinite **amōre** of 5 (in the same suspenseful position in the verse), personified in **callidus . . . nocet** (6), here becomes Love himself, i.e., Cupid, as the speaker recognizes that he has been smitten by the god.

9 **Cēdimus**: *Do I surrender?* Note the sound- and word-play with **accendimus** and **cēdāmus** (identically positioned in 10).

    subitus, -a, -um, *sudden, unexpected.*

        subitum: a deliberate play on **subit** (6), emphasizing the suddeness of Love's assault.

    luctandō: *by resisting.*

    accendimus ignem: for the metaphor of love's fiery passion, cf. 43–46 below and *Met.* I.495–96 above.

10 **leve . . . onus**: a famous **sententia**, already a proverb in Ovid's day; cf. *Met.* VIII.633–34 above.

11 **Vīdī . . . vīdī** (12): anaphora encourages the reader's visualization.

    iactātās mōtā face: freely, *fanned by the movement of a torch*, but what images do the line's action verbs compel us to visualize; for the word order, see on 4 and cf. 20, 42.

AMORES I.2

"The Triumph of Love"

1	Esse quid hoc dīcam, quod tam mihi dūra videntur
2	strāta, neque in lectō pallia nostra sedent,
3	et vacuus somnō noctem (quam longa!) perēgī,
4	lassaque versātī corporis ossa dolent?
5	Nam, puto, sentīrem, sī quō temptārer amōre—
6	an subit et tēctā callidus arte nocet?
7	Sīc erit: haesērunt tenuēs in corde sagittae,
8	et possessa ferus pectora versat Amor!
9	Cēdimus, an subitum luctandō accendimus ignem?
10	Cēdāmus: leve fit, quod bene fertur, onus.
11	Vīdī ego iactātās mōtā face crēscere flammās,
12	et vīdī nūllō concutiente morī;

Discussion Questions

1. Comment on the dramatic and visual elements in the poem's opening lines (1–4); what is the mental state of the speaker? How does this opening scene set the stage for what follows?

2. In what ways do the next two couplets (5–8) connect this poem with the preceding one?

3. Why does Ovid describe Cupid's arrows as **tenuēs** (7)?

4. In view of the reference to **sagittae** in 7 and the military imagery that dominates the rest of the poem, what do you regard as the best interpretation of **possessa** and **ferus** in 8? How does word order enhance Ovid's point here?

---

flammās: subject of both **crēscere** and **morī** (12).

12   **concutiō, concutere, concussī, concussus**, *to shake, agitate.*
      concutiente: supply **ignem**.

13 **verber, verberis,** n., usually pl., *whip; beating; lash, blow* (from a whip or a stick).

 ferunt: the subject is **bovēs**; the prose arrangement would be **Bovēs prēnsī, dum iuga prīma dētractant, plūra verbera ferunt, quam (bovēs) quōs ūsus arātrī iuvat.**

 quōs . . . arātrī: freely, *who delight in the work of the plow* (lit., *whom use of the plow delights*).

 iuvō, iuvāre, iūvī, iūtus, *to help; to delight, give pleasure to.*

 *arātrum, -ī, n., *plow.*

14 **dētractō, -āre, -āvī, -ātus,** *to refuse to undertake; to recoil from.*

 prēnsī: here, *when they have been rounded up.*

 iugum, -ī, n., *yoke* (by which a plow is drawn).

15 **contundō, contundere, contudī, contūsus,** *to pound; to bruise, make sore.*

 ōra: acc. of respect with **contunditur;** cf. *Met.* I.484 above.

 lupāta, -ōrum, n. pl., *toothed bit* (used with horses difficult to manage).

16 **frēnum, -ī,** n., *bridle, rein.*

 ad arma facit: *adapts to the harness* (lit., *acts with regard to its gear*).

18 **quī:** supply **eōs** as antecedent and object of **urget.**

 servitium, -ī, n., *slavery, service.*

 Amor: subject of **urget,** suspensefully delayed; the two instances of the word, here and at the end of 8 (each at the end of its sentence and its verse), neatly frame the argument in 9–18, which now, in the speaker's view, has been resolved.

19 **ēn,** interj., *behold, look!*

 cōnfiteor, cōnfitērī, cōnfessus sum, *to admit, confess.*

  cōnfiteor: the word deliberately looks back to **fatentur** (18).

 praeda: the word clarifies **servitium**—the speaker is not just Love's slave, he is his prisoner of war!

 Cupīdō: from this point to the end of the poem, the speaker addresses Cupid directly.

20 **porrigō, porrigere, porrēxī, porrēctus,** *to stretch forth, extend.*

 ad tua iūra: i.e., I surrender myself *to your control.*

21 **Nīl:** = **Nōn.**

 bellō: abl. with **opus est.**

22 *laus, laudis, f., *praise, glory, reputation; praiseworthy act, honor.*

  laus: predicate nom.

 victus: the image of the poet as victim of Love's assault (cf. **victās** 20) is taken up again in the poem's closing lines (cf. **victor** 50 and **vīcit, victōs** 52).

 *inermis, -is, -e, *unarmed, defenseless.*

  armīs . . . inermis: for the wordplay, cf. *Am.* I.9.22 below.

23 **nectō, nectere, nexī, nexus,** *to weave; to bind, tie.*

  Necte . . . columbās: with its repeated **n/m** sounds, the line is highly alliterative and is perhaps meant to suggest the hushed cooing of the doves.

 myrtō: see on *Am.* I.1.29 above.

13   verbera plūra ferunt quam quōs iuvat ūsus arātrī,
14   dētractant prēnsī dum iuga prīma, bovēs;
15   asper equus dūrīs contunditur ōra lupātīs:
16   frēna minus sentit, quisquis ad arma facit.
17   Ācrius invītōs multōque ferōcius urget,
18   quam quī servitium ferre fatentur, Amor.
19   Ēn ego, cōnfiteor, tua sum nova praeda, Cupīdō;
20   porrigimus victās ad tua iūra manūs.
21   Nīl opus est bellō—veniam pācemque rogāmus—
22   nec tibi laus, armīs victus inermis, erō.
23   Necte comam myrtō, māternās iunge columbās;

Discussion Questions

1.   What is the "rhetorical" purpose of the three couplets in 11–16? Comment on the relation of these lines to the point made in 17–18.

2.   How do verses 21–22 in particular evoke the opening of *Am.* I.1?

māternus, -a, -um, *of a mother, maternal.*
    māternās iunge columbās / . . . currum . . . dabit (24) **/ . . . datō**
      currū (25) **. . . adiūnctās . . . avēs** (26): the extended chiasmus, and
      the correspondence between the verbs and the perfect participles that
      imply their realization, suggest the swiftness of the action as the poet
      imagines it.
    iunge: *yoke* (i.e., to the triumphal chariot described in the following lines).
    columbās: like the myrtle, doves were sacred to Venus, Cupid's mother—but
      these are very special doves indeed, capable of drawing their young
      master's chariot (like the sparrows who drew Aphrodite's chariot in a
      poem by the Greek lyric poetess Sappho).

24   **quī deceat**: supply **tē**; a relative clause of purpose, describing **currum**.
     *currus, -ūs, m., *chariot*.
     vītricus, -ī, m., *stepfather*.
        vītricus ipse: probably Vulcan is meant, Venus' husband, god of the
        forge; though she had cuckolded him in a relationship with Mars (cf.
        Am. I.9.39-40 below), Venus could charm him into crafting weapons
        for her son Aeneas (as she did in *Aeneid* VIII) or, here, a chariot for
        her other son Cupid (whose real father, according to some accounts,
        was Jupiter).

25   **triumphum**: for the triumphal procession of a victorious general, see on *Met.*
     I.560.

26   **adiungō, adiungere, adiūnxī, adiūnctus**, *to connect; to yoke, harness*.
     movēbis: here, *you will direct*.

27   **Dūcentur . . . puellae**: the slow initial spondees and the ordered anaphora
     suit the description of this majestic procession of youths and maidens who
     have become (both literally and figuratively) Love's captives.

28   **haec . . . triumphus**: for the interlocked order, see on 8.

29   **Ipse . . . recēns**: the poet imagines himself as one of the **iuvenēs captī** in the
     god's procession.
     factum modo: *freshly inflicted*; note the chiasmus in **praeda recēns, factum**
     modo vulnus, and for **praeda** cf. 19 above.

31   **Mēns Bona . . . / et Pudor** (32): personifying the virtues of *Good Sense and*
     Chastity, Ovid imagines them as deities (there were shrines to both in
     Rome) taken prisoner, like himself, by Love and his wild
     companions—*Sweet-talk, Miscalculation, and Madness* (35)—and paraded
     through the streets of Rome in the god's triumphal procession. In part this
     is a humorous reversal of the scene in *Aeneid* I.292-96, where Jupiter
     prophecies the victory of Fidelity (**Fidēs**) over Madness (**Furor**), who is
     similarly depicted with hands bound **post tergum**.
     retorqueō, retorquēre, retorsī, retortus, *to twist around, pull backward*.

32   ***castra, -ōrum**, n. pl., *military camp*.
        castrīs: the military imagery continues—and cf. the reference to Love's
        camp in *Am.* I.9.1 and 44 below.
     obsum, obesse, obfuī + dat., irreg., *to be a hindrance* (to), *be a nuisance*
     (to).

33   **tē . . . tē**: frequent use of the second-person pronoun punctuates the
     speaker's lengthy address to Cupid, which continues to the end of the poem
     (see on 19). Here placement of the word under the ictus heightens the
     effect of the anaphora.

34   ***vulgus, -ī**, n., *the common people, the multitude*.
     iō, interj., *oh!* (a ritual shout with **triumphe**—see on *Met.* I.560 above).

35   **error, errōris**, m., *wandering; error, mistake* (here personified).

36   **assiduē**, adv., *continually, constantly*.
        assiduē . . . tuās: the entire participial phrase is in apposition to the
        subjects of the preceding verse; English would use a relative clause
        (freely, *a mob that has constantly trouped along with your party—but*

24   quī deceat, currum vītricus ipse dabit;
25   inque datō currū, populō clāmante triumphum,
26   stābis et adiūnctās arte movēbis avēs.
27   Dūcentur captī iuvenēs captaeque puellae;
28   haec tibi magnificus pompa triumphus erit.
29   Ipse ego, praeda recēns, factum modo vulnus habēbō
30   et nova captīvā vincula mente feram.
31   Mēns Bona dūcētur manibus post terga retortīs
32   et Pudor et castrīs quidquid Amōris obest.
33   Omnia tē metuent; ad tē sua bracchia tendēns,
34   vulgus "Iō" magnā vōce "triumphe" canet.
35   Blanditiae comitēs tibi erunt Errorque Furorque,
36   assiduē partēs turba secūta tuās.
37   Hīs tū mīlitibus superās hominēsque deōsque;
38   haec tibi sī dēmās commoda, nūdus eris.

Discussion Questions

1. In what respect is the interlocked order of 30 particularly apt?

2. How are the sound effects and the word order in 35 especially effective?

---

what is the literal translation?). The series of sibilants and dentals suggests the tittering of this *Passion Brigade* (Peter Green's irresistible translation!).

partēs: here with the sense of *partisans* or even a rollicking, quasi-political "Cupid for President" *party*; all these folks are Love's groupies.

37   **Hīs . . . mīlitibus**: abl. of accompaniment, with **cum** omitted (as is common in military contexts).

hominēsque deōsque: the polysyndeton (cf. **Errorque Furorque** 35) adds epic effect; Cupid is master of both heaven and earth!

38   **haec tibi**: a deliberate echo of **Hīs tū** (37), to underscore the contrasting ideas; **tibi** is dat. of reference with both **dēmās** and **commoda**, *if someone should take from you these allies (who are) so advantageous to you*.

sī dēmās . . . eris: a mixed future condition, tentative in the protasis (hence the generalizing 2nd pers. verb), more vivid in the apodosis.

nūdus: figuratively, *defenseless*, but also with a play on Cupid's usual attire—his birthday suit!

39   **Laeta . . . Olympō**: for the interlocked order, see on verse 8 above; we are
    reminded for the second time of Venus (cf. **māternās . . . columbās** 23),
    who rejoices here, like any good mother, in her son's triumph.
      triumphō, -āre, -āvī, -ātūrus, *to celebrate a triumph.*
        triumphantī: supply **tibi**, dat. with **plaudet.**
40   **plaudō, plaudere, plausī, plausus**, *to clap, applaud* (for).
      appositus, -a, -um, *nearby, at one's side.*
41   **pinna, -ae**, f., *feather, wing* (Cupid was regularly depicted with wings).
      pinnās . . . capillōs: both nouns are objects of the abl. absolute **gemmā
        variante**; instead of the pl., which might be expected, **gemmā** is
        repeated to intensify the image.
      variō, -āre, -āvī, -ātus, *to adorn with various colors.*
42   **in aurātīs . . . rotīs**: synecdoche (not just *on golden wheels*, but *in your
    golden chariot*—cf. *Am.* I.12.14).
43   **Tunc quoque . . . / tunc quoque** (44): i.e., even as he advances in his
    triumphal chariot; anaphora underscores the point.
      nōn paucōs: i.e., *many* (cf. **multa** 44); litotes.
    *__nōscō, nōscere, nōvī, nōtus__, *to get to know, find out, learn*; perf. forms
    with pres. sense, *to know, know how/be able* (to).
      nōvimus: again pl. for sing.—see on **nostra** (2).
    ūrēs: the vivid metaphor in 43–46 of lovers wounded by Cupid's assault with
    fire and arrows purposely recalls the poem's earlier imagery (especially in
    7–9 and 29).
45   **licet ipse velīs**: a concessive subjn. clause, *even though you . . .* ; even
    Cupid cannot control the forces he has unleashed.
46   **fervidus, -a, -um**, *intensely hot, blazing.*
      fervida . . . nocet: the arrows themselves are aflame and their searing
        heat burns not only those who are struck but any who are too close to
        their path. The repetition of **v** is perhaps meant to suggest
        onomatopoetically the whooshing of the arrows through the air (cf. on
        Met. I.528 above); Vergil uses the same alliteration for the sound of
        rushing winds when he describes Aeneas' vain attempt at embracing
        Creusa's ghost in *Aeneid* II.794, **pār levibus ventīs volucrīque
        simillima somnō**, an effect brilliantly replicated in C. Day Lewis'
        translation, *it was like grasping a wisp of wind or the wings of a
        fleeting dream.*
      vīcīnō . . . vapōre: *when its heat comes too close.*
47   **Bacchus, -ī**, m., *Bacchus* (god of vegetation, and especially of wine and its
    effects on men).
    Gangētis, Gangētidis, f. adj., *of the Ganges* (a river of India, the eastern
      boundary of Alexander's conquests and Bacchus'—after establishing his
      cult there, the god returned to Greece in a chariot drawn by leopards).
      domitā . . . Gangētide terrā: abl. absolute.
48   **tū . . . ālitibus, tigribus ille**: chiasmus; take **gravis** (here, *powerful* or
    majestic) also with the second clause and supply **es** with the first.
49   **Ergō**: the conjunction here, along with the series of spondees, emphatically

39   Laeta triumphantī dē summō māter Olympō
40   plaudet et appositās sparget in ōra rosās.
41   Tū—pinnās gemmā, gemmā variante capillōs—
42   ībis in aurātīs aureus ipse rotīs.
43   Tunc quoque nōn paucōs (sī tē bene nōvimus) ūrēs;
44   tunc quoque praeteriēns vulnera multa dabis.
45   Nōn possunt, licet ipse velīs, cessāre sagittae;
46   fervida vīcīnō flamma vapōre nocet.
47   Tālis erat domitā Bacchus Gangētide terrā—
48   tū gravis ālitibus, tigribus ille fuit.
49   Ergō, cum possim sacrī pars esse triumphī,
50   parce tuās in mē perdere, victor, opēs.

Discussion Questions

1.   What are the most striking elements of diction, word order, and sound effect in 41–42? Why is the elaborate structure of this couplet so appropriate to its context?

2.   Compare the imagery of 43–44 with that of *Met.* I.493–96 above. How are the two passages alike, and in what significant respects do they differ?

3.   Consider Ovid's purposes for the seemingly abrupt comparison of Cupid with Bacchus in 47–48, the final couplet in the description of the god's triumph. In what ways were the two deities alike? How were they different? Ovid's audience knew the story of Bacchus' exploits in India and of his procession in a chariot drawn by leopards; how does Ovid emphasize Cupid's contrasting image in 48, and what is the effect of the contrast?

      marks the transition to the poet's epilogue.

      sacrī: a key word, reminding us that Cupid is really a god, not a general, and that his "prisoners" are in fact his devotees; it is in this capacity that Ovid closes with what seems a political entreaty but is instead a prayer.

50   **parce**: with the infin. **perdere**, this verb is essentially equivalent to **nōlī**, *do not waste*.

51   **cognātus, -ī,** m., *kinsman.*

  Caesar, Caesaris, m., *Caesar* (a cognomen of the **gēns Iulia** and of the emperors, here Caesar Augustus).

    cognātī . . . Caesaris: the Iulii traced their lineage through the legendary Iulus and his father Aeneas to Venus, mother of both Aeneas (by Anchises) and of Cupid (see, e.g., *Aeneid* I.256–88).

52   **quā: manū** is antecedent.

    quā vīcit, victōs: spondees and the deliberate juxtaposition underscore Ovid's point.

  prōtegō, prōtegere, prōtēxī, prōtēctus, *to cover; to protect.*

  ille: identical positioning of the demonstrative here and in 48 leaves the reader wondering about the nuance of a link between Augustus and Bacchus, both of whom are compared with Cupid in the poem's conclusion.

Prima Porta Augustus, with Cupid
Late 1st century B.C.
Vatican Museums, Vatican State

51   Aspice cognātī fēlīcia Caesaris arma:
52   quā vīcit, victōs prōtegit ille manū.

Discussion Questions

1. Within the context of the poet's entire address to Cupid, what do you see as the rhetorical function of the two closing couplets?

2. Comment on the image of victor and vanquished as developed in these concluding lines (49–52). How does the image compare with that in 19–22? What is the relation of verses 23–48 to these framing couplets?

3. What is Ovid's purpose in introducing the reference to Augustus into his final couplet? What is its effect on the mood established throughout the rest of the poem? How do these lines compare, in intent and effect, with the Augustan references in *Met.* I.560–65?

4. Explore the possibility of an intentional link between Bacchus and Augustus in the ways they are associated with Cupid. What might Ovid's point be? In what ways are the two figures analogous? How might Augustus himself have responded to the connection with Cupid or Bacchus?

In the hexameter rises the fountain's silvery column;
In the pentameter aye falling in melody back.

Samuel Taylor Coleridge (translated from Schiller)
"The Ovidian Elegiac Metre Described and Exemplified"

1   **iūsta**: i.e., *justice.*
     quae: as often in verse, the antecedent (**puella**, subject of **amet** and **faciat**) is delayed.
     praedor, -ārī, -ātus sum, *to acquire loot, plunder; to take as plunder.*
         praedāta puella est: at last we meet Ovid's **puella**, cast in the role of a conqueror who has captured him in war; the line's harsh alliteration emphasizes the point.

2   **faciat**: with **cūr**, *let her actions give me a reason why*; i.e., he wants his mistress to treat him well enough to earn his love.

3   **ā**, interj. expressing strong emotion, *ah.*
     nimium voluī: i.e., in the wishes he has expressed in the preceding verse.
     patiātur amārī: i.e., **puella patiātur sē amārī**.

4   **audierit**: = **audīverit**; probably fut. perf. indic., apodosis of the conditional notion in the prior clause (though, alternatively, it may be perf. subjn., jussive like **patiātur**).
     tot: a more intense substitution for **multās**.
     Cytherēa, -ae, f., *the Cytherean* (Venus, who was according to some legends born on the Aegean island of Cythera).

5   **Accipe . . . / accipe (6)**: something like **tālem virum** is understood, *accept a man who would. . . .*; the construction conveys an idea of result or characteristic, hence the subjn. in the following rel. clauses.
     dēserviō, dēservīre, *to devote oneself* (to), *serve.*
         dēserviat: continuing the image in line 1, the word suggests enslavement, a notion intensified by the prefix **dē-**.

6   **nōrit**: = **nōverit**, perf. subjn.

7   **veterum**: with **parentum**, i.e., of ancient lineage; the poet makes a stronger claim for his genealogy in *Am.* III.15.5 below.
     commendō, -āre, -āvī, -ātus, *to entrust; to recommend.*

8   **auctor, auctōris**, m., *originator, founder.*
     *****eques, equitis**, m., *horseman; knight, equestrian* (a member of the wealthy Roman equestrian class).
         auctor eques: supply **est**; Ovid was proud of his equestrian heritage (cf. *Am.* III.15.5–6 below), but here imagines that his mistress may be unimpressed.

9   **renovātur**: this verb is commonly used of the reconditioning or cultivation of farmland.

10   **temperō, -āre, -āvī, -ātus**, *to exercise restraint; to moderate, control.*
         temperat et: anastrophe.
     sūmptus, -ūs, m., *the spending of money, expenditure.*
     parcus, -a, -um, *thrifty, economical.*

11   **comitēs novem**: the Muses.
     repertor, repertōris, m., *discoverer, inventor.*
         vītisque repertor: Bacchus, here in his role as a patron of poets.

12   **hāc faciunt**: i.e., **hāc ex parte faciunt**, *act on this side*, i.e., *on my behalf*; the verb has eight subjects, the three nom. nouns in line 11 and the five in 12–14.

AMORES I.3

"My Love Is My Song"

1 Iūsta precor: quae mē nūper praedāta puella est,
2   aut amet aut faciat cūr ego semper amem.
3 Ā, nimium voluī: tantum patiātur amārī,
4   audierit nostrās tot Cytherēa precēs.
5 Accipe, per longōs tibi quī dēserviat annōs;
6   accipe, quī pūrā nōrit amāre fidē.
7 Sī mē nōn veterum commendant magna parentum
8   nōmina, sī nostrī sanguinis auctor eques,
9 nec meus innumerīs renovātur campus arātrīs,
10   temperat et sūmptūs parcus uterque parēns,
11 at Phoebus comitēsque novem vītisque repertor
12   hāc faciunt et mē quī tibi dōnat Amor
13 et nūllī cessūra fidēs, sine crīmine mōrēs,

Discussion Questions

1. How is the prayer in verse 3 a retreat from those expressed in 2?

2. What imagery in the preceding poem is evoked here in verses 1–5? What specific verbal echoes can you find?

3. Comment on the word order in line 9.

---

    et . . . Amor: the prose order would be **et Amor quī tibi mē dōnat**; as he proclaimed in the preceding poem, Ovid is the slave of Amor, who can do with him what he wants.

13   **cessūra**: again Ovid uses a participle where we might expect a rel. clause, *that will yield. . . .*

14 *simplicitās, simplicitātis, f., *unity; simplicity, sincerity; lack of sophistication, ignorance.*

purpureus: here, *blushing.*

fidēs . . . mōrēs (13) / . . . simplicitās . . . pudor: Ovid's enumeration of his virtues is forcefully punctuated through internal rhyme, alliteration, and especially the positioning of each abstract noun at the end of its phrase.

15 mīlle: supply puellae.

dēsultor, dēsultōris, m., *horse-jumper* (a circus performer who jumped from one horse to another while performing).

dēsultor amōris: a mild obscenity, evoking the image of a philanderer leaping off one lover and onto another and perhaps meant to connect humorously with eques in 8 ("I may be an equestrian, but I don't jump from horse to horse!"); the same word had been used by Ovid's patron Messalla of an unreliable politician who kept jumping from one faction to another, a metaphor that perhaps inspired the poet's own more rambunctious imagery.

16 sī qua fidēs: supply est; qua = quae, indefinite after sī, *any.* Fidelity is a major theme of the poem; cf. lines 6 and 13.

cūra: for the sense of the word used here, cf. *Met.* VIII.724 above.

perennis, -is, -e, *lasting through the years, eternal.*

17 quōs: the antecedent annōs, acc. of time with vīvere, has been attracted into the rel. clause, a common device in Latin verse.

sorōrum: the three Fates (the Parcae), Clotho, Atropos, and Lachesis, who were pictured in myth as weaving the tapestry of each man's life and then cutting the thread at his death.

18 contingō, contingere, contigī, contactus, *to come into contact with, touch;* impers. + dat. + infin., *it falls to* (someone's) *lot, is granted to* (someone to do something).

vīvere contingat: supply mihi.

19 in carmina: i.e., *for my.* . . .

20 prōveniō, prōvenīre, prōvēnī, prōventūrus, *to come forth, be produced.*

prōvenient: a metaphor for birth, continuing the biological metaphor in fēlīcem; the offspring of Ovid's union with his mistress will be his poetry.

causā . . . suā: here, *their inspiration,* i.e., the girl herself or rather the māteriem fēlīcem into which she has been depersonalized.

21 Carmine: *From poetry* or *Thanks to poetry.*

nōmen: a key word in this last section, repeated in the closing verse.

habent: the subjects are Io and the other two mythical heroines alluded to in 22–24.

exterreō, exterrēre, exterruī, exterritus, *to frighten, terrify.*

Īō, acc., Īō, f., *Io* (daughter of Inachus, loved by Jupiter and transformed by him into a cow, so that he, in the form of a bull, could continue their affair without Juno's knowledge).

exterrita . . . Īō: in telling Io's story at *Met.* I.638–41, Ovid describes her terror at her own transformed appearance and bestial voice.

14	nūdaque simplicitās purpureusque pudor.
15	Nōn mihi mīlle placent, nōn sum dēsultor amōris:
16	tū mihi, sī qua fidēs, cūra perennis eris;
17	tēcum, quōs dederint annōs mihi fīla sorōrum,
18	vīvere contingat tēque dolente morī.
19	Tē mihi māteriem fēlīcem in carmina praebē;
20	prōvenient causā carmina digna suā.
21	Carmine nōmen habent exterrita cornibus Īō,

Discussion Questions

1. Analyze and comment in detail on the purpose and structure of the lengthy sentence in 7–14; what are its two major divisions, what are the individual elements of each, and how are the elements interconnected?

2. What features of Ovid's language give the impression that the four abstract virtues in 13–14 are personified? How is this personification more subtle than that in the preceding poem, at lines 31–36?

3. How is the poet's use of anaphora in 15–16 especially effective?

4. What is particularly apt in the word order of verse 18?

5. What is especially appropriate and effective in Ovid's use of personal pronouns in 15–19?

22 **quam . . . ave**: supply **ea** as antecedent and subject of **habent**; the allusion is
to Leda, with whom Jupiter coupled, this time in the form of a swan,
fathering Pollux and perhaps Castor and Helen.

flūmineus, -a, -um, *(of a) river.*

  flūmineā . . . ave: abl. of description, *in the form of a. . . .*

adulter, adulterī, m., *illicit lover, adulterer.*

23 **pontus, -ī,** m., *sea, ocean.*

vecta: with **super pontum**; Europa, daughter of the Phoenician king
Antenor, was seduced by Jupiter in the form of a bull and carried over the
sea to Crete.

iuvencus, -ī, m., *young bull, bullock.*

24 **virgineus, -a, -um,** *of a virgin/maiden, virginal.*

vārus, -a, -um, *bent outwards, curving.*

25 **pariter**: some take the adverb to mean that their fame will match that of
Jupiter and his loves, but this would duplicate the point of **quoque**,
whereas the intent here and in the last verse is that the two "lovers," poet
and **puella**, shall be immortalized together and equally.

26 **nōmina nostra tuīs**: a final alliterative flourish. Despite the true pl. **Nōs** (*We*
= "You and I") in 25, **nostra** here, as often, = **mea**, poetic pl. by
attraction to **nōmina**—*our names shall be forever joined, mine with yours.*

"Zeus and the Cow Io"
Red-figure Attic stamnos
5th century B.C.
Kunsthistorisches Museum
Vienna, Austria

22	et quam flūmineā lūsit adulter ave,
23	quaeque, super pontum simulātō vecta iuvencō,
24	virgineā tenuit cornua vāra manū.
25	Nōs quoque per tōtum pariter cantābimur orbem,
26	iūnctaque semper erunt nōmina nostra tuīs.

Discussion Questions

1. Identify all the poem's references to the passage of time. How do they all interconnect thematically and culminate in the point of the final couplet?

2. Similarly identify all the references to mythological characters. What is Ovid's purpose in introducing each of them, and how do they function overall in integrating and advancing the poem's themes? What several circumstances do the last three characters in particular have in common with each other and with Ovid's **puella**? How might their circumstances connect with Ovid's denial in verse 15 that he is a **dēsultor amōris**?

3. Why in the end does the poem's **puella** remain nameless? How does she compare with Pygmalion's nameless creation?

1   **mīlitō, -āre, -āvī, -ātūrus**, *to serve as a soldier, perform military service.*
      Mīlitat omnis amāns . . . mīlitat omnis amāns: repetition of this entire
         clause at the beginning and end of the opening couplet emphatically
         announces the metaphor (a variant of the love/war metaphor in *Am.*
         I.2) which the rest of the poem elaborates.
      amāns: here, as elsewhere, = **amātor** (cf. *Met.* I.474 above).
      castra: cf. *Am.* I.2.32 above.

2   **Atticus, -ī, m.,** *Atticus* (the poem's addressee, named in a few of Ovid's
         other poems but not certainly identifiable).

3   **quae:** the rel. pron. and its antecedent **aetās** frame the line in a type of
         chiasmus.
      habilis, -is, -e + dat., *useful* (to), *suited* (for).
      Venerī: the goddess represents love in general, of course, just as **bellō**
         suggests Mars, the god of war; cf. 29 below.
      convenit: here essentially = **est habilis.**

4   *****turpis, -is, -e**, *offensive, foul, disgusting; shameful, disgraceful.*
      turpe . . . amor: supply **est;** the n. adj., *a loathsome thing*, reduces the
         aged soldier and the aged lover to objects.
      senīlis amor: a neat (and metrically convenient) variation for **senex amāns.**

5   **Quōs petiēre . . . / hōs petit** (6): rhyme and anaphora underscore the
         parallel Ovid is drawing.
      petiēre: for the form, see on *Met.* I.478 above.
      animōs: take with both **quōs** and **hōs** (6).
      fortī: prolepsis; i.e., once the soldier has **animōs**, then he will be **fortis.**

6   *****socius, -a, -um**, *keeping company* (with another), (in the role of) *companion;
      allied.*
      bellus, -a, -um, *beautiful, lovely, charming.*
         bella puella: a favorite phrase in the poetry of Catullus; in this context
            the adj. is likely a pun on **bellum**, *war* (cf. on **bella** 45).

7   **pervigilō, -āre, -āvī, -ātūrus**, *to stay awake all night.*
      terrā: supply **in.**

8   **forēs . . . servat:** with both **ille . . . dominae** and **ille ducis;** the
         lover/soldier *guards the entranceway*, i.e., by sleeping on the ground
         outside the girlfriend's house or the commander's tent.

9   **via:** here, *march.*
      mitte: = **ēmitte** (on the use of simple for compound verbs, see on *Met.*
         X.283 above), *send the girl forth*, i.e., on some mission; the imper. is
         often used in place of the indic. in the protasis of conditional sentences.

10 **strēnuus . . . amāns:** the adj./noun phrase is aptly extended from the
         beginning of the verse to the end—another neat Ovidian word-picture,
         suggesting the *long march* (**longa . . . via** 9) that the *hardy lover* is willing
         to endure.
      eximō, eximere, exēmī, exēmptus, *to take out, remove.*
         exēmptō fīne: = **sine fīne**, i.e., to the ends of the earth.

11 **ībit in:** lit., *he will go up against*, though one might consider the expression
         a kind of zeugma, i.e., *he will climb* (**montēs**) and *he will ford* (**flūmina**).

AMORES I.9

"Make Love, Not War!"

1	Mīlitat omnis amāns, et habet sua castra Cupīdō;
2	Attice, crēde mihī, mīlitat omnis amāns!
3	Quae bellō est habilis, Venerī quoque convenit aetās:
4	turpe senex mīles, turpe senīlis amor.
5	Quōs petiēre ducēs animōs in mīlite fortī,
6	hōs petit in sociō bella puella virō.
7	Pervigilant ambō, terrā requiēscit uterque;
8	ille forēs dominae servat, at ille ducis.
9	Mīlitis officium longa est via: mitte puellam,
10	strēnuus exēmptō fīne sequētur amāns.
11	Ībit in adversōs montēs duplicātaque nimbō

Discussion Questions

1. In what ways does the poem's opening couplet (1–2) resume the imagery of *Am*. I.2?

2. Comment on the anaphora and the word order in 4. What are the intended effects? *unappealing of older man, both as leader & lover emphasizing*

3. Some manuscripts have **annōs** for **animōs** in 5. In view of the context both immediately preceding and following, why is **animōs** more likely what Ovid wrote? *youthful in spirit*

4. How are the word order and sound effects in 6 especially appropriate to the image? *bella → beautiful → wars   in socio (   ) viro → in company of men*

5. Comment on the arrangement of the several love/war images in 1–6.
   war is on left, war on right

every lover in arms (weapons / embrace)

duplicātus, -a, -um, *doubled in size* (here = *swollen*).
nimbus, -ī, m., *rain-cloud; rain*.

12   **congestus, -a, -um**, *piled up, accumulated.*
    exterō, exterere, exterīvī, exterītus, *to rub away, wear down; to crush.*
    *****nix, nivis**, f., *snow.*

13   **fretum, -ī**, n., *strait, channel;* sing. or pl., *the sea.*
        freta pressūrus: i.e., as he is about to set sail.
    tumidōs: here, *violent.*
    causor, causārī, causātus sum, *to plead a case; to plead* (about something)
        as an excuse (here, as an excuse not to sail).
    eurus, -ī, m., *east wind.*

14   **verrō, verrere, versūrus**, *to remove dust, sweep; to sweep over, skim the*
    surface of.
        aptaque verrendīs sīdera . . . aquīs: *stars suited for . . .* , i.e., skies
        propitious for sailing; the interlocked order and the sound effects—both
        the roaring **r**'s and the assonant **-īs/sī-/-īs**—help us see and hear the
        ship's oars dipping into and out of the sea.

15   **frīgus, frīgoris**, n., *cold, chill;* often pl., *cold spells, frosts.*

16   **dēnsō . . . nivēs**: a golden line (see on *Met.* I.484 above and cf. 23 below).
    perferet: for the intensifying prefix cf. **pervigilant** (7).

17   **Mittitur**: the verb is often used of military missions; cf. **mitte** (9).
    Mittitur . . . tenet (18): the entire couplet is an elaborate ABCDEEDCBA
    chiasmus, with the corresponding elements **Mittitur/tenet**, **īnfestōs/ut**
    hoste, alter/alter, speculātor/oculōs, in hostēs/in rīvāle.
    īnfestus, -a, -um, *hostile; savage, violent.*
        īnfestōs . . . hostēs: within the extended chiasmus Ovid uses another
        favorite chiastic arrangement, with adjs. first, nouns following, in
        acc./nom./nom./acc. order; the *savage foe* "surrounds" the *observer.*
    speculātor, speculātōris, m., *observer, scout, spy.*

18   **in . . . tenet**: the prose order would be **alter oculōs in rīvāle, ut hoste,**
    tenet.
    rīvālis, rīvālis, m., *a rival* (especially in love—the word means, lit., *one who*
    shares with another the use of a stream, **rīvus**, a fascinating etymology!).
    oculōs . . . tenet: English has the same idiom, he *keeps his eyes on* . . . .

19   **Ille . . . hic . . . hic . . . ille** (20): chiasmus; the roles assigned to the
    different demonstratives are reversed.
    gravēs: with **urbēs**, *mighty.*
    līmen: this and other words for doors or pathways often have a sexual double
    entendre in Latin erotic verse; Ovid may intend such a nuance in this
    couplet. Cf. on **arma** (26).

20   **ille forēs**: cf. **ille forēs** (8); there the lover was guarding his mistress' door,
    here he is breaking it down.

21   **sopōrātus, -a, -um**, *lulled to sleep, asleep.*
    invādō, invādere, invāsī, invāsus, *to assault, attack.*

22   **caedō, caedere, cecīdī, caesus**, *to strike; to attack, slaughter.*
        caedere et: = **et caedere**; anastrophe.
    armātā vulgus inerme manū: note the assonance, the etymologizing
    wordplay in **armātā/inerme** (cf. *Am.* I.2.22), and the arrangement which

12	flūmina; congestās exteret ille nivēs;
13	nec, freta pressūrus, tumidōs causābitur eurōs
14	aptaque verrendīs sīdera quaeret aquīs.
15	Quis, nisi vel mīles vel amāns, et frīgora noctis
16	et dēnsō mixtās perferet imbre nivēs?
17	Mittitur īnfestōs alter speculātor in hostēs;
18	in rīvāle oculōs alter, ut hoste, tenet.
19	Ille gravēs urbēs, hic dūrae līmen amīcae
20	obsidet; hic portās frangit, at ille forēs.
21	Saepe sopōrātōs invādere prōfuit hostēs
22	caedere et armātā vulgus inerme manū:
23	sīc fera Thrēiciī cecidērunt agmina Rhēsī,

Discussion Questions

1. How do each of the specific circumstances described in 7–16 support the assertion of 5–6?

2. How are the meter and word order in 16 suited to the action?

3. What is the point of the chiasmus in 17–18?

4. Comment on the word order and the anaphora in 19–20.

has the *unarmed throng* positioned within the grip, so to speak, of the *armed hand* (cf. 26 below) or (with a different sense of **manus**) surrounded by an *armed band*.

23   **fera . . . Rhēsī**: another golden line (cf. 16 above).

     Thrēicius, -a, -um, *Thracian, of Thrace* (a region of Greece east of Macedon).

     agmen, agminis, n., *stream*; sing. or pl., *army*.

     Rhēsus, -ī, m., *Rhesus* (a Thracian ally of Priam, killed by Ulysses and Diomedes in a night raid).

24   **captī . . . equī**: voc. case. An important purpose of the mission against
       Rhesus was to steal his horses; the apostrophe to those horses here adds a
       touch of mock pathos. The adj./noun placement, producing internal rhyme
       at the pentameter's caesura and line's end, is a favorite Ovidian device, as
       we have seen before (cf. 6 and 14 above, 38, 42, and 44 below).

25   **nempe**, *of course, to be sure.*
       ūtor, ūtī, ūsus sum + abl., *to use, take advantage of.*

26   **sua . . . arma movent**: *they brandish their own weapons*; here, as often in
       Latin, **arma** is intended as a metaphor for the lover's sexual apparatus, a
       point emphasized by **sua** (cf. the similar use of the word in **sua castra** 1
       and **castrīs . . . suīs** 44). For the double entendre, see on **līmen** (19); and
       for the word order, cf. 22.
       sōpītus, -a, -um, *overcome by sleep, sleeping.*
          sōpītīs hostibus: abl. absolute.

27   **vigil, vigilis**, m., *guard, sentry.*

28   **mīlitis . . . opus**: supply **est**, *it is the task of the soldier* (+ infin.).
       miserī: read with **mīlitis** as well as **amantis**.

29   **Mars dubius, nec certa Venus**: chiasmus; for Mars and Venus, cf. 3 above
       and 39–40 below.
       nec certa: litotes for **dubia**.
       victīque . . . / quōsque (30): correlative conjunctions (*both . . . and*)
       connect the two clauses; the verbs are each set at the end of the verse for
       end-rhyme and to underscore the contrasting images (which again carry a
       sexual double entendre).
       resurgō, resurgere, resurrēxī, resurrēctūrus, *to rise again.*

30   **quōsque**: acc. subject of the indirect statement; supply **illī**, *and those who
       you would say could never lie in defeat.*
       negēs: potential subjn.

31   **Ergō**: a strong transition word, introducing a central argument of the poem.
       dēsidia, -ae, f., *laziness, idleness; leisure.*
          dēsidiam . . . amōrem: **vocābat** takes a double acc., *whoever was
           calling love a vacation*; placement of the nouns at opposite ends of the
           clause emphasizes the polarity, and the **dēsidiam/dēsinat** (32)
           soundplay underscores the prohibition.
       vocābat: the indic. mood implies some actual character (the Atticus of line 2,
       perhaps), who has been accusing the poet, or the lover in general, of idling
       away his life.

32   **dēsinō, dēsinere, dēsīvī, dēsitus**, *to cease, desist; to stop talking.*
       experiēns, experientis, *enterprising, active.*
          ingeniī . . . experientis: gen. of description, in place of a predicate
           nom., *of an enterprising nature* (we might say instead, *Love has an
           enterprising nature*).
       Amor: because of the characterization here and the references to Mars and
       Venus in 29, we are probably meant to think of Cupid (cf. **Cupīdō** 1) and
       not just **amor** in general.

33   **abdūcō, abdūcere, abdūxī, abductus**, *to lead away, carry off.*

24   et dominum captī dēseruistis equī;
25   nempe marītōrum somnīs ūtuntur amantēs
26   et sua sōpītīs hostibus arma movent.
27   Custōdum trānsīre manūs vigilumque catervās
28   mīlitis et miserī semper amantis opus.
29   Mars dubius, nec certa Venus: victīque resurgunt,
30   quōsque negēs umquam posse iacēre, cadunt.
31   Ergō, dēsidiam quīcumque vocābat amōrem,
32   dēsinat—ingeniī est experientis Amor!
33   Ardet in abductā Brīsēide maestus Achillēs
34   (dum licet, Argeās frangite, Trōes, opēs);

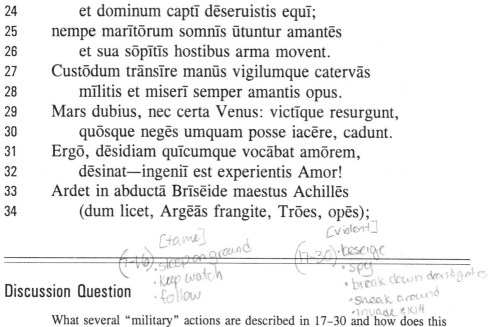

[tame]
(1-16): sleep on ground
· keep watch
· follow

[violent]
(17-30): besiege
· spy
· break down doors & gates
· sneak around
· invade & kill

Discussion Question

What several "military" actions are described in 17–30 and how does this
section of the poem compare with 7–16?

Brīsēis, Brīsēidos, abl., **Brīsēide**, f., *Briseis* (Achilles' captive mistress in
the Trojan war—for the name's Greek case endings, see on **Pēnēis**, *Met.*
I.472 above, and cf. **Priamēide** 37 below).
maestus, -a, -um, *unhappy, sad, sorrowful.*
Achillēs, Achillis, m., *Achilles* (son of Peleus and Thetis, Greek prince in
the Trojan war).
   Ardet . . . Achillēs: in a story best known from *Iliad* I, Achilles
   ultimately withdrew from fighting the Trojans because of
   Agamemnon's seizure of his slave-girl Briseis; in this display of
   dēsidia (31) he is, some readers object, an inappropriate example for
   Ovid here. But Achilles' first impulse, in a fit of anger, was to slay
   the king—hence **ardet**, which implies his hostility toward the Greek
   chieftain as much as his passion for Briseis.
34 **dum licet**: we might say, *while you can* (which was not long, of course, as
    Troy was doomed to destruction, once Achilles returned to battle).
Argēus, -a, -um, *Argive, of Argos* (an important city of the Greek
    Peloponnese); *Greek.*
Trōs, Trōis, nom. and voc. pl. **Trōes**, m., *a Trojan.*
   frangite, Trōes: for the epic apostrophe, cf. 24 above; the exhortation
   here adds a dash of emotion to Ovid's catalog of heroes.
opēs: here, *defenses* (a reference to the walls of the Greek camp at Troy).

35   **Hector, Hectoris**, m., *Hector* (the chief Trojan prince, eldest son of Priam and Hecuba).

        Hector . . . arma: the famous scene of Hector's farewell to Andromache before rushing off to battle is in Homer *Iliad* VI.

    Andromachē, Andromachēs, f., *Andromache* (daughter of Eëtion and wife of Hector—the Greek case endings are the same as those of **Daphnē** and **Thisbē** above).

    complexus, -ūs, m., *embrace, lovemaking*.

36   **galea, -ae**, f., *helmet*.

    quae daret: a rel. clause of pupose, with **uxor** as antecedent; the prose order would be **uxor erat quae capitī galeam daret**, *he had a wife to place his helmet on his head* (an elaboration of Homer's account).

37   **summa ducum**: = **summus dux**, *the ultimate leader* (in apposition to **Atridēs**), but Ovid's substantive use of the n. pl. adj. is more striking, *the quintessence of leaders*.

    Atridēs, Atridae, m., *son of Atreus* (king of the powerful Greek city of Mycenae, father of both Menelaus and, here, Agamemnon).

    Priamēis, Priamēidos, abl., **Priamēide**, f., *daughter of Priam* (here, the prophetess Cassandra).

        vīsā Priamēide: the abl. absolute is best translated as a temporal clause.

    fertur: *is said*, + infin.

38   **Maenas, Maenadis**, f., *a Maenad, Bacchante* (a female devotee of Bacchus); *a frenzied woman*.

        Maenadis . . . comīs: Cassandra resembled a Maenad as she wildly tossed her long, flowing hair in one of her oracular trances; the alliteration of **s** was perhaps meant to suggest the hissing of her frenzied prophetic utterances.

    effūsus, -a, -um, *loose, flowing*.

        effūsīs . . . comīs: dat. with the compound **obstipuisse**.

    obstipuisse: i.e., in amazement at Cassandra's beauty.

39   **Mars . . . sēnsit**: Mars and Venus were caught in adultery by the goddess' husband, the blacksmith god Vulcan, who ensnared them in a bronze net and hung them on display for all the other Olympians to see and ridicule; Ovid tells the story in *Met.* IV, and see on *Am.* I.2.24 above.

    dēprēndō, dēprēndere, dēprēndī, dēprēnsus, *to seize, catch; to catch in the act*.

        dēprēnsus . . . sēnsit: placement of these two words at the caesura and line's end accentuates both the assonance and the point that Mars had been "caught" both literally and figuratively.

    fabrīlis, -is, -e, *of a workman, an artisan's, a blacksmith's*.

40   **fābula nūlla fuit**: note the assonance with **fabrīlia vincula sēnsit** in the preceding line, especially the play on **fabrīlia/fābula**, both deliberately positioned to follow the caesura.

41   **Ipse ego**: the pronouns make an effective transition.

    sēgnis, -is, -e, *inactive, lazy, sluggish*.

        sēgnis: the word looks back to the charge of **dēsidia** in 31; in military

35　Hector ab Andromachēs complexibus ībat ad arma,
36　　et galeam capitī quae daret, uxor erat;
37　summa ducum, Atridēs, vīsā Priamēide, fertur
38　　Maenadis effūsīs obstipuisse comīs;
39　Mars quoque dēprēnsus fabrīlia vincula sēnsit—
40　　nōtior in caelō fābula nūlla fuit!
41　Ipse ego sēgnis eram discīnctaque in ōtia nātus;
42　　mollierant animōs lectus et umbra meōs.
43　Impulit ignāvum fōrmōsae cūra puellae

Discussion Question

What is the purpose of the four epic allusions in 33–40? How do they relate to the ideas presented in 1–2 and 31–32? In what respects are the references alike and in what ways do they differ? What significance do you see in the order of presentation?

　　　contexts, both **sēgnitia** and **dēsidia** implied dereliction of duty.
discīnctus, -a, -um, *in loose-fitting attire; easygoing, undisciplined.*
ōtium, -ī, n., often pl. for sing., *leisure.*
　　discīncta . . . ōtia: there is a military allusion here, as **ōtium** often referred to the status enjoyed by one discharged from the army and the adj. (here a transferred epithet) was used of soldiers who were unarmed and had unbelted their tunics. Readers of Catullus might compare his poem 51 on the perils of **ōtium**.
nātus: supply **sum**; + **in**, *I was born for* or *I was naturally inclined to.*
42　**animōs . . . meōs**: here, continuing the military metaphor in **animōs** (5), *my fighting spirit*; note the internal rhyme (and cf. **castrīs . . . suīs** 44).
lectus et umbra: hendiadys, *my shaded lounge* (where the poet would often recline to write his verse); **umbra** was a common metaphor for leisured retirement (cf. our expression, "to have it made in the shade").
43　**Impulit ignāvum**: supply **mē** here and with **iussit . . . merēre** (44).
cūra: subject of both **impulit** and **iussit**; with the objective gen. **puellae** the word means *love* or *affection*, but the military double entendre is continued (as is clear from **castrīs** 44), since **cūra** + the objective gen. often referred to the command of an army or responsibility for some military assignment.

44 **iussit et**: anastrophe.

  castrīs . . . suīs: the reflex. adj. here refers to **cūra** = **amor**; cf. **habet sua castra Cupīdō** (1).

  aes, aeris, n., *copper, bronze; money* (here with specific reference to the **aera mīlitāria**, *army pay*).

  mereō, -ēre, -uī, -itus, *to receive* (as a wage), *earn* (money).

   merēre: the verb was regularly used of earning money for sexual favors (hence the noun **meretrīx**, *prostitute*), a nuance doubtless intended here.

45 **vidēs**: with the 2nd pers. verb we are reminded of the poem's (rather generalized) addressee (Atticus, line 2).

  agilis, -is, -e, *swift, agile; active*.

   agilem . . . gerentem: supply **mē**; the adj. **agilis** is related to **agere**, and hence implies the opposite of **sēgnis** (41) and **dēsidiōsus** (46).

  bella: *wars*, but perhaps with a play on the adj., *lovely (activities)*; cf. on **bella puella** (6).

46 **Quī . . . amet**: a final, stirring "call to arms," based on the arguments the poet has presented.

  dēsidiōsus, -a, -um, *idle, lazy*.

   dēsidiōsus: cf. **dēsidiam** (31).

"Venus Awaits the Return of Mars"
Lambert Sustris, ca. 1570, Louvre, Paris

44   iussit et in castrīs aera merēre suīs:
45   inde vidēs agilem nocturnaque bella gerentem.
46   Quī nōlet fierī dēsidiōsus, amet!

Discussion Questions

1.   Comment on the word-picture in 44. *gold is in the camp*

2.   What is the function of the last three couplets (41–46)? What specific images does this section recall from earlier in the poem?

3.   How is this poem, in its structure and its argumentation, like a miniature speech of persuasion? Which lines constitute the prologue and epilogue, and what specific functions do those sections serve? What principal point does the speaker hope to prove? Summarize his major arguments. Are they convincing? Are they meant to be?

Briseis taken from Achilles
Pompeii, 1st century A.D.
Museo Archeologico Nazionale
Naples, Italy

1   **Colligere . . . et . . . pōnere:** construe both infinitives with **docta,** *skilled at.*
       incertōs: here, *disarrayed, disheveled.*

2   **doctus, -a, -um,** *learned, wise; expert, skilled* (at).
       docta: this epithet and the series of adjectives and participles in each of
          the several phrases following (through **reperta** 5) are vocatives in
          agreement with **Napē;** calling the girl *learned* in this context adds a
          comic touch.
       neque . . . habenda: *and not one to be considered.*
       ancillās inter: anastrophe; Nape is no ordinary slave-girl, as we shall see.
       Napē, Napēs, f., *Nape* (a female name).
          The slave-girl in this little drama has a common Greek name, and the
          role she plays as go-between is typical of the maids in Roman comedy.

3   **ministerium, -ī,** n., *activity* (of a slave)*, service; duty.*
       fūrtīvus, -a, -um, *stolen; secret, clandestine.*
          fūrtīvae: here, as often, a transferred epithet, logically referring to
          ministeriīs, but more imaginatively applied to **noctis.**

4   **ūtilis:** predicate adj. with **cognita** (3), *known (to be) useful (in);* cf. **fīda**
       reperta (6). Note the identical, and emphatic, positioning of **docta** (2) and
       ūtilis; "intellect" and "pragmatism" are wonderfully complementary
       virtues!
       dandīs . . . notīs: the gerundive phrase is dat. of reference or purpose with
       ingeniōsa; for the internal rhyme, cf. 6, 12, and 28, and for the word
       order (modifier at caesura, noun at line's end), common in Ovid's
       pentameters, cf. 6, 8, 14, etc.
       ingeniōsus, -a, -um, *clever, gifted, talented* (at).

5   **saepe . . . / saepe** (6): the anaphora adds emotional intensity, as the past
       services Ovid recalls come nearer and nearer to the purpose of his request
       on the present occasion.
       hortāta: lit., *having urged,* but freely, *you who have urged;* in prose the verb
       takes an **ut** clause, but in verse an infinitive is common.
       Corinna, -ae, f., *Corinna* (the name of a Greek lyric poetess, used by Ovid
       for the mistress of his *Amores*).

6   **labōrantī . . . mihī:** dat. with **fīda** (cf. **FĪDĀS SIBI** 27); English would use
       a clause, not a participle, *whenever I was laboring* or *having difficulty* (in
       love).
       fīda: for the usage, see on **ūtilis** (4).
       reperta: freely (cf. **hortāta** 5), *(you who have been) found (to be).*

7   **accipe . . . / perfer . . . pelle** (8): the series of three imperatives (the first
       two in initial line position) stresses the urgency of the speaker's request.
       dominam: Corinna was both Nape's *mistress* and Ovid's.
       perarō, -āre, -āvī, -ātus, *to plow through; to incise, inscribe.*
       māne: with **perarātās . . . tabellās** (not **perfer**).
    *tabella, -ae, f., *board, tablet;* pl., *writing tablet* (a common type of
       notebook, consisting of two boards with wax surfaces for inscribing
       messages with a stilus and hinged so that the tablet could be closed and
       sealed with the writing inside).

AMORES I.11
"A Letter to Corinna"

1	Colligere incertōs et in ōrdine pōnere crīnēs
2	docta, neque ancillās inter habenda, Napē,
3	inque ministeriīs fūrtīvae cognita noctis
4	ūtilis, et dandīs ingeniōsa notīs,
5	saepe venīre ad mē dubitantem hortāta Corinnam,
6	saepe labōrantī fīda reperta mihī,
7	accipe et ad dominam perarātās māne tabellās
8	perfer, et obstantēs sēdula pelle morās.

Discussion Questions

1. How is the word order in verse 1 appropriate to the image described?

2. What is the rhetorical purpose of Ovid's lengthy characterization of Nape in 1–6?

3. How does the function of Nape as addressee differ from that of Atticus in *Am.* I.9?

4. If you are familiar with the poetry of Catullus, compare the function and organization of this poem's opening lines (1–7) with verses 1–16 of his poem 11. In what other respects are the two poems alike?

---

tabellās / . . . morās (8): note the end-line rhyme and cf. 25–28; **morās** (*delays*) is deliberately "delayed," and **tabellās** in particular is emphatically placed, as it is (in the same case and number) in 15 and 25.

8   **perfer**: the prefix plays on **perarātās** (7) and has its full force here, *carry straight to* (i.e., straight through to the addressee without delay).
      sēdula: the adj. here, as commonly in Latin, has an adverbial force.

9   **Nec . . . nec . . . / nec** (10): anaphora intensifies the tricolon crescens.

       silicum: for the commonplace metaphor, cf. *Met.* X.242.

       vēnae . . . ferrum / . . . simplicitās (10): all are subjects of **adest** (sing. in agreement with the nearest of the three), with **tibi**, dat. of possession, *you have neither.* . . .

10   **ōrdine maior**: *greater than (usual in) your class*. This point, like the next, seems a backhanded compliment—Nape is no more ignorant than others of her (low) social station! (Alternatively, as McKeown has suggested, one might accept the reading **et** for **nec** and take **simplicitās** in a positive sense, *integrity*, but this would undercut the anaphora, the tricolon, and, most importantly, the humor: Ovid pays more respect, as the drama develops, not to the maid but to his tablet!)

11   **crēdibilis, -is, -e**, *believable, credible, conceivable*.

       crēdibile est et tē: another backhanded compliment, *it is conceivable that even you* (have been in love)!

       et: = **etiam**.

       arcūs: metonymy for **sagittās**; for Cupid's bow and arrows, see *Met.* I.456–73 and *Am.* I.2.7–8 above.

12   *****mīlitia, -ae**, f., *military service*.

       signa: here, military *standards* (of the sort carried by Roman legions); for the military imagery cf. especially *Am.* I.9 above.

       tuēre: imper., *defend*; the point is that both Nape and Ovid are "soldiers" in the same army—Cupid's—and so each should look after the other's interests.

13   **quaeret**: Corinna is the understood subject.

       quaeret . . . dīcēs: note the aptly chiastic arrangement for query and reply; **dīc** might be expected in the apodosis, but **dīcēs** is more vivid.

       quid agam: idiom—not *what* but *how I am doing*.

       spē: abl. of means, but we would say *in hope*.

       noctis: not only *of the night* but also its pleasures (cf. **furtīvae . . . noctis** 3).

       vīvere: supply **mē** as subject of the indirect statement.

14   **cētera**: i.e., *other* (more intimate) *details* of his condition; the assonance in **cētera/cēra**, accentuated through positioning the words at the beginning of the verse and after the caesura, helps draw our attention to the shift of focus from Nape (**dīcēs**) to the tablet itself (**cētera fert . . . cēra**).

       blandā: transferred epithet; it is the message itself, rather than the hand that wrote it, which is *coaxing*, but Ovid's phrasing is more imaginative and more sensual.

15   **vacuae**: supply **dominae**; i.e., approach her when she isn't busy.

       bene: in the sense of *quite* or *thoroughly*, the adv. may modify **vacuae**, or with **redde** it may be taken to mean *opportunely* or *in timely fashion*, or (as Kenney suggests) it may be taken in common with both words.

16   **vērum**, conj., *but*.

       continuō, adv., *immediately, without delay* (here with **legat**).

       fac . . . legat: i.e., **fac ut illa legat**, *see to it that she reads them*; a

9   Nec silicum vēnae, nec dūrum in pectore ferrum,
10   nec tibi simplicitās ōrdine maior adest;
11   crēdibile est et tē sēnsisse Cupīdinis arcūs—
12   in mē mīlitiae signa tuēre tuae.
13   Sī quaeret quid agam, spē noctis vīvere dīcēs;
14   cētera fert blandā cēra notāta manū.
15   Dum loquor, hōra fugit—vacuae bene redde tabellās,
16   vērum continuō fac tamen illa legat!
17   Aspiciās oculōs mandō frontemque legentis
18   (et tacitō vultū scīre futūra licet).

Discussion Questions

1.   How are 9–12 comparable in function to 1–5, and how do they differ?

2.   Compare the speaker's comments to Nape in 11–12 with Orpheus' remarks to the gods of the Underworld in *Met.* X.27–29 above. How are the remarks similar in both content and purpose?

3.   Comment on the multiple sound effects in verse 12.

4.   How does meter suit meaning in line 15?

---

       substantive volitive (or jussive noun) clause.
17   **Aspiciās . . . mandō**: = **Mandō ut aspiciās**, another volitive clause.
       oculōs . . . frontemque: take both with **legentis**, freely, *her eyes and face as she reads.*
       mandō, -āre, -āvī, -ātus, *to hand over, consign*; + **ut**, *to order, request.*
18   **et**: = **etiam**. Some editors favor the manuscript reading **ē**; but in addition to the other arguments for **et** is its contribution to the staccato sound effects (the alliterative **t**'s, the **et/licet** rhyme, and the assonant **-tō/-tū/-tū-** syllables, each under the ictus).
       tacitus, -a, -um, *silent, speechless.*
       scīre: with **licet**, *one may learn* (lit., *it is permitted to know*).
       futūrum, -ī, n., *the future*; pl., *future events.*

19 **Nec mora:** = **Sine morā.**

  perlēctīs: supply **tabellīs,** abl. absolute; again (cf. **perfer** 8) the prefix has its full intensive force (*thoroughly read*).

  rescrībat . . . iubētō: = **iubētō ut rescrībat** (cf. **aspiciās . . . mandō** 17); the future imper. has a stern, legalistic tone, reminding us at once of poor Nape's humble rank and of the impropriety of her "ordering" her mistress to do anything (little surprise that Nape never responds through this entire drama, which is more a harangue than a dialogue).

20 **ōdī, ōdisse, ōsus,** defective verb with perf. forms and pres. meanings, *to have an aversion to, hate, dislike.*

  lātē, adv., *over a large area, largely, widely.*

   ōdī, cum lātē: the short words, hard consonants, and spondees pound out Ovid's indignation.

  splendidus, -a, -um, *bright, shiny; splendid, brilliant.*

21 **comprimō, comprimere, compressī, compressus,** *to compress, squeeze; to pack densely;* with **ōrdō,** *to close up* (the ranks of an army).

   Comprimat . . . morētur: chiasmus intensifies the hortatory verbs and neatly juxtaposes Corinna's (hoped-for) lines and Ovid's eyes.

  ōrdinibus: supply **in** and cf. **in ōrdine** (1)—Corinna's anticipated letter will be arranged in orderly fashion, just like her hair and like the soldiers in a Roman battalion. Nape's **simplicitās** is also "orderly"—see line 10—a very tidy poem in every respect!

  versūs: here the *lines* of Corinna's letter.

  oculōs . . . meōs (22): note the word-picture—Ovid's eyes are in fact *delayed,* not *at the margin's edge,* but at the extremities of the clause.

22 **extrēmus, -a, -um,** *at the edge, outermost.*

  littera: Ovid often uses the sing. for an *epistle* and not just a letter of the alphabet (cf. *Am.* I.12.2 below). Ovid's switch from Corinna to the **littera** itself as subject anticipates his sharpening focus on the **tabellae** in the closing couplets.

  ****rādō, rādere, rāsī, rāsus,** *to scrape, scratch; to erase; to pass, move (closely) past.*

   rāsa: here probably *inscribed,* rather than *erased* (which, if correct, would imply a letter that Corinna had labored over, erasing and correcting). But McKeown's suggested emendation **arāta,** *inscribed,* is also attractive (cf. **perarātās** 7).

23 **digitōs . . . graphiō lassāre tenendō:** interlocked order; the entire infin. phrase complements **Quid . . . opus est,** *Why is it necessary.*

  graphium, -ī, n., *stylus* (the Greek word for the Latin **stilus,** the pointed instrument used for writing on wax tablets).

  lassō, -āre, -āvī, -ātus, *to make tired, tire, fatigue.*

24 **Hoc . . . scrīptum:** in apposition to **VENĪ,** which is set in capital letters here, just as Corinna might have written the word (and like the dedicatory inscription in 27–28).

  scrīptum, -ī, n., *inscription; writing.*

  tōta tabella, "VENĪ!": the highly alliterative verse and the strong diaeresis

19	Nec mora, perlēctīs rescrībat multa iubētō—
20	ōdī, cum lātē splendida cēra vacat!
21	Comprimat ōrdinibus versūs, oculōsque morētur
22	margine in extrēmō littera rāsa meōs.
23	Quid digitōs opus est graphiō lassāre tenendō?
24	Hoc habeat scrīptum tōta tabella, "VENĪ!"
25	Nōn ego victrīcēs laurō redimīre tabellās
26	nec Veneris mediā pōnere in aede morer.

Discussion Questions

1. Why might we expect the epithet **victrīcēs** (25) to be applied to Nape? What is the effect of applying it instead to **tabellās**? What might we imagine as Nape's response? Why does she not respond?

2. In what several ways does Ovid gradually but emphatically shift his focus from Nape to the writing tablets in the second half of the poem (especially 15–26)?

following **tabella** prepare us for the brief message itself, which is suspended to line's end for further emphasis; Ovid pictures the single word inscribed in huge letters and filling the entire tablet.

25   **Nōn ego**: for this transition to the poem's closing section, cf. **ipse ego** (I.9.41).

    victrīx, victrīcis, f. adj., *victorious;* (associated with or denoting) *victory.*

      victrīcēs . . . tabellās: letters to the Roman senate announcing a military victory (the so-called **litterae laureātae**) were wreathed with laurel, but here the letter is itself pictured as *victorious*—a continuation of the military imagery in 21. For the laurel's association with triumphs and triumphant warriors, see the Daphne and Apollo story above, especially *Met.* I.558–61.

  redimiō, redimīre, redimiī, redimītus, *to (encircle with a) garland, wreathe.*

    redimīre . . . / nec . . . pōnere (26): complementary infins. with **morer**, a potential subjn.

  tabellās / . . . morer (26) **/ . . . MINISTRĀS** (27) **/ . . . ACER** (28): note the ABAB end-line rhyme, one function of which (besides mere assonance) is to underscore the personifying link between **tabellās** and **ministrās**.

26   **aedēs, aedis**, f., *house; temple, shrine.*

27 **subscrībō, subscrībere, subscrīpsī, subscrīptus,** *to write at the bottom, append.*

> **Subscrībam**: possibly another potential subjn., but more likely a vivid fut. indic., suggesting, along with the inscription following, the poet's heightened confidence in the success of his letter and the realization of his fantasy. Votive offerings to the gods were often accompanied by inscriptions on dedicatory **tabellae**—these were not usually love-letters, obviously, but this is Venus' temple, after all!

Nāsō, Nāsōnis, m., *Naso* (Ovid's cognomen, with the final **-o** shortened here).

ministra, -ae, f., *female servant, maid.*

> **FĪDĀS . . . MINISTRĀS**: with these words the personification of the tablets, implied earlier, is now complete; cf. **ministerium** (3).

28 **dēdicō, -āre, -āvī, -ātus,** *to declare; to dedicate, consecrate* (to).

> **DĒDICAT. AT**: the abrupt diaeresis, harsh sound effects, and the unexpected adversative conjunction all prepare us for the poem's odd closure (which itself anticipates the following poem).

NŪPER . . . ACER: internal rhyme further accentuates this final image. The tablets are alive; Ovid addresses them (**fuistis**); they have become his trusty maid-servants. But in this last curious flourish, he reminds these servants, as he had Nape, of their lowly station.

acer, acris, n., *maple tree; maple wood.*

An ancient reader,
with writing implements,
from a Roman sarcophagus

27   Subscrībam, "VENERĪ FĪDĀS SIBI NĀSO MINISTRĀS
28   DĒDICAT. AT NŪPER VĪLE FUISTIS ACER."

Discussion Question

What similarities of characterization, both positive and negative, do you see between the **tabellae** in 25–28 and Nape in 1–12? What is the dramatic effect of these associations?

Portraits (with tabella and scroll), Pompeii, 1st century A.D.
Museo Archeologico Nazionale, Naples, Italy

1   **Flēte**: the pl. imper. immediately engages the audience.

    tristēs rediēre tabellae: the alliterative opening line makes it clear that this poem is a sequel—and a most unhappy one—to *Am.* I.11. And the vivid personification developed at the end of that poem bursts into action here: these tablets (not Nape) do the walking (**rediēre**) and the talking (**negat** 2)!

2   **īnfēlīx littera**: both *ill-omened* and *unproductive*, an elaboration of **tristēs . . . tabellae** (1); for the sing. form, cf. *Am.* I.11.22.

    posse negat: supply **Corinnam** as subject of **posse**, and **venīre** (from *Am.* I.11.24) as complement.

3   **Ōmina**: the reference adds mock solemnity.

    aliquid: i.e., *something significant* (cf. the English idiom "that really is something!").

    cum discēdere vellet: **vellet** here serves essentially as an auxiliary, *when she was wanting to* (i.e., *was about to*) *leave*.

4   **ad līmen**: tripping was regarded as a bad omen by the Romans, but tripping *at a threshold* was even worse.

    digitōs: acc. of respect with the reflexive **icta**, *having stubbed her toes* (for the syntax, see on **ōra**, *Met.* I.484 above).

    digitōs restitit icta: the alliteration has onomatopoetic effect.

5   **Missa . . . pedem** (6): regarded by some editors as an interpolation, this couplet is an effective apostrophe to poor Nape, who is ordered about and insulted, in absentia, just as she is in the preceding poem. For the opening participial phrase, English would use a clause, *Whenever you are sent*.

    līmen . . . pedem (6): the chiastic arrangement is appropriate to the action proposed, since it suggests a reversal of Nape's earlier, allegedly careless departure.

    meminī, meminisse, defective verb, *to keep in mind, remember* (the fut. imper. here has the same stern tone as **iubētō**, *Am.* I.11.19)

6   **cautē**, adv., *in a cautious manner, carefully*.

    cautius: both the enjambement, as McKeown observes, and the strong diaeresis suggest Nape's stumbling across the threshold.

    sōbrius, -a, -um, *not intoxicated, sober*.

    sōbria: another humorously indelicate aspersion on Nape's character.

7   **Īte hinc**: the abrupt spondaic phrase, accentuated by elision and diaeresis, looks back to **rediēre** (1) and, following the prologue of 1–6, dramatically commences Ovid's curse.

    difficilēs: here, *troublesome, unhelpful*; the alliteration with **fūnebria** suggests Ovid's angry, hissing tone.

    fūnebria ligna: voc., in apposition to the enclosing phrase, **difficilēs . . . tabellae**; Ovid may mean that the tablet's wooden frame is good only for burning on a funeral pyre, but more generally the description anticipates the funereal images in 17–18.

    tabellae: cf. line 1; the poem's focal word is neatly set at the end of the first verse of each of the two principal sections (prologue and curse).

8   **tūque**: quite in the manner of ancient curses against persons, Ovid singles out the tablet's individual parts; cf. **vōsque** (14).

AMORES I.12

"Return to Sender!"

1	Flēte meōs cāsūs: tristēs rediēre tabellae;
2	īnfēlīx hodiē littera posse negat.
3	Ōmina sunt aliquid: modo cum discēdere vellet,
4	ad līmen digitōs restitit icta Napē.
5	(Missa forās iterum, līmen trānsīre mementō
6	cautius atque altē sōbria ferre pedem!)
7	Īte hinc, difficilēs, fūnebria ligna, tabellae,
8	tūque, negātūrīs cēra referta notīs,

Discussion Questions

2/2

1. How does the tone of the opening couplet (1–2) differ from the close of I.11? What key words in 1–2 set the tone, and where has Ovid positioned those words?

2. Why does Ovid make such a point about the **līmen** in 3–6? What symbolic function can the word have?

3. Comment on the word order and sound effects in **negātūrīs . . . notīs** (8) and compare the image with that of *Am.* I.11.24.

> Ovid is the surest guide
> You can name, to show the way
> To any woman, maid, or bride
> Who resolves to go astray.

"Written in an Ovid"
Matthew Prior

negātūrīs . . . notīs: cf. **littera . . . negat** (2).
refertus, -a, -um, *crowded, packed* (with).

9   **puto:** the final **-o** is shortened by systole (cf. on *Am.* I.2.5); the verb implies that this theory of the wax's origin is only Ovid's (spiteful) conjecture.

   dē . . . Corsica (10): the prose order would be **dē flōre longae cicūtae sub melle īnfāmī collēctam;** the entire participial phrase modifies **quam,** object of **mīsit.**

   cicūta, -ae, f., *the hemlock plant.*

      longae . . . cicūtae: the adj./noun separation is appropriate to the image of the *long-stemmed hemlock.* The hemlock plant was the source of poison used in executions (notably that of Socrates), so that there is an allusion here comparable to those in 17–18; elsewhere (*Am.* III.7.13) Ovid refers to the drug's depressant effect on sexual drive, a further nuance probably intended here.

10   **īnfāmis, -is, -e,** *notorious, ill-reputed.*

      melle . . . īnfāmī: Corsican honey was noted for its bitterness, which, together with the reference to poison here, accounts for the strong epithet; the honeycomb would be collected along with the honey but would settle to the bottom of the container, hence **sub.**

   Corsicus, -a, -um, *Corsican, of Corsica* (an island off Italy's west coast, noted for its honey, wax, and other exports).

   mīsit: here, *exported;* supply **Rōmam.**

   apis, apis, f., *bee.*

      The tiny insect is comically imagined here, with **mīsit,** shipping the wax and honey off to Rome all by itself!

11   **At:** i.e., unlike Corsican wax.

   minium, -ī, n., *cinnabar* (a substance used both as a source for red pigment and as a medication).

   penitus, adv., *deep inside; deep(ly), thoroughly.*

   medicātus, -a, -um, *treated, medicated* (with); *dyed* (with).

      In view of the context's references, not only to cinnabar, but also to death and poisoning, the word here means at once *colored* and *drugged;* cf. on **sanguinulentus** (12).

   rubeō, rubēre, *to be(come) red; to blush.*

      rubēbās: the wax used for writing tablets was generally dark, and often had a reddish hue; but in view of the personification here, the better translation is *you were red-faced* (i.e., because of guilt over your failure).

12   **ille:** here, like **iste,** in a pejorative sense.

   sanguinulentus, -a, -um, *of blood, bloody; blood-red.*

      sanguinulentus erat: the wax was crimson both with the "blood" that flushed its guilty face and, given the funereal associations of verses 7 and 17–18, with the blood of death.

13   **prōiciō, prōicere, prōiēcī, prōiectus,** *to cast forth, throw out.*

      Prōiectae: supply **tabellae,** voc. with the jussive **iaceātis;** English would more likely use two verbs, *may you be cast forth and lie . . . .*

   trivium, -ī, n., often pl., *a crossroads.*

      triviīs: supply **in;** like our "street-corner" or "gutter," a place for

9   quam, puto, dē longae collēctam flōre cicūtae
10   melle sub īnfāmī, Corsica mīsit apis.
11   At, tamquam miniō penitus medicāta, rubēbās—
12   ille color vērē sanguinulentus erat!
13   Prōiectae triviīs iaceātis, inūtile lignum,
14   vōsque rotae frangat praetereuntis onus.
15   Illum etiam, quī vōs ex arbore vertit in ūsum,
16   convincam pūrās nōn habuisse manūs;
17   praebuit illa arbor miserō suspendia collō,

---

    worthless persons or things—and certainly not a charming final resting-place!

inūtilis, -is, -e, *useless.*

    inūtile lignum: voc., in apposition to the understood **tabellae**, like **fūnebria ligna** (7) and cf. **VĪLE . . . ACER** (I.11.28); contrast **ūtilis,** of Nape, in I.11.4 and **ūsum** below (15).

14   **vōsque**: see on **tūque** (8).

    rotae: synecdoche for cart (cf. *Am.* I.2.42); Ovid wants us to focus on the wheel itself as it rolls over and shatters the tablet.

    praetereuntis: a slight echo of the identically placed pentasyllable **sanguinulentus** (12); in a message sent to Lesbia, Catullus (poem 11) uses the same word of a plow that crushes a flower in its path, a symbol of the love the poet's mistress has callously destroyed.

    onus: here the *weight* of a loaded cart.

15   **Illum**: subject of **habuisse** (16) in the indirect statement governed by **convincam**.

    quī . . . ūsum: i.e., the craftsman who made the tablet; in a poem Ovid has in mind here (*Odes* 2.13), Horace similarly curses both a tree that fell on him and the man who planted it.

    ūsum: here, *something useful.*

16   **convincō, convincere, convīcī, convictus,** *to overcome; to prove.*

    pūrās . . . manūs: this charge, that the carpenter was a villain, anticipates the tree's association with suicides and criminals in the next couplet.

17   **praebuit illa . . . praebuit illa** (18): careful positioning intensifies the anaphora.

    suspendium, -ī, n., *hanging* (i.e., death, especially suicide, by hanging).

    suspendia: pl. for sing.

18 **carnifex, carnificis**, m., *executioner*.
dīrus, -a, -um, *grim, terrifying, horrible*.
crux, crucis, f., *cross* (crucifixion was a common punishment for criminals).

19 **turpēs . . . umbrās**: through a chiastic word-picture (acc./abl./abl./acc.) the owls are enveloped by *loathsome darkness*; the epithets come first, holding the complete image in suspense to the end.
raucus, -a, -um, *hoarse; raucous, noisy*.
būbō, būbōnis, m., *eagle-owl, horned owl* (a bird of ill omen, like the vulture and the screech-owl in the following line).
 raucīs būbōnibus: both words are onomatopoetic, the latter especially (in its assonance with **umbrās**) suggesting the doleful moan of the owl.

20 **vultur, vulturis**, m., *vulture*.
strix, strigis, f., *screech-owl* (a mythic bird associated with vampires and ghouls).

21 **Hīs**: supply **tabellīs**; cf. **hae . . . cērae** (23).
ego . . . amōrēs: the interlocked order highlights the speaker's dismay.
īnsānus, -a, -um, *crazed, insane*.

23 **capiant**: potential subjn., *would hold*.
vadimōnium, -ī, n., *bond, recognizance* (a legal document guaranteeing a person's appearance in court.
 vadimōnia: an irony here, in view of Corinna's message that she cannot honor Ovid's "summons."
garrulus, -a, -um, *chatty, wordy*.
cērae: i.e., **tabellae**.

24 **quās**: the word agrees with **cērae**, though **vadimōnia** is strictly the more logical antecedent.
aliquis . . . ōre: interlocked order; **dūrō . . . ōre**, besides suggesting harsh legal language, is a deliberate play on **mollia . . . verba** (22). This criticism of legalistic language and maneuvering recalls Ovid's own rejection of the law as his profession.
cognitor, cognitōris, m., *legal representative, lawyer*.
legat: subjn. by attraction to the imagined action of **capiant**; cf. **flēret** (26).

25 **inter . . . iacērent**: the quick dactylic rhythms of both this hexameter line and verse 23 help underscore the contemptuous tone of the two parallel couplets.
ephēmeris, ephēmeridis, acc. pl., **ephēmeridās**, f., *(daily) account book*.
melius . . . iacērent: potential subjn., like **aptius . . . capiant** (23).
tabulās: here, *account-books* or *ledgers*; the image, like many others in Ovid, is inspired by a passage from an earlier elegist (Propertius 3.23.19–20).

26 **avārus, -a, -um**, *greedy, avaricious; miserly*.

27 **Ergō ego vōs**: the conj. and strong pronouns, especially the shift back to 2nd pers. address (contrast **hīs ego** 21), mark the transition to the curse's denouement.
vōs . . . duplicēs: supply **esse**; indirect statement with **sēnsī**.
rēbus: abl. of respect; with **prō nōmine**, *in fact as well as in name*.

18	carnificī dīrās praebuit illa crucēs;
19	illa dedit turpēs raucīs būbōnibus umbrās,
20	vulturis in rāmīs et strigis ōva tulit.
21	Hīs ego commīsī nostrōs īnsānus amōrēs
22	molliaque ad dominam verba ferenda dedī?
23	Aptius hae capiant vadimōnia garrula cērae,
24	quās aliquis dūrō cognitor ōre legat;
25	inter ephēmeridās melius tabulāsque iacērent,
26	in quibus absūmptās flēret avārus opēs.
27	Ergō ego vōs rēbus duplicēs prō nōmine sēnsī—

Discussion Questions

1. **Dīrās** is a widely accepted conjecture for the manuscript reading **dūrās** in verse 18. What several arguments can you think of both for and against the two readings?

2. What specifically does Ovid curse in 9–12? in 13–20? How do these sections relate to 7–8?

3. Comment on the imagery in 17–20. Where is this imagery first anticipated? How is it appropriate to the overall tone of the poem?

4. What is the rhetorical function of 21–22? What is the emotional tone?

5. How is Ovid's use of demonstrative pronouns in 12–23 especially effective?

6. Comment on the word-picture in 23.

7. What is the function of 23–26? In what ways do these lines have an affinity to satire?

8. Explore fully the image of "doubleness" and "duplicity" evoked in line 27. In what ways does the image serve as a kind of metaphor for the entire drama contained in *Am.* I.11–12? Why is it especially appropriate that this drama be enacted in a diptych, rather than within a single poem?

duplex, duplicis, *double, folded over; two-faced, deceitful, duplicitous.*
  duplicēs: Ovid plays on both senses of the word here, the literal and the figurative, a point which the interlocked order helps to underscore.

28 **auspiciī . . . bonī**: gen. of description in place of a predicate nom. after
    erat; the chiastic golden-line arrangement (cf. **immundō . . . sitū** 30) suits
    the image of the folding tablet itself.

29 **precer**: deliberative subjn.
    nisi: supply **ut**, *except that*, introducing a jussive noun clause after **precer**.
    cariōsus, -a, -um, *decayed, rotten*.
    senectūs, senectūtis, f., *old age*.
        The reference suggests a time of life devoid of love, as both Ovid and
        the tablet must now be.

30 **rōdō, rōdere, rōsī, rōsus**, *to gnaw; to eat away, erode*.
    immundus, -a, -um, *unclean, foul*.
    situs, -ūs, m., *neglect, disuse; rot, mold*.

Medieval statue of Ovid
Liceo d'Ovidio
Sulmona, Abruzzi

28   auspiciī numerus nōn erat ipse bonī!
29   Quid precer īrātus, nisi vōs cariōsa senectūs
30   rōdat, et immundō cēra sit alba sitū?

Discussion Questions

1.   Where else in the poem, besides verse 28, is there a reference to unfavorable *leading to death of relation*
      omens? What are the functions of this repeated notion, both structurally and *of relation*
      thematically? *Nope stubs toe, using death words, crossroads, unpure hands, birds nested*

2.   Comment on the final image in 29–30. What do we see happening to the
      tablet itself and, on the symbolic level, to the "person" the tablet has become
      in the poet's imagination? How does the reference to color function here?
      Where else in the poem does Ovid refer to the color of the wax, and what is
      the significance of the shift? *tablet no longer useful*

3.   In what way does the little drama enacted in this poem affect our
      interpretation of the sentiment expressed in the closing line of I.11?

4.   If you are familiar with Catullus' poetry, what elements does this poem have
      in common with his second sparrow poem (poem 3)?

P. OVIDI NASONIS AMORVM

EPIGRAMMA IPSIVS

Quī modo Nāsōnis fuerāmus quīnque libellī,
   trēs sumus; hoc illī praetulit auctor opus.
Ut iam nūlla tibī nōs sit lēgisse voluptās,
   at levior dēmptīs poena duōbus erit.

Preface to the second edition of the Amores

1 **novum . . . Amōrum**: the alliteration of **m** and especially the assonance in **-ovum/-ōrum/-ōrum** add an aptly delicate sound effect.

māter Amōrum: Venus, mother of Cupid (cf. 15 below), and the goddess who inspired Ovid's *Amores*.

2 **rāditur . . . meīs**: English would more likely use an active construction, *my elegies are moving closely round the final turning post*, a metaphor from chariot racing; but what is the literal translation?

*****elegī, -ōrum**, m. pl., *elegiac verses, elegies.*

    elegīs . . . meīs: poetry often omits the prep. **ab** in the abl. of agent construction; for the internal rhyme, a favorite Ovidian effect, cf. verses 4, 16, and 18, and note the soundplay between **-tima/mēta/me-** and **māter** in verse 1.

3 **Quōs**: here = **Eōs**, *These (elegies).*

*****Paelignus, -a, -um**, *Paelignian, of the Paelignians* (a tribe of central Italy).

rūs, rūris, n., *country, countryside.*

alumnus, -ī, m., *nursling, child; native.*

    alumnus: in apposition to **ego**, as are **hērēs** (5) and **eques** (6).

4 **nec . . . dēdecuēre**: a not immodest litotes, but perhaps also defensive, in view of criticism Ovid's erotic verse had brought him from some quarters.

dēlicia, -ae, f., usually pl., *pleasure, delight, any pleasurable activity.*

    dēliciae: i.e., his poetry—Ovid's greatest pleasure.

dēdecet, dēdecēre, dēdecuit, *it disgraces, dishonors.*

5 **sī quid id est**: a self-deprecating aside, *if this is anything*, i.e., if his background is of any interest to his audience. This same line appears in Ovid's autobiographical poem, *Tristia* IV.10 (verse 7).

proavus, -ī, m., *great-grandfather; ancestor, forefather.*

vetus . . . hērēs: while strictly modifying **hērēs**, the adj. logically applies to **ōrdinis**, *descendant of an ancient (equestrian) family.*

hērēs, hērēdis, m., *successor, heir.*

6 **nōn . . . eques**: i.e., he was born an equestrian, not merely elevated to the rank as a consequence of wealth gained from the latest war (cf. *Am.* I.3.7–8 above); but, with an eye to the imagery of verses 2 and 18, Ovid means us to think of the literal meaning of **eques** (*horseman*) as well (see on **ārea** 18).

turbō, turbinis, m., *spinning top* (or other spinning object); *whirlwind* (either literal or figurative).

7 **Mantua, -ae**, f., *Mantua* (a town in Cisalpine Gaul, birthplace of the poet Vergil).

Vērōna, -ae, f., *Verona* (another city of Cisalpine Gaul, birthplace of Catullus).

8 **Paelignae . . . ego**: alliteration of hard **g** adds emphasis to Ovid's boast.

9 **honestus, -a, -um**, *honorable.*

arma: here, as often, metonymy for *war.*

10 **sociās . . . manūs**: note the word-picture, with *fearful Rome* "surrounded by" the *allied forces*; the Paeligni took a leading role in the Social War of 91–87 B.C.

AMORES III.15

"And Now, Farewell to Love"

1   Quaere novum vātem, tenerōrum māter Amōrum:
2   rāditur haec elegīs ultima mēta meīs!
3   Quōs ego composuī, Paelignī rūris alumnus—
4   nec mē dēliciae dēdecuēre meae—
5   sī quid id est, usque ā proavīs vetus ōrdinis hērēs,
6   nōn modo mīlitiae turbine factus eques.
7   Mantua Vergiliō gaudet, Vērōna Catullō;
8   Paelignae dīcar glōria gentis ego,
9   quam sua lībertās ad honesta coēgerat arma,
10   cum timuit sociās anxia Rōma manūs.
11 Atque aliquis spectāns hospes Sulmōnis aquōsī

Discussion Questions

1. Comment on the appropriateness of the metaphor in line 2. How does the word-picture enhance the image?

2. What are the most striking sound effects in 4?

3. Comment on the word order in 7–8. What is the significance of Ovid's associating himself with Catullus and Vergil in particular?

---

anxius, -a, -um, *uneasy, anxious.*
11 **hospes:** here, *visitor, traveler.*
  Sulmō, Sulmōnis, m., *Sulmo* (a town of the Paeligni—see on verse 3—and Ovid's birthplace, modern Sulmona).
  aquōsus, -a, -um, *abounding in water, well-watered.*
    Sulmōnis aquōsī: so called because of the region's many streams.

12 **moenia, moenium,** n. pl., *(defensive) walls.*
campī: here, *its territory* (cf. **campō** 16).
tenent: here, *encircle, protect.*

13 **Quae**: the antecedent is **vōs** (14), i.e., the **moenia**, synecdoche for the city of
Sulmo itself.
tantum: with **poëtam**, a deliberate contrast with **quantulacumque** (14); the
line's initial spondees add weight to the characterization.

14 **quantuluscumque, -acumque, -umcumque,** *however small, tiny.*
quantulacumque: a massive word, extended by the elision with **estis,**
for so tiny an image—doubtless a deliberate effect.

15 ***cultus, -a, -um,** *cultivated; beautiful; elegant.*
Culte . . . cultī: the line's elaborate chiastic structure, its anaphora and
assonance, and the quick dactylic rhythms all mark a transition to the
poem's epilogue—a farewell to elegy, to its inspiring divinities Cupid
and Venus (who are recalled from line 1), and to its Muse, along with
an expression of confidence in the work's survival.
Amathūsius, -a, -um, *Amathusian, of Amathus* (a town in Cyprus, Venus'
birthplace).

16 **aurea . . . signa**: naturally the military standards carried by Venus and her
conquering son are golden!
campō: we should read the word both literally, looking back to **campī** (12),
and figuratively, of the poet's *field* of literary interest; cf. the nearly
identical double entendre in **ārea** (18).
vellō, vellere, vulsī, vulsus, *to pull out, pull up*; with **signa**, *to pull up the
standards* (of an army), i.e., as a signal to break up camp and move on.

17 **corniger, cornigera, cornigerum,** *having horns, horned.*
increpō, increpāre, increpuī, increpitus, *to make a loud noise; to strike
noisily.*
thyrsus, -ī, m., *thyrsus* (a staff, tipped with a pine-cone, ivy, or grape-
leaves, carried by Dionysus and his followers and often symbolizing, as
here, poetic inspiration).
Lyaeus, -ī, m., *Lyaeus* ("the Liberator," a cult-title of Dionysus/Bacchus).
Corniger . . . Lyaeus: according to a legend well-known from
Euripides' *Bacchae*, Dionysus was born out of Zeus' thigh with the
horns of a bull; frequently depicted in Roman art as a youth with bull's
horns, he is invoked here in his role as inspirer of poets (cf. *Am.*
I.2.47–48 above).

18 **ārea**: with a double entendre comparable to those in **campō** (16) and in
eques (6), which is deliberately echoed by **equīs** in the same metrical
position here, the word means both a *field* over which one might literally
drive a team of horses and a *field of endeavor*. The same imagery is used
by Ovid in his *Fasti* (IV.10), which, along with the *Metamorphoses*, he
must have in mind here; work was begun on both these poems shortly after
publication of the second edition of the *Amores*.
magnīs . . . maior: the two epithets play on the imagery of size introduced
in 12–14.

12   moenia, quae campī iūgera pauca tenent,
13   "Quae tantum," dīcet, "potuistis ferre poētam,
14   quantulacumque estis, vōs ego magna vocō."
15   Culte puer puerīque parēns Amathūsia cultī,
16   aurea de campō vellite signa meō.
17   Corniger increpuit thyrsō graviōre Lyaeus:
18   pulsanda est magnīs ārea maior equīs.
19   Imbellēs elegī, geniālis Mūsa, valēte—
20   post mea mānsūrum fāta superstes opus!

Discussion Questions

1. How is word order appropriate to image in verse 16?

2. What metaphor introduced earlier in the poem is resumed in 18? How are the images alike and in what ways are they different? Compare also the similarities between verses 1 and 19. How do these connections contribute to the poem's unity?

3. Discuss Ovid's use of military imagery in this poem, including the brief mention in verse 6, the references to the Paelignians' role in the Social War, the allusions to Cupid and Venus, and the final characterization of his elegies as **imbellēs** (19). Compare the love/war imagery in other selections from the *Amores* which you have read.

4. How does Ovid's language here at the close of his final elegy (19–20) correspond with the last lines of his opening poem (*Am.* I.1.27–30)? What is the purpose of these correspondences? How does word order enhance theme in verse 20?

---

19   **imbellis, -is, -e,** *not suited to war, unwarlike.*
     Imbellēs . . . valēte: this closing farewell to elegy and Muse balances the opening invocation of Venus as **māter Amōrum** (1).
   geniālis, -is, -e, *of one's soul; jovial, genial.*
     geniālis Mūsa: not just *friendly (congenial) Muse,* but *soul-inspiring Muse*; in Roman belief, the **genius** was a man's soul, his spiritual essence, and the seat of his intellect and talent.
20   **mānsūrum . . . opus:** voc., in apposition to **elegī**; English would use a relative clause, in place of the participle, *work that will remain. . . .*
   superstes, superstitis, *surviving, alive.*

VOCABULARY

This vocabulary lists all words that are not glossed in the running vocabularies (these are in general common items that most students will be familiar with from prior study), as well as those that are glossed and marked with an asterisk at their initial occurrence; since asterisked vocabulary items occur more than once in the text, students should memorize such entries when they are first encountered.

A

ā or **ab**, prep. + abl., *from*

abeō, abīre, abiī, abitūrus, irreg., *to go away*

absum, abesse, āfuī, āfutūrus, irreg., *to be away, be absent, be distant*

absūmō, absūmere, absūmpsī, absūmptus, *to use up; to wear out, exhaust*

ac, conj., *and*

accendō, accendere, accendī, accēnsus, *to kindle, ignite; to make hotter, intensify*

accipiō, accipere, accēpī, acceptus, *to receive, get, welcome*

ācer, ācris, ācre, *keen*

ācriter, adv., *fiercely*

acūtus, -a, -um, *sharp, pointed*

ad, prep. + acc., *to, toward, at, near*

adeō, adv., *so much, to such an extent*

adeō, adīre, adiī, aditus, irreg., *to come to, approach*

adhūc, adv., *still, as yet*

adiuvō, adiuvāre, adiūvī, adiūtus, *to help, assist*

admoveō, admovēre, admōvī, admōtus, *to move toward*

adsum, adesse, adfuī, *to be present, near*

adversus, -a, -um, *opposite (to), facing, turned toward*

āēr, āeris, m., *air*

aetās, aetātis, f., *age, time of life*

aethēr, aetheris, acc., **aethera**, n., *the upper regions of space, heaven*

aevum, -ī, n., *time, age*

afferō, afferre, attulī, allātus, irreg., *to bring, bring to, bring in*

agō, agere, ēgī, āctus, *to do, drive*

ait, *he/she says, said*

āla, -ae, f., *wing*

albus, -a, -um, *white*

aliquis, aliquid, *someone, something*

aliter, adv., *otherwise, differently*

alter, altera, alterum, *the other (of two), another, a second, the one*

altus, -a, -um, *tall, high; deep*

ambō, ambae, ambō, *both*

amictus, -ūs, m., *mantle, cloak*

amīcus, -a, -um, *friendly, loving; of a friend/lover*

amō, -āre, -āvī, -ātus, *to love, like*

amor, amōris, m., *sexual passion, love*; pl., *the object of love, a lover; a love affair*

Amor, Amōris, m., *Cupid (the god of love)*

amplector, amplectī, amplexus sum, *to embrace*

an, conj., *whether, or, if*

ancilla, -ae, f., *slave-woman*

anima, -ae, f., *air, breath; soul, life; spirit, ghost*

animus, -ī, m., *mind*

annus, -ī, m., *year*

ante, adv., *in front; previously, before*

ante, prep. + acc., *before, in front of*

anus, -ūs, f., *old woman*

aperiō, aperīre, aperuī, apertus, *to open*

aptō, -āre, -āvī, -ātus, *to place, fit*

aptus, -a, -um, *tied, bound*; + dat., *suitable (for)*

aqua, -ae, f., *water*

āra, -ae, f., *altar*

arātrum, -ī, n., *plow*

arbor, arboris, f., *tree*

arcus, -ūs, m., *a bow*

ārdeō, ārdēre, ārsī, *to burn, blaze*

arduus, -a, -um, *tall, towering; steep, precipitous*

ārea, -ae, f., *open space, area*

arma, -ōrum, n. pl., *arms, weapons*

armātus, -a, -um, *armed*

ars, artis, f., *skill*

artus, -ūs, m., *joint of the body; arm, leg, limb*

arvum, -ī, n., *field*

asper, aspera, asperum, *rough, harsh* (to the touch); *wild, uncultivated*

aspiciō, aspicere, aspexī, aspectus, *to look at, observe; to consider, think about*

at, conj., *but, nevertheless*

āter, ātra, ātrum, *black, dark*

atque, conj., *and, also*

attollō, attollere, *to raise, lift up*

attonitus, -a, -um, *astonished, astounded*

audāx, audācis, *bold*

audeō, audēre, ausus sum, *to dare*

auferō, auferre, abstulī, ablātus, irreg., *to carry away, take away*

augeō, augēre, auxī, auctus, *to increase*

aura, -ae, f., *breath of air, breeze*

aurātus, -a, -um, *golden*

aureus, -a, -um, *golden*

auris, auris, f., *ear*

aurum, -ī, n., *gold*

auspicium, -ī, n., *omen, augury*

aut, conj., *or*

avis, avis, m./f., *bird*

B

baca, -a, f., *berry, nut; pearl, bead*

baculum, -ī, n., *stick, staff*

Baucis, Baucidis, acc., **Baucida,** f., *Baucis* (the old wife of Philemon)

bellum, -ī, n., *war*

bene, adv., *well*

blanditia, -ae, f., *flattery, alluring speech;* often pl. with sing. meaning

blandus, -a, -um, *coaxing, flattering; persuasive, enticing*

bonus, -a, -um, *good*

bōs, bovis, gen. pl. **boum,** m./f., *ox, cow*

bracchium, -ī, n., *forearm*

brevis, -is, -e, *short*

bustum, -ī, n., often pl. for sing., *funeral pyre, ash; grave-mound, tomb*

C

cacūmen, cacūminis, n., *peak, top*

cadō, cadere, cecidī, cāsūrus, *to fall*

caedēs, caedis, f., *killing, slaughter; blood, gore*

caelō, -āre, -āvī, -ātus, *to engrave, emboss*

caelum, -ī, n., *sky, heaven*

callidus, -a, -um, *expert, wise; clever, crafty*

campus, -ī, m., *plain, field*

candidus, -a, -um, *white, fair-skinned, beautiful*

canō, canere, cecinī, cantus, *to sing, chant; to sing about, celebrate*

cantō, -āre, -āvī, ātus, *to sing*

capillī, -ōrum, m. pl., *hair*

capiō, capere, cēpī, captus, *to take, capture*

captīvus, -a, -um, *captured, captive*

captō, -āre, -āvī, -ātus, *to try to touch, grasp at*

caput, capitis, n., *head*

careō, carēre, caruī, caritūrus + abl., *to need, lack*

carmen, carminis, n., *ritual utterance, chant, hymn; song, poem*

carpō, carpere, carpsī, carptus, *to pluck, gather; to tear at; to travel, pursue*

cārus, -a, -um, *dear, beloved*

casa, -ae, f., *hut, cottage*

castra, -ōrum, n. pl., *military camp*

cāsus, -ūs, m., *fall; mishap, misfortune, accident; occurrence;* pl., *experiences, fortune*

caterva, -ae, f., *crowd*

causa, -ae, f., *reason*

cēdō, cedere, cessī, cessūrus, *to go, proceed;* + dat., *to yield to, be inferior to*

celeber, celebris, celebre, *busy* (with), *frequented* (by); *famous*

celer, celeris, celere, *quick, swift*

cēra, -ae, f., *beeswax, wax; writing tablet*

Cerēs, Cereris, f., *Ceres* (goddess of grain)

certus, -a, -um, *certain, unerring*

cervīx, cervīcis, f., often pl. for sing., *the neck*

cessō, -āre, -āvī, -ātūrus, *to be idle, do nothing, delay*

cēterī, -ae, -a, *the rest, the others*

cingō, cingere, cīnxī, cīnctus, *to surround, encircle*

cithara, -ae, f., *lyre*

citus, -a, -um, *swift, rapid*

clāmō, -āre, -āvī, -ātūrus, *to shout*

claudō, claudere, clausī, clausus, *to shut, close*

clīvus, -ī, m., *sloping ground, slope;*

hillside; inclined surface

coeō, coīre, coiī, coitus, irreg., *to come together, meet; to form an alliance*

coepī, coepisse, coeptus, *to begin*

cognōscō, cognōscere, cognōvī, cognitus, *to find out, learn, hear of*

cōgō, cōgere, coēgī, coāctus, *to compel, force*

colligō, colligere, collēgī, collēctus, *to gather (together); to arrange*

collis, collis, m., *hill*

collum, -ī, n., *neck*

colō, colere, coluī, cultus, *to cultivate, worship*

color, colōris, m., *color*

columba, -ae, f., *pigeon, dove*

coma, -ae, f., *hair*

comes, comitis, m./f., *companion*

comitō, comitāre, comitāvī, comitātus, *to accompany*

committō, committere, commīsī, commissus, *to bring together, entrust*

commodus, -a, -um, *pleasant*

commūnis, -is, -e, *common*

cōmō, cōmere, cōmpsī, cōmptus, *to make beautiful, adorn; to dress, arrange, comb*

compōnō, compōnere, composuī, compositus, *to compose*

concha, -ae, f., *shellfish; shell, pearl*

concidō, concidere, *to fall down*

concipiō, concipere, concēpī, conceptus, *to receive; to conceive, develop; to express, compose* (in words); *to pronounce solemnly* (a prayer, oath)

condō, condere, condidī, conditus, *to found, establish*

cōnfugiō, cōnfugere, cōnfūgī, *to flee for refuge*

coniūnx, coniugis, m./f., *spouse*

cōnspiciō, cōnspicere, cōnspexī, cōnspectus, *to catch sight of, see*

cōnstō, cōnstāre, cōnstitī, cōnstātūrus, *to take up a position, stand upon, stand firmly*

conterminus, -a, -um + dat., *bordering (upon), close (to)*

cōnūbium, -ī, n., often pl. for sing.; *marriage, wedding rites*

conveniō, convenīre, convēnī, conventūrus, *to assemble, meet*; + dat., *to be suited (to), befit, harmonize (with)*

cor, cordis, n., *heart*

cornū, -ūs, n., *animal's horn, object made of horn*

corpus, corporis, n., *body*

cortex, corticis, m., *bark* (of a tree)

crātēr, crātēris, acc., **crātēra**, m., *mixing-bowl* (usually for wine)

crēdō, crēdere, crēdidī, crēditus + dat., *to trust, believe*

creō, -āre, -āvī, -ātus, *to beget, create*

crēscō, crēscere, crēvī, crētūrus, *to be born, arise; to increase, change into* (by growing); *to grow, bud*

crīmen, crīminis, n., *charge, accusation; misdeed, crime*

crīnis, crīnis, m., *lock of hair*; pl. or collective sing., *hair*

crūdēlis, -is, -e, *cruel*

cruor, cruōris, m., *blood* (from a wound); *slaughter.*

cultus, -a, -um, *cultivated; beautiful; elegant*

cum, prep. + abl., *with*

cum, conj., *when, since, whenever, although*

cūnctus, -a, -um, *all*

Cupīdō, Cupīdinis, m., *Cupid* (Venus' son and the god of physical love)

cupiō, cupere, cupīvī, cupītus, *to desire, want*

cūr, adv., *why?*

cūra, -ae, f., *care*

cūrō, -āre, -āvī, -ātus, *to look after, attend to*

currō, currere, cucurrī, cursus, *to run*

currus, -ūs, m., *chariot*

cuspis, cuspidis, f., *sharp point, tip*

custōs, custōdis, m./f., *guard*

D

Daphnē, Daphnēs, f., *Daphne*

dē, prep. + abl., *down from, concerning, about*

dēbeō, -ēre, -uī, -itus, *to owe,* (one) *ought*

decet, decēre, decuit, *to adorn; to be right for* (+ acc.); impers., *it is right, suitable*

dēferō, dēferre, dētulī, dēlātus, *to bring/carry down; to award, grant*

dēfleō, dēflēre, dēflēvī, dēflētus, *to weep for, mourn*

dēmittō, dēmittere, dēmīsī, dēmissus, *to let down, suspend*

dēmō, dēmere, dēmpsī, dēmptus, *to remove, take away; to cut off*

dēnsus, -a, -um, *thick, dense; frequent*

dēpōnō, dēpōnere, dēposuī, dēpositus, *to lay down, put aside, set down*

dēscendō, dēscendere, dēscendī, dēscēnsūrus, *to come* or *go down, climb down*

dēserō, dēserere, dēseruī, dēsertus, *to leave, desert*

deus, deī, nom. and voc. pl., **deī, diī, dī,** dat. and abl. pl., **deīs, dīs,** m., *god*

dextra, -ae, f., *right hand*

dīcō, dīcere, dīxī, dictus, *to say, tell*

dicta, -ōrum, n. pl., *words*

diēs, diēī, m. (f.), *day*

difficilis, -is, -e, *difficult*

digitus, -ī, m., *finger*

dignus, -a, -um, *suitable, appropriate;* + abl., *worthy* (of)

dīmittō, dīmittere, dīmīsī, dūnissus, *to send away*

discēdō, discēdere, discessī, discessūrus, *to leave, go away, depart*

discrīmen, discrīminis, n., *distinction*

diū, adv., *for a long time*

dīversus, -a, -um, *opposite; different; separate*

dō, dare, dedī, datus, *to give*

doceō, docēre, docuī, doctus, *to teach*

doleō, -ēre, -uī, -itūrus, *to be sorry, be sad, hurt*

dolor, dolōris, m., *grief, pain*

domina, -ae, f., *mistress, lady of the house*

dominus, ī, m., *master, owner*

domō, domāre, domuī, domitus, *to subdue, tame; to conquer*

domus, -ūs, abl., **domō,** acc. pl., **domōs,** f., *house*

dōnec, conj., *until, as long as*

dōnō, -āre, -āvī, ātus, *to give; to present somebody* (acc.) *with something* (abl.)

dōnum, -ī, n., *gift*

dubitō, -āre, -āvī, -ātus, *to be in doubt/be uncertain* (with **an** + indirect question); *to waver, hesitate*

dūcō, dūcere, dūxī, ductus, *to lead, take, bring*

dum, adv. and conj., *while, as long as*

duo, duae, duo, *two*

dūrus, -a, -um, *hard, firm; harsh*

dux, ducis, m., *leader, commander, general*

E

ē, ex, prep. + abl., *from, out of*

ebur, eboris, n., *ivory;* by synecdoche, *an object made of ivory*

ecce, interj., *look! look at . . . !*

ēdō, ēdere, ēdidī, ēditus, *to give forth, emit; to utter sollemnly; to narrate, publish*

ego, pl. **nōs,** *I, we*

ēgredior, ēgredī, ēgressus sum, *to go out, leave, disembark*

elegī, -ōrum, m. pl., *elegiac verses; elegies*

enim, conj., *for;* with **sed,** *but in fact*

ēnsis, ēnsis, m., *sword*

eō, īre, iī, itūrus, irreg., *to go*

epulae, -ārum, f. pl., *banquet, feast*

eques, equitis, m., *horseman; knight, equestrian* (a member of the wealthy Roman equestrian class)

equus, -ī, m., *horse*

ergō, conj., *therefore*

ēripiō, ēripere, ēripuī, ēreptus, *to snatch from, rescue*

errō, -āre, -āvī, -ātūrus, *to wander, be mistaken*

et, adv. and conj., *and, also*

etiam, conj., *also, even*

Eurydicē, Eurydicēs, acc., **Eurydicēn,** f., *Eurydice* (wife of Orpheus)

excēdō, excēdere, excessī, excessūrus, *to go out, leave*

excipiō, excipere, excēpī, exceptus, *to welcome, receive, catch*

exeō, -īre, -iī, -itūrus, *to go out*

exiguus, -a, -um, *small, slight*

expallēscō, expallēscere, expalluī, *to grow pale*

extendō, extendere, extendī, extentūrus, *to hold out*

exstinguō, exstinguere, exstīnxī, exstīnctus, *to put out, extinguish*

F

fābula, -ae, f., *story*

faciēs, faciēī, f., *outward appearance; face; shape, form*

faciō, facere, fēcī, factus, *to make, do*

fallō, fallere, fefellī, falsus, *to deceive,*

trick; to disappoint; (of time) to while away, beguile

falsus, -a, -um, *untrue, false; misleading, deceptive*

fāma, -ae, f., *news, report; tradition, story*

fateor, fatērī, fassus sum, *to acknowledge, admit, confess; to accept*

fātum, -ī, n., *prophecy; destiny, fate; Fate* (as a deity); *doom, death* (often pl. for sing.)

fax, facis, f., *torch; material used for a torch; flame of love.*

fēlix, fēlīcis, *fertile, productive; lucky, happy, fortunate*

fēmina, -ae, f., *woman*

fera, -ae, f., *wild animal, beast*

ferō, ferre, tulī, lātus, irreg., *to carry, bring, bear*

ferōx, ferōcis, *fierce*

ferrum, -ī, n., *iron;* by synecdoche, *weapon, sword*

ferus, -a, -um, *wild, ferocious, savage*

fervēns, ferventis, *boiling; warm*

fēstus, -a, -um, *festive;* with **diēs** (and often pl.), *holiday, festival*

fētus, -ūs, m., *giving birth; fruit; offspring*

fidēs, fideī, f., *good faith, reliability, trust*

fīdus, -a, -um, *faithful, loyal, devoted*

fīgō, fīgere, fīxī, fīxus, *to drive in, insert; to transfix, pierce; to fix, press*

figūra, -ae, f., *form, composition; outward appearance*

fīlia, -ae, f., *daughter*

fīlius, -ī, m., *son*

fīlum, -ī, n., *thread*

fīniō, -īre, -īvī, -ītus, *to finish*

fīnis, -is, m., *end*

fīō, fierī, factus sum, irreg., *to become, be made, be done, happen*

fistula, -ae, f., *tube, pipe; shepherd's pipe*

flamma, -ae, f., *flame*

flāvēns, flāventis, *golden, yellow*

flāvus, -a, -um, *yellow, golden; fair-haired, blonde*

flectō, flectere, flexī, flexus, *to bend, curve; to turn*

fleō, flēre, flēvī, flētus, *to weep, cry; to weep for, lament*

flōs, flōris, m., *flower*

flūmen, flūminis, n., *stream, river*

focus, -ī, m., *hearth, fireplace*

fōns, fontis, m., *spring, spring-water*

forās, adv., *out of doors, forth, out*

foris, foris, f., *door, entrance* (of a building or room); pl., *double-doors*

fōrma, -ae, f., *form, shape; beauty*

fōrmōsus, -a, -um, *beautiful, lovely*

fors, fortis, f., *chance, destiny*

forte, adv., *by chance*

fortis, -is, -e, *brave*

frangō, frangere, frēgī, fractus, *to break*

frondeō, frondēre, *to sprout leaves*

frōns, frondis, f., *leafy part of a tree, foliage*

frōns, frontis, f., *forehead*

frūstrā, adv., *in vain*

fuga, -ae, f., *running away, flight*

fugiō, fugere, fūgī, fugitūrus, *to flee*

fugō, -āre, -āvī, -ātus, *to drive away, dispel, banish*

fūmus, -ī, m., *smoke*

fūnebris, -is, -e, *funereal*

fungor, fungī, fūnctus sum + abl., *to perform; to experience, suffer* (with **morte** and similar words, *to die*)

furca, -ae, f., *forked stick, fork*

furor, furōris, m., *frenzy*

G

gaudeō, gaudēre, gāvīsus sum, *to be glad, rejoice*

gelidus, -a, -um, *cold, cool, chilly*

geminus, -a, -um, *twin-born, twin; twofold, double*

gemma, -ae, f., *jewel, gem*

gena, -ae, f., *the side of the face, cheek;* pl., *the area around the eyes, the eyes*

genitor, -ōris, m., *father, creator*

gēns, gentis, f., *family, clan*

gerō, gerere, gessī, gestus, *to wear, carry on*

glōria, -ae, f., *fame, glory*

gradus, -ūs, m., *step, pace; phase, stage* (in a process)

grātus, -a, -um, *pleasing, dear* (to), *loved* (by)

gravis, -is, -e, *heavy, serious*

H

habeō, -ēre, -uī, -itus, *to have, hold*

habitō, -āre, -āvī, -ātus, *to live, dwell*

haereō, haerēre, haesī, haesus, *to stick, cling; to be hesitant, be uncertain*

harundō, harundinis, f., *reed; fishing rod; shaft of an arrow.*

haud, adv., *not, by no means*

hauriō, haurīre, hausī, haustus, *to drain, to draw in*

herba, -ae, f., *small plant, herb; grass*

hērōs, hērōos, m., *hero*

heu, interj., *alas!*

hic, haec, hoc, *this*

hīc, adv., *here*

hinc, adv., *from this place; from/on this side*

hodiē, adv., *today*

holus, holeris, n., *vegetable*

homō, hominis, m., *man*

hōra, -ae, f., *hour*

hortor, hortārī, hortātus sum, *to encourage, urge*

hortus, -ī, m., *garden*

hospes, hospitis, m., *friend, host, guest*

hostis, hostis, m./f., *enemy*

hūc, adv., *here, to here*

hūmānus, -a, -um, *human*

humilis, -is, -e, *humble*

I

iaceō, iacēre, iacuī, iacitūrus, *to lie, be lying down*

iaciō, iacere, iēcī, iactus, *to throw*

iam, adv., *now, already*

ibi, adv., *there*

Īcarus, -ī, m., *Icarus (the son of Daedalus)*

īciō, īcere, īcī, ictus, *to strike*

īdem, eadem, idem, *the same*

ignārus, -a, -um, *ignorant, unknowing, unaware*

ignāvus, -a, -um, *cowardly, lazy*

ignis, ignis, m., *fire*

ignōtus, -a, -um, *unknown, unfamiliar*

ille, illa, illud, *that; he, she, it; that famous*

imber, imbris, m., *rain*

immēnsus, -a, -um, *boundless, vast*

impediō, -īre, -īvī, -ītus, *to hinder, prevent*

impellō, impellere, impulī, impulsus, *to strike, beat against; to motivate*

impōnō, impōnere, imposuī, impositus, *to place on, put*

īmus, -a, -um, *lowest, bottommost; (at the) lowest part of, bottom of, base of;* n. pl.,

substantive, *the Underworld*

in, prep. + acc. and abl., *into, toward, until; in, on, among*

incēdō, incēdere, incessī, incessūrus, *to march, go*

incertus, -a, -um, *not fixed; uncertain, doubtful; disarranged*

incola, -ae, m./f., *inhabitant, tenant*

incumbō, incumbere, incubuī + dat., *to bend over; to throw oneself (on), fall (on), lie down (on)*

inde, adv., *from there, then*

indignus, -a, -um, *unworthy (of), not deserving (to)* + infin.; *innocent*

indūcō, indūcere, indūxī, inductus, *to lead on/into*

inermis, -is, -e, *unarmed, defenseless*

iners, inertis, *lazy, lifeless*

īnfēlīx, īnfēlīcis, *unfertile, unproductive; disastrous, ill-fated, unfortunate*

ingenium, -ī, n., *intelligence, ingenuity*

ingēns, ingentis, *huge, big*

innīxus, -a, -um + abl., *leaning (on)*

innumerus, -a, -um, *countless, innumerable*

inquit, *(he/she) says, said*

īnsequor, īnsequī, īnsecūtus sum, *to pursue, chase*

īnstruō, īnstruere, īnstrūxī, īnstrūctus, *to build, construct;* + abl., *to equip, furnish (with); to instruct, teach*

īnsula, -ae, f., *island*

inter, prep. + acc., *between, among*

intereā, adv., *meanwhile*

inveniō, invenīre, invēnī, inventus, *to come upon, find*

invītus, -a, -um, *unwilling, unwillingly*

ipse, ipsa, ipsum, *-self, very*

īra, -ae, f., *anger*

īrātus, -a, -um, *angry*

is, ea, id, *he, she, it; this, that*

iste, ista, istud, *that, that . . . of yours*

ita, adv., *thus, so, in this way, in such a way*

iter, itineris, n., *journey, road, path, way*

iterum, adv., *again, a second time*

iubeō, iubēre, iussī, iussus, *to order, bid*

iūgerum, -ī, n., *a measure of land;* pl., *an expanse of land, fields, acres*

iungō, iungere, iūnxī, iūnctus, *to join*

Iuppiter, Iovis, m., *Jupiter (the Roman sky-god, father of Apollo by Latona)*

iūs, iūris, n., *law, legal sanction; legal authority, right*

iūstus, -a, -um, *lawful, legitimate; rightful, proper, deserved*

iuvenis, iuvenis, m., *young man*

L

labor, labōris, m., *work, toil*

lābor, lābī, lāpsus sum, *to slip, stumble*

labōrō, -āre, -āvī, -ātūrus, *to work*

lacertus, -ī, m., *the arm,* especially *the upper arm*

lacrima, -ae, f., *tear*

laedō, laedere, laesī, laesus, *to harm, hurt, wound*

laetus, -a, -um, *happy, glad, joyful*

laniō, -āre, -āvī, -ātus, *to wound savagely; to tear, shred, mutilate*

lapis, lapidis, m., *stone*

lateō, latēre, latuī, *to lie in hiding, hide*

laudō, -āre, -āvī, -ātus, *to praise*

laurus, -ī, f., *laurel tree, bay; sprig/branch of laurel; garland of laurel*

laus, laudis, f., *praise, glory, reputation; praiseworthy act, honor*

lectus, -ī, m., *bed, couch*

legō, legere, lēgī, lēctus, *to gather, collect, select; to read*

leō, leōnis, m., *lion*

lepus, leporis, m., *rabbit*

lētum, -ī, n., *death, destruction*

levis, -is, -e, *light* (in weight); *nimble; gentle; unsubstantial, thin*

levō, -āre, -āvī, -ātus, *to lift, raise up*

lēx, lēgis, f., *law; rule, regulation, order*

licet, licēre, licuit, impers., + dat., *it is allowed;* + subjn., *although*

lignum, -ī, n., *firewood; wood; stump; shaft*

līmen, līminis, n., *threshold, doorway*

littera, -ae, f., *letter* (of the alphabet); pl., *letter, epistle, literature*

locus, -ī, m. (pl., **loca, -ōrum,** n.), *place*

longus, -a, -um, *long*

loquor, loquī, locūtus sum, *to speak, talk*

luctor, luctārī, luctātus sum, *to wrestle; to struggle, resist*

lūdō, lūdere, lūsī, lūsūrus, *to play* (with, at)

lūmen, lūminis, n., *light; eye* (especially pl.), *vision, gaze, glance* (sing. or pl.)

lupus, -ī, m., *wolf*

lūx, lūcis, f., *light*

lyra, -ae, f., *lyre*

M

madēscō, madēscere, maduī, *to become wet*

magis, comp. adv., *more*

magnificus, -a, -um, *magnificent*

magnus, -a, -um, *big, great*

mālum, -ī, n. *apple*

mālus, -a, -um, *bad, evil*

māne, adv., *early in the day, in the morning*

maneō, manēre, mānsī, mānsūrus, *to remain, stay*

manus, -ūs, f., *hand; band* (of men)

margō, marginis, m., *wall; border, edge; margin*

marītus, -ī, *husband*

Mars, Martis, m., *Mars* (Roman god of war)

māter, mātris, f., *mother*

māteria, -ae, or **māteriēs, -ēī,** f., *wood* (as a building material); *material, subject-matter*

mātūrus, -a, -um, *ripe; advanced in age*

medicīna, -ae, f., *medicine*

medius, -a, -um, *mid-, middle of*

mel, mellis, n., *honey*

membrum, -ī, n., *part of the body, limb, member*

mēns, mentis, f., *mind*

mēnsa, -ae, f., *table*

mēta, -ae, f., *mark, goal, turning-point*

metuō, metuere, metuī, metūtus, *to fear, be afraid of*

metus, -ūs, m., *fear*

meus, -a, -um, *my, mine*

micō, micāre, micuī, *to move quickly to and fro, flash*

mīles, mīlitis, m., *soldier*

mīlitia, -ae, f., *military service*

mīlle, indecl. adj., *thousand*

Minerva, -ae, f., *Minerva* (virginal goddess of wisdom and warfare, the Roman counterpart to the Greek's Athena)

minimus, -a, -um, *very small, smallest*

minor, minor, minus, gen., **minōris,** *smaller*

minuō, minuere, minuī, minūtus, *to lessen, reduce, decrease*

mīrābilis, -is, -e, *wonderful*

mīror, mīrārī, mīrātus sum, *to wonder*

mīrus, -a, -um, *wonderful, marvelous, strange*

misceō, miscēre, miscuī, mixtus, *to mix*

miser, misera, miserum, *unhappy, miserable, wretched*

miserābilis, -is, -e, *miserable, wretched*

mittō, mittere, mīsī, missus, *to send, let go*

moderātus, -a, -um, *temperate, moderate, restrained*

modo, adv., *only; only recently, just now;* **modo . . . modo,** *at one time . . . at another*

modus, -ī, m., *way, method*

molliō, -īre, -īvī-/-iī, mollītus, *to make soft, soften; to weaken, make effeminate*

mollis, -is, -e, *soft, tender; gentle*

moneō, monēre, monuī, monitus, *to advise, warn*

mōns, montis, m., *mountain, hill*

mora, -ae, f., *delay*

morior, morī, mortuus sum, *to die*

moror, morārī, morātus sum, *to delay, remain, stay*

mors, mortis, f., *death*

morsus, -ūs, m., *bite* (of an animal); pl., by metonymy, *teeth, jaws*

mortalis, -is, -e, *subject to death, mortal*

mōs, mōris, m., *custom,* pl., *character*

moveō, movēre, mōvī, mōtus, *to move, shake*

mox, adv., *soon, presently*

multus, -a, -um, *much;* pl. *many*

mūnus, mūneris, n., *a required task; tribute, offering* (to a deity); *gift* (with **prō,** *as a gift*); *favor, service*

murmur, murmuris, n., *murmur, ramble*

mūrus, -ī, m., *wall*

mūtō, -āre, -āvī, -ātus, *to exchange; to change, replace; to transform*

mūtuus, -a, -um, *mutual*

myrtus, -ī, m./f., *myrtle*

N

nam, conj., *for*

nārrō, -āre, -āvī, -ātus, *to tell* (a story)

nāscor, nāscī, nātus sum, *to be born*

nātālis, -is, -e, *of/belonging to birth*

nātūra, -ae, f., *nature*

nātus, -ī, m. *son*

nē, conj. (+ subjn.), *in case, to prevent, not to, so that . . . not*

nec, conj., *and . . . not*

necō, -āre, -āvī, -ātus, *to kill*

negō, -āre, -āvī, -ātus, *to say (that) not; to refuse*

neque, conj., *and . . . not*

nēquīquam, adv., *with no effect, to no avail, in vain*

nervus, -ī, m., *muscle, nerve; cord* (made of such material), *string* (of a musical instrument or a bow)

nesciō, -īre, -īvī, -ītus, *to be ignorant, not know*

nēve or **neu,** conj., *nor; and so that . . . not*

nex, necis, f., *death, murder*

niger, nigra, nigrum, *black*

nīl, n., indecl., *nothing*

nimis, adv., *too much*

nimium, adv., *too much, excessively*

nisi, conj., *unless, if . . . not, except*

niveus, -a, -um, (consisting) *of snow; snow-white, snowy*

nix, nivis, f., *snow*

noceō, -ēre, -uī, -itūrus + dat., *to harm*

nocturnus, -a, -um, *happening during the night*

nōlō, nōlle, nōluī, irreg., *to be unwilling, not wish, refuse*

nōmen, nōminis, n., *name*

nōminō, -āre, āvī, -ātus, *to name, call by name*

nōn, adv., *not*

nōndum, adv., *not yet*

noster, nostra, nostrum, *our*

notō, -āre, -āvī, -ātus, *to mark, brand; to scar; to notice; to inscribe*

nōtus, -a, -um, *known*

novem, *nine*

novus, -a, -um, *new*

nox, noctis, f., *night*

nūdus, -a, -um, *naked; unadorned*

nūllus, -a, -um, *no, none*

nūmen, nūminis, n., *nod* (of assent); *divine power, supernatural influence*

numerō, -āre, -āvī, -ātus, *to count*

numerus, -ī, n., *number*

nunc, adv., *now*

nūper, adv., *recently*

nūtriō, -īre, -īvī, -ītus, *to feed at the breast; to support, nourish*

nux, nucis, f., *nut*

O

ō, interj., *oh!*

obscūrus, -a, -um, *dark, obscure; shadowy; hidden from sight*

observō, -āre, -āvī, -ātus, *to watch, pay attention to*

obsideō, obsidēre, obsēdī, obsessus, *to besiege*

obstipēscō, obstipēscere, obstipuī, *to be stunned, dazed, awestruck*

obstō, obstāre, obstitī, obstātūrus + dat., *to face; to stand in the way (of); obstruct*

occupō, -āre, -āvī, -ātus, *to seize*

ōcior, ōcior, ōcius, compar. adj., *swifter, more fleeting*

oculus, -ī, m., *eye*

officium, -ī, n., *official ceremony, duty*

ōlim, adv., *once (upon a time), one day*

ōmen, ōminis, n., *omen, augury, sign*

omnis, -is, -e, *all, the whole, every, each*

onus, oneris, n., *load, burden*

opācus, -a, -um, *shaded; shadowy, dark, dim*

ops, opis, f., *power, ability; resources; aid*

optō, -āre, -āvī, -ātus, *to wish*

opus, operis, n., *work, task; function, purpose*; opus est + abl., idiom, *there is need of* (something)

ōra, -ae, f., *shore, coast*

orbis, orbis, m., *disc, any disc-shaped object; wheel; orb* (of the sun or moon); *the world*

ōrdō, ōrdinis, m., *row, line; social status, class; order, arrangement*

ōrnō, -āre, -āvī, -ātus, *to decorate, equip*

ōrō, -āre, -āvī, -ātus, *to beg*

ōs, ōris, n., *mouth, face, expression* (pl. common for s. in verse)

os, ossis, n., *bone*

ōsculum, -ī, n., *little mouth;* (most commonly) *kiss* or, pl., *lips*

ostendō, ostendere, ostendī, ostentus, *to show, point out*

ōvum, -ī, n., *egg*

P

Paelignus, -a, -um, *Paelignian, of the Paelignians* (a tribe of central Italy)

palūster, palūstris, palūstre, *marshy; of/living in marshes*

parcō, parcere, pepercī + dat., *to spare*

parēns, parentis, m./f., *parent*

pareō, parēre, paruī + dat., *to obey*

pariēs, parietis, m., *wall*

pariter, adv., *together; at the same time*

parō, -āre, -āvī, -ātus, *to prepare*

pars, partis, f., *part*

parvus, -a, -um, *small*

passus, -ūs, m., *step, pace, stride*

pāstor, pāstōris, m., *shepherd*

pateō, -ēre, -uī, *to be open; to be visible; to be revealed*

pater, patris, m., *father*

patrius, -a, -um, *of a father, a father's*

patior, patī, passus sum, *to suffer, endure; to allow, permit*

patrius, -a, -um, *of a father, father's*

paucī, -ae, -a, *few*

paulatim, adv., *gradually, little by little*

paulum, adv., *a little, little*

pauper, pauperis, *poor*

pāx, pācis, f., *peace*

pectus, pectoris, n., *chest, breast*

pellō, pellere, pepulī, pulsus, *to beat against, strike; to drive away, banish, expel*

pendeō, pendēre, pependī, *to be suspended, hang; to hang down (upon/over)*

Pēnēis, Pēnēidos, abl. sing. Pēnēide, voc. sing. Pēnēi, acc. pl. Pēnēidas, *of the river Peneus, descended from the river-god Peneus*

Pēnēius, -a, -um, *of Peneus, child of Peneus*

penna, -ae, f., *wing; feather*

per, prep. + acc., *through, along, over*

peragō, peragere, perēgī, perāctus, *to chase; to complete; to go through* (space or time); *to live out, complete* (a period of time)

percutiō, percutere, percussī, percussus, *to strike; to beat, shake violently*

perdō, perdere, perdidī, perditus, *to destroy, ruin; to waste*

perferō, perferre, pertulī, perlātus, irreg., *to report; to endure, to carry* (to someone)

perīculum, -ī, n., *danger*

perlegō, perlegere, perlēgī, perlēctus, *to read through*

perveniō, pervenīre, pervēnī, perventūrus, + ad + acc., *to arrive (at), reach*

pēs, pedis, m., *foot*

petō, petere, petīvī, petītus, *to seek, look for, aim at, attack*

pharetra, -ae, f., *quiver*

Philēmōn, Philēmonis, acc., **Philēmona,** m., *Philemon* (a poor Phrygian farmer, husband of Baucis)

Phoebē, -ēs, f., *Diana* (sister of Phoebus Apollo and virgin goddess of the moon)

Phoebus, -ī, m., *Phoebus* (Apollo, god of the sun and the arts)

pila, -ae, f., *ball*

pius, -a, -um, *dutiful, worshipful*

placeō, placēre, placuī, placitūrus + dat., *to please*

plēnus, -a, -um, *full*

plūma, -ae, f., *feather; feather cushion, pillow*

plumbum, -ī, n., *lead*

pōculum, -ī, n., *cup*

poena, -ae, f., *punishment, penalty*

poēta, -ae, m., *poet*

pollex, pollicis, m., *thumb*

polliceor, pollicērī, pollicitus sum, *to promise*

pompa, -ae, f., *ceremonial procession*

pōmum, -ī, n., *fruit-tree; fruit*

pōnō, pōnere, posuī, positus, *to put, place*

populus, -ī, m., *people*

porta, -ae, f., *gate*

portō, -āre, -āvī, -ātus, *to carry*

poscō, poscere, poposcī, *to ask for, demand*

possideō, possidēre, possēdī, possessus, *to have in one's control; to take control of, seize*

possum, posse, potuī, irreg., *to be able*

post, prep. + acc., *after*

posterus, -a, -um, *next, following*

postis, -is, m., *door-post; doorway*

postquam, conj., *after*

potentia, -ae, f., *power, potency*

praebeō, -ēre, -uī, -itus, *to display, show, provide*

praeceptum, -ī, n., *instruction, order*

praeda, -ae, f., *booty, plunder; prey, game*

praeferō, praeferre, praetulī, praelātus, irreg., *to carry in front, prefer*

praetereō, praeterīre, praeteriī, praeteritus, irreg., *to go past*

precor, -ārī, -ātus sum, *to pray for, beg*

premō, premere, pressī, pressus, *to press, press upon; to cover; to oppress*

prēndō, prēndere, prēndī, prēnsus, *to grasp, seize, take hold of; to catch, capture*

prex, precis, f., *entreaty, prayer*

prīmum, adv., *first, at first*

prīmus, -a, -um, *first*

prior, prius, *first (of two), previous*

prō, prep. + abl., *for, on behalf of, as*

probō, -āre, -āvī, -ātus, *to approve, commend;* with acc. + infin., *to consider it proper* (for someone to do something)

procul, adv., *in the distance, far off*

prōdūcō, prōdūcere, prōdūxī, prōductus, *to bring forth, lead out, produce*

prōnus, -a, -um, *face down*

properō, -āre, -āvī, -ātus, *to act with haste, be quick; to hurry, rush*

prōsum, prōdesse, prōfuī + dat., irreg., *to be of use to, benefit, help;* + infin., *to be beneficial* (to do something)

prōtinus, adv., *immediately*

pudor, pudōris, m., *sense of shame; decency, chastity*

puella, -ae, f., *girl*

puer, -ī, m., *boy*

pulcher, pulchra, pulchrum, *beautiful, handsome*

pulsō, -āre, -āvī, ātus, *to strike, beat*

purpureus, -a, -um, *purple*

pūrus, -a, -um, *spotless, clean*

putō, -āre, -āvī, -ātus, *to think, consider*

Pygmaliōn, Pygmaliōnis, m., *Pygmalion* (a sculptor from Cyprus)

Pȳramus, -ī, m., *Pyramus* (a Babylonion youth)

Q

quaerō, quaerere, quaesīvī, quaesītus, *to seek, look for, ask* (for)

quantus, -a, -um, *how big . . . ? how much . . . ?*

-que, enclitic conj., *and*

quercus, -ūs, f., *oak tree; oak garland*

queror, querī, questus sum, *to complain (about), protest*

quī, quae, quod, *who, which, that;* after **sī, nisi, nē, num,** *some(one/thing), any(one/thing)*

quīcumque, quaecumque, quodcumque, indefinite adj. or pron., *whoever, whatever*

quid, adv., *why?*

quidem, adv., *indeed*

quīnque, indecl., *five*

quis, quid, pron., *who . . . ? what . . . ?*
quisque, quaeque, quidque, each
quisquis, quidquid, indefinite rel. pron.,
any who, whoever, whatever
quondam, adv., *once, formerly*
quoniam, conj., *since*
quoque, adv., *also*

R

radius, -ī, m., *ray of light*
rādīx, rādīcis, f., *root* (of a plant or trȇe)
rādō, rādere, rāsī, rāsus, *to scrape,
scratch; to erase; to pass, move (closely)
past*
rāmus, -ī, m., *branch*
recēns, recentis, *recent, newly arrived;
newly shed; recently caught*
recipiō, recipere, recēpī, receptus, *to
receive*; **sē recipere**, *to go, return*
reddō, reddere, reddidī, redditus, *to give
back, return*
redeō, redīre, rediī, reditūrus, irreg., *to
return, go back*
referō, referre, rettulī, relātus, irreg., *to
bring back*
rēgia, -ae, f., *palace, royal house*
rēgnō, -āre, -āvī, -ātus, *to rule, govern,
reign*
rēgnum, -ī, n., *kingdom*
regō, regere, rēxī, rēctus, *to rule*
relinquō, relinquere, relīquī, relictus, *to
leave*
removeō, removēre, removī, remōtus, *to
remove, move aside*
renovō, -āre, -āvī, -ātus, *to renew, revive*
reperiō, reperīre, repperī, repertus, *to
find, discover; to find* (someone,
something) *to be*
repetō, repetere, repetīvī, repetītus, *to seek
again; to repeat; to pick up, recover*
requiēs, requiētis, acc. usually **requiem**, f.,
rest, respite
**requiēscō, requiēscere, requiēvī,
requiētūrus**, *to rest, lie at rest*
requīrō, requīrere, requīsīvī, requīsītus, *to
ask, inquire*
rēs, reī, f., *thing, matter, situation*
rescrībō, rescrībere, rescrīpsī, rescrīptus,
to write back; reply
resistō, resistere, restitī, *to pause in one's*

journey, halt, stop
respiciō, respicere, respexī, respectus, *to
look back (at)*
**respondeō, respondēre, respondī,
respōnsūrus**, *to reply*
retrō, adv., *toward the rear, backwards,
behind*
revocō, -āre, -āvī, -ātus, *to recall, call back*
Rhodopēius, -a, -um, *of Mt. Rhodope* (in
Thrace)
rīdeō, rīdēre, rīsī, rīsūrus, *to laugh, smile*
rīma, -ae, f., *crack*
rogō, -āre, -āvī, -ātus, *to ask*
Rōma, -ae, f., *Rome*
rosa, -ae, f., *rose*
rota, -ae, f., *wheel*
rumpō, rumpere, rūpī, ruptus, *to burst*
rūrsus, adv., *again*

S

sacer, sacra, sacrum, *sacred, religious*
saepe, adv., *often*
saevus, -a, -um, *fierce, savage*
sagitta, -ae, f., *arrow*
salignus, -a, -um, *made of willow-wood*
sanguis, sanguinis, m., *blood; family, class*
satis, adv., *enough*
saxum, -ī, n., *stone, rock, boulder*
scindō, scindere, scidī, scissus, *to cut, split,
carve*
sciō, scīre, sciī, scītus, *to know*
sē or **sēsē** (acc. and abl.), gen., **suī**, dat.,
sibi, *himself, herself, oneself, itself,
themselves*
secundus, -a, -um, *second*; **secundae
mēnsae, -ārum**, f. pl., *second course,
dessert*
sed, *but*
sedeō, sedēre, sēdī, sessūrus, *to sit*
sēdēs, sēdis, f., *seat; home; place, position*
sēdulus, -a, -um, *attentive, careful,
painstaking, sedulous*
semper, adv., *always*
senex, senis, m. and adj., *old man; old*
senīlis, -is, -e, *of an old man, old man's; in
old age, aged*
sepeliō, sepelīre, sepelīvī, sepultus, *to bury*
septem, indecl., *seven*
sepulcrum, -ī, n., *tomb*
sequor, sequī, secūtus sum, *to follow*

sermō, sermōnis, m., *conversation, talk*
sērō, adv., *late*
serpēns, serpentis, m., *snake, serpent*
servō, -āre, -āvī, -ātus, *to save, keep, protect*
sex, indecl., *six*
sī, conj., *if*
sīc, *thus, in this way*
siccus, -a, -um, *dry*
sīdus, sīderis, n., *star, planet;* usually pl., *the stars*
signum, -ī, n., *signal, sign; (military) standards*
silentium, -ī, n., *silence*
silex, silicis, m., *hard stone, flint*
silva, -ae, f., *woods, forest*
similis, -is, -e, *like, similar (to)*
simplicitās, simplicitātis, f., *unity; simplicity, sincerity; lack of sophistication, ignorance*
simul, adv., *together, at the same time*
simulācrum, -ī, n., *likeness; image, statue; phantom, ghost*
simulō, -āre, -āvī, -ātus, *to pretend; to produce, simulate; to take the form of*
sine, prep. + abl., *without*
sinō, sinere, sīvī, situs, *to allow*
sitis, sitis, acc. **sitim**, f., *thirst*
socius, -a, -um, *keeping company* (with another), (in the role of) *companion; allied*
sōl, sōlis, m., *the sun; Sol* (god of the sun)
soleō, solēre, solitus sum + infin., *to be accustomed* (to), *be in the habit of*
sōlus, -a, -um, *alone*
solūtus, -a, -um, *unbound, loosened; opened; weakened*
somnium, -ī, n., *dream*
somnus, -ī, m., *sleep*
sordidus, -a, -um, *dirty*
soror, sorōris, f., *sister*
spargō, spargere, sparsī, sparsus, *to scatter, strew; to allow to stream out*
spectō, -āre, -āvī, -ātus, *to watch, look at*
spērō, -āre, -āvī, -ātus, *to hope*
spēs, speī, f., *hope*
sternō, sternere, strāvī, strātus, *to lay out, spread; to strike down, defeat*
stipula, -ae, f., *stalk* (of a grain plant); *stubble* (left in a field once the grain has been harvested), *straw*
stō, stāre, stetī, statūrus, *to stand*

strātum, -ī, n., *bedding, coverlet;* (often in pl.) *bed*
strēnuus, -a, -um, *active, energetic*
stringō, stringere, strīnxī, strīctus, *to bind, secure; to draw tight; to draw* (a sword); *to draw close to, touch*
stupeō, -ēre, -uī, -itus, *to be amazed, gape; to be paralyzed*
sub, prep. + acc. and abl., *under, beneath*
subeō, subīre, subiī, subitus, irreg., *to go underneath; to come upon* (someone) *stealthily, sneak up on* (a person)
submissus, -a, -um, *lowered; quiet, subdued, soft*
sum, esse, fuī, futūrus, irreg., *to be*
summus, -a, -um, *very great, the greatest, the top of*
super, prep. + acc., *over, above*
superbus, -a, -um, *proud, arrogant*
superus, -a, -um, *above, upper;* **superī**, m. pl., *the gods above*
surgō, surgere, surrēxī, surrēctūrus, *to get up, rise*
surripiō, surripere, surripuī, surreptus, *to steal*
sustineō, sustinēre, sustinuī, *to hold up, support; to sustain;* (+ infin.) *to be able* (to do something) *without relenting*
suus, -a, -um, *his, her, its, their (own)*

T

tabella, -ae, f., *board, tablet;* pl., *writing tablet*
tabulae, -ārum, f. pl., *tablets, records*
taeda, -ae, f., *torch*
tālis, -is, -e, *such, like this, of this kind*
tam, adv., *so*
tamen, conj., *however, nevertheless*
tamquam, adv., *just as, as if, as though*
tandem, adv., *at last, at length*
tangō, tangere, tetigī, tāctus, *to touch*
tantum, adv., *only; so much*
tantus, -a, -um, *so great, such a big*
tardus, -a, -um, *slow*
tēctum, -ī, n., *roof, ceiling; house, dwelling*
tegō, tegere, tēxī, tēctus, *to cover; to hide, conceal*
tellūs, tellūris, f., *land, earth*
temerārius, -a, -um, *rash, reckless, bold*
templum, -ī, n., *temple*

temptō, -āre, -āvī, -ātus, *to try*

tempus, temporis, n., *time*

tendō, tendere, tetendī, tentus, *to extend, stretch forth; to proceed*

teneō, tenēre, tenuī, tentus, *to hold*

tener, tenera, tenerum, *soft, tender; immature, young*

tenuis, -is, -e, *slender, thin*

tepeō, tepēre, tepuī, *to be warm; to have the warmth of a human body*

tergeō, tergēre, tersī, tersus, *to dry, wipe*

tergum, -ī, n., *back, rear; flank* (of meat)

terra, -ae, f., *earth, ground*

tertius, -a, -um, *third*

Thisbē, Thisbēs, f., *Thisbe* (a Babylonian maiden)

tigris, tigris, m./f., *tiger*

timeō, -ēre, -uī, -itūrus, *to be afraid; to fear;* + dat., *to fear for*

timidus, -a, -um, *fearful, timorous*

timor, timōris, *fear*

tingō, tingere, tīnxī, tīnctus, *to wet, soak, moisten; to dye, stain, color*

tollō, tollere, sustulī, sublātus, *to lift, raise*

torus, -ī, m., *couch, bed; marriage bed*

tot, indecl. num. adj., *so many*

tōtus, -a, -um, *all, the whole*

tractō, -āre, -āvī, -ātus, *to keep pulling, dragging; to handle, rub, stroke*

trādō, trādere, trādidī, trāditus, *to hand over*

trahō, trahere, trāxī, tractus, *to drag, pull*

trānseō, trānsīre, trānsiī, trānsitūrus, irreg., *to cross*

tremō, tremere, tremuī, *to tremble*

trepidō, -āre, -āvī, -ātus, *to panic; to tremble, quiver*

trēs, trēs, tria, *three*

tristis, -is, -e, *sad*

triumphus, -ī, m., *the ritual shout "triumphe"; triumph* (ritual procession of a triumphant general); *victory celebration; victory*

tū, pl. vōs, *you*

tueor, tuērī, tuitus sum, *to look at, observe; to watch over, protect*

tum, adv., *at that moment, then*

tumidus, -a, -um, *swollen; enraged, violent*

tumulus, -ī, m., *burial mound, tomb*

tunc, adv., *then*

turba, -ae, f., *crowd, mob*

turpis, -is, -e, *offensive, foul, disgusting; shameful, disgraceful*

tūtus, -a, -um, *safe, secure*

tuus, -a, -um, *your* (sing.)

U

ubi, adv. and conj., *where, when*

ūllus, -a, -um, *any*

ultimus, -a, -um, *last*

umbra, -ae, f., *shadow, shade* (of the dead)

umerus, -ī, m., *shoulder*

umquam, adv., *ever*

unda, -ae, f., *wave, water*

ūnus, -a, -um, *one; alone, only;* ūnā, adv., *together*

urbs, urbis, f., *city*

urgeō, urgēre, ursī, *to press, insist*

urna, -ae, f., *pitcher, urn*

ūrō, ūrere, ussī, ustus, *to destroy by fire, burn*

ūsque, adv., *all the way to/from; continuously*

ūsus, -ūs, m., *use, employment; the right to use/enjoy; potential for use, utility; marriage* (one type of Roman marriage)

ut, conj. + indic., *as, when;* + subjn., *so that, that, to*

uterque, utraque, utrumque, *each* (of two), *both*

ūtilis, -is, -e, *useful*

ūva, -ae, f., *grape, bunch of grapes*

uxor, uxōris, f., *wife*

V

vacō, -āre, -āvī, -ātūrus, *to be empty, unfilled; to be free from, take a rest from*

vacuus, -a, -um, *empty, hollow; carefree, fancy-free;* + abl., *devoid* (of), *free* (from)

valeō, -ēre, -uī, *to be strong, be well*

vapor, vapōris, m., *steam*

vātēs, vātis, m., *prophet; bard, poet*

-ve, enclitic conj., *or*

vehō, vehere, vexī, vectus, *to carry;* pass., *to be carried, travel*

vel, adv. and conj., *or, if you prefer, at least*

vēlāmen, vēlāminis, n., *veil, shawl*

velut, *just as*

vēna, -ae, f., *blood-vessel, vein; vein, streak* (of some stone or mineral)

venia, -ae, f., *favor, kindness, blessing ; forgiveness, pardon; reprieve, remission*

veniō, venīre, vēnī, ventūrus, *to come*

ventus, -ī, m., *wind*

Venus, Veneris, f., *Venus* (goddess of love and Cupid's mother)

verbum, -ī, n., *word*

vereor, verērī, veritus sum, *to be afraid, fear*

Vergilius, -ī, m., *Vergil*

versō, -āre, -āvī, -ātus, *to turn, spin; to turn back and forth, twist*

versus, -ūs, m., *line* (of poetry or prose)

vertō, vertere, vertī, versus, *to* (cause to) *turn, spin; to reverse, change*

vērus, -a, -um, *true;* **vērō,** *truly*

vester, vestra, vestrum, *your* (pl.)

vēstīgium, -ī, n., *track, footprint, trace*

vestis, vestis, f., *clothing, garment*

vetō, vetāre, vetuī, vetitus, *to forbid, tell not to*

vetus, veteris, *old*

via, -ae, f., *road, street*

viātor, viātōris, m., *traveler*

vīcīnia, -ae, f., *nearby area, vicinity; nearness, proximity*

vīcīnus, -a, -um, *neighboring, adjacent; near, close*

victor, victōris, m., *conqueror, victor*

videō, vidēre, vīdī, vīsus, *to see*

vīlis, -is, -e, *cheap, worthless; contemptible, of inferior rank*

vīlla, -ae, f., *country house*

vincō, vincere, vīcī, victus, *to win, conquer, overcome*

vinculum, -ī, n., *chain;* usually pl., *shackles*

vīnum, -ī, n., *wine*

vir, virī, m., *man*

virgō, virginis, f., *maiden*

vīs, vīs, f., *force;* pl. **vīrēs,** *strength*

vīta, -ae, f., *life*

vītis, vītis, f., *grapevine*

vitium, -ī, n., *defect, fault; flaw, imperfection; vice*

vītō, -āre, -āvī, -ātus, *to avoid*

vitta, -ae, f., *ribbon, headband*

vīvō, vīvere, vīxī, vīctūrus, *to live*

vix, adv., *scarcely, with difficulty, only just*

vocō, -āre, -āvī, -ātus, *to call, invite*

volō, -āre, -āvī, -ātus, *to fly*

volō, velle, voluī, irreg., *to wish, want, be willing*

volucris, volucris, f., *winged creature, bird*

vōtum, -ī, n., *vow; prayer, wish*

vōx, vōcis, f., *voice*

vulgus, -ī, n., *the common people, the multitude*

vulnus, vulneris, n., *wound*

vultus, -ūs, m., *face, expression*